Ione Chase   Dorothy Hamon Gardner   Molly McGuire Grothaus

S. Lockwood   Harriet McMahon Turtell   Jane C. Scott

Betty H. Blake   Anne C. Carr   Ione Chase

Jocelyn Horder   Marion Prince Hosmer   Lockwood

Louise Agee Wrinkle   Louise Richardson Allen   Betty H. Blake

Molly McGuire Grothaus   Polly Hill   Jocelyn Horder

Turtell   Jane C. Scott   Eleanor Brinckerhoff Spingarn   Louise Agee Wrinkle

Ione Chase   Dorothy Hamon Gardner   Molly McGuire Grothaus

S. Lockwood   Harriet McMahon Turtell   Jane C. Scott

Betty H. Blake   Anne C. Carr   Ione Chase

Jocelyn Horder   Marion Prince Hosmer   Harrietta E. S. Lockwood

Louise Agee Wrinkle   Louise Richardson Allen   Betty H. Blake

Molly McGuire Grothaus   Polly Hill   Jocelyn Horder

EARTH
ON HER
HANDS

EARTH ON HER HANDS

The American Woman in Her Garden

BY STARR OCKENGA

CLARKSON POTTER/PUBLISHERS
NEW YORK

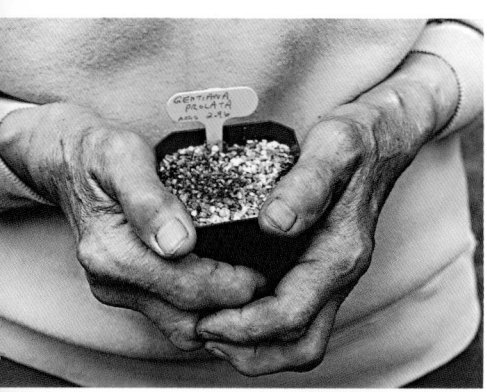

PAGES 2–3: Molly McGuire
Grothaus's garden; PAGE 4: Jane
P. Overesch with *Hypericum* ×
moserianum 'Tricolor'; THIS PAGE:
Eleanor Brinckerhoff Spingarn
with *Gentiana prolata*; PAGE 9:
Dorothy Hannon Gardner's gar-
den; PAGE 10: Jane P. Overesch's
garden; PAGE 12: Joanna
McQuail Reed's garden; PAGE 14
(LEFT): *Clematis* 'Carnaby';
(RIGHT): *Canna* 'Pretoria';
PAGE 234: Betty H. Blake with
Iris lacustris.

All photographs are by Starr Ockenga except: page 50 (except top left and second from top right) and 51 by Molly Grothaus; page 129 (below) by Cynthia Hosmer.

USDA Plant Hardiness Zone Map appears on page 240.

Published by Clarkson N. Potter, Inc., 201 East 50th Street, New York, New York 10022.
Member of the Crown Publishing Group.
Random House, Inc. New York, Toronto, London, Sydney, Auckland
www.randomhouse.com

Clarkson N. Potter, Potter, and colophon are trademarks of Random House, Inc.

Printed in China

Design by Kayo Der Sarkissian

Library of Congress Cataloging-in-Publication Data
Ockenga, Starr.
    Earth on her hands: the American woman in her garden / by Starr Ockenga. — 1st ed.
    1. Gardens—United States. 2. Women gardeners—United States. 3. Landscape gardening—United States. 4. Gardening—United States. I. Title.
    SB466.U6028   1998
    635.9'082—dc21   98-6323

ISBN 0-517-70561-3

10 9 8 7 6 5 4

The photograph of my mother was taken in our mountain vegetable garden by my father in the fall of 1949. The garden was dug out of a rocky field next to our New Hampshire farmhouse. The tomato teepees are saplings cut from the forest; the ties, strips torn from worn-out bedsheets. Tomatoes rarely ripened on the vine at that altitude and latitude; they lined our kitchen windowsills after the first frost. My mother also planted old-fashioned flowers, iris, columbine, tansy, daylily, phlox, by the porch. A panorama of the White Mountains—134 peaks, including Mt. Washington, according to my father's count—lay at our feet. When the rainbows spread from end to end of the valley, which they did with frequency, we believed we owned the pot of gold.

Acknowledgments

To the eighteen women who welcomed me into their gardens and their homes, who gave freely of their gardening knowledge, their personal stories, their hospitality and warmth, I offer my deepest gratitude. The experience of making this book has been one of the high points of my life—because of each of you.

The only way a project like this can succeed is through the thoughtful recommendations from a network of gardeners and representatives of institutions from coast to coast. We believed that to present a picture of what American women have been doing in their gardens over the last five decades, we needed national representation. Graciously, each of you took the time for phone conversations, sometimes at great length. Many of you called me back with further ideas and suggestions. The names of grand American gardeners assembled with your help is long and venerable. Choosing only eighteen women from such august company was a difficult task.

I wish to thank The American Horticultural Society, The Garden Club of America, The Garden Conservancy, The Hardy Plant Society, The New York Botanical Garden, The Philadelphia Horticultural Society, Smithsonian Institution Archives of American Gardens, The Southern Garden History Society, The St. Louis Botanical Garden.

I am especially appreciative to: Antonia F. Adezio, Virginia Almand, Darel Apps, Ingrid Baramki, Susan Bodin, Deanna Braeger, Nancy Peterson Brewster, Harry Butler, Flora Ann Bynum, Frederick Case, Margaraet Culp, Nancy Chute, Carol Donnelly, Gay Estes, Jane Flynn, Flora French, Florence Griffin, Betsy Gullan, Margaret Hall, Lois Himes, Penny Horne, Juliette Hubbard, Nancy Lee Kemper, Peachy Kohler, Beatrice and Peter Nessen, Jane Mandel, Sara Mauritz, Carol McConomy, Nan Patternotte, Janet Meakin Poor, Joanna Reed, Cynthia B. Richards, Robyn A. Shapiro, Patti Scheuning, Kay Steffe, Mary Anne Streeter, Nancy Swanson, Bonnie Trowbridge, Carl Totemeier, Genevieve Tremble, Chip Tynan, Ann Vogel, Calista Washburn, Rosemary Wilson.

I am indebted to those who so carefully prepared plant lists: Diane Clarke (the Scott garden), Gail Griffin (the Carr garden), Rosina McIvor (the Chase garden), Robin Zitter (the Lockwood garden).

Finally, I am deeply grateful to:

Pamela Krauss, my editor and friend, who, quite simply, makes everything better.

Margot Schupf, who keeps all wheels turning.

Kayo Der Sarkissian, the designer, who took my photographs and a few words about these women—strength, simplicity, individuality, history—and turned the many parts into an elegant context that enforces these women's collective voice.

All those at Clarkson Potter Publishers, especially Lauren Shakely, Maggie Hinders, Mark McCauslin, and Jane Searle, who contributed to making the process of producing this book such a pleasure.

Barbara Hogenson, my agent, who believed in the idea of this book from the beginning.

Jacques Charlas of Black and White on White, who made the luminous prints of the portraits of the women.

Cassie Sigler, who, while I am at the computer, takes home management to a new level.

Gary Kettelle, who provides tender care to my garden when I am away.

Aldryth Ockenga, my sister, and John Ockenga, my brother, who are my dear companions.

Robin Oury, my son, who lights up my life.

Donald Forst, my helpmate, who serves as my wise sounding board.

And to Donald and Robin, cheerful "undergardener" help, I thank you for your support and love—and for encouraging me to spend time in our garden.

Contents

"We come and go, but the land will always be here.

Those people who love and understand it are the only ones who really own it—for a while."

WILLA CATHER, *O PIONEERS!*

Introduction

The gardens gathered here have been created by eighteen exceptional women. Each is a hands-on, longtime gardener, many the product of a deep family history of gardening. None of the gardens resembles another, and each woman's vision and the story of developing her personal signature is different. Yet common threads are woven through this tapestry of paths and plants. To paraphrase John Bartram's eighteenth-century observation about Mistress Martha Logan, their gardens are their delight.

These women are not professionals. None is a garden designer; none has owned a nursery. Their gardens are private, created to be enjoyed by themselves alone or with families and friends. Yet the women are warm and generous with their knowledge, their experience—even their plants. They share their dreams, their ambitions, their mistakes, their successes. They demonstrate the use of cold frames, lath houses, greenhouses, and explain methods of plant culture. They stress the importance of participating in horticultural organizations, recalling the pleasures they've derived from communities of kindred spirits. Cumulatively, their words form a remarkable resource of a half century of everyday gardening across America—from Maine to California, from Georgia to Michigan. As Louise Wrinkle says, "The things you learn

from other people, things that have worked for them, those are often the most valuable lessons of all."

These gardens, which have ripened over decades, often began at the kitchen door. Joanna Reed remembers her first little garden, begun in 1940, which predicted a lifelong interest in herbs. She says, "The first fall and winter we built a retaining wall, making a flat area adjacent to the kitchen door. The bed was laid out in an elongated U shape, edged with brick, with simple treillage for background. It was a pleasing, utilitarian spot featuring culinary herbs." Most of these women love to cook; even the most ornamental garden, like Dorothy Gardner's formal parterre, has a spot designated to grow herbs and vegetables. Marion Hosmer, asked to name her favorite plants, opens her arms to her orchard. To Georgie Erskine, a garden would be barren without citrus. Marianna Paulson's vegetable garden on a Midwest prairie feeds more than her family; at harvest she welcomes friends to share the bounty.

Many have built their gardens, including the hardscaping, with their own hands. Ellie Spingarn has crafted more than 600 feet of stone walls throughout her property, and maintains extensive rock gardens without any help. Ione Chase moved rocks and poured concrete to make reflecting pools.

from meticulous handwritten ledgers to fact-filled entries on computer data bases. Marion Hosmer's loose-leaf notebooks stretch back through sixty-five years of gardening. Netta Lockwood knows every plant that has entered her garden. Jocey Horder can tell a plant's bloom date with the punch of the "enter" key—or give an updated list of plants that have "croaked" with suspected reasons for their demise. Photography is part of record keeping; slides of plants, carefully labeled, fill file cabinets.

All experiment. They grow plants from seed, many participating in exchanges through their memberships in organizations that offer seeds from far-flung areas of the world. They subscribe to explorer seed programs. They collect seeds from their own plants and from endangered plants in the wild. They take cuttings of rare or precious plants and nurture them to maturity. They hybridize and select fine strains. Some, like Ellie Spingarn, Molly Grothaus, and Betty Blake, have had plants named in their honor. Polly Hill has made a forty-year career of growing and selecting azaleas, ilex, and stewartias for use in American gardens;

she has introduced more than seventy-five plants, many into the nursery trade, without ever accepting a dollar for her work.

But their gifts to gardening have spread far beyond their own boundaries. Some, like Louise Allen in Atlanta, have been instrumental in organizing and raising funds for the establishment of public gardens, often with a focus on native plants. Anne Carr rallied her garden club to the founding of a major horticultural library, the Cherokee Garden Library. Molly Grothaus worked with a small dedicated group of women to establish a regional seed bank. They have used their writing skills, too. Louise Wrinkle acted in research and editorial capacity in the production of a book on conservation of plants in their natural habitats, and Molly Grothaus edited the newsletter for the American Rhododendron Society. They, like Joanna Reed, who was the president of the Herb Society of America, or Dorothy Gardner and Louise Wrinkle on the board of the Garden Conservancy, have served as officers in organizations; they even have been

Jane Scott says, "Every tree, every stone, I have put here." They have grown strong through hard work. Their energy seems boundless. To this day Jane Overesch will not allow anyone else to pull a weed in her garden.

Highly motivated, many of these women are self-taught gardeners. However, they say their formal education, which varies from art to French literature to nursing, has contributed to the way they work their gardens. The desire to learn spurred them to assemble fine libraries on garden design, history, and horticulture, with concentrations from alpines to bonsai weighing down shelves. The women are well read and current on plant discoveries or changes in taxonomy. Catalogs from specialty nurseries across the country are dog-eared from use. Over the years the women have enrolled in courses in botany and horticulture, often squeezing classes between domestic duties. A few earned related certificates or degrees. Joanna Reed was a member of the first class at the Barnes Foundation Arboretum, Betty Blake has a bachelor's degree in botany, and Hattie Purtell went back to school when her children were grown to earn her master's degree in botany. Most favor botanical names over common ones, for as Jocey Horder says, "It is too difficult to learn both, and Latin is descriptive and exact."

These women keep precise garden records; they range

instrumental in initiating organizations, friends of botanical gardens or chapters of national organizations in their regions.

They speak of evolution and change as part of gardening. Sometimes it takes the intervention of nature—the loss of a great tree in the case of Georgie Erskine, Netta Lockwood, and Anne Carr—which sets their gardens on other courses. At such times outside influences—lectures, the awakening of interests in particular plants, visits to other gardens—may spur reevaluation. Confronted with the necessity of modification, Georgie Erskine pulled particular features of gardens in Spain from her memory bank and adapted them in the reconstruction of her own; Netta Lockwood turned a once shaded area into a rocky Mediterranean garden, and Anne Carr created a white garden. Generally the seeds of change will have been germinating for a long time.

Most of the women have traveled. Many have climbed mountains or hiked to remote lakes to see plants in their native habitats. The major gardens of this country and the historical homes of the illustrious, like Jefferson and Washington, have made indelible impressions. The lush plantings, the formal designs of England, France, Italy, Spain, as well as the spare gardens of Japan are cited as influences. But, great gardens aside, it is visiting private gardens that each woman believes helped shape her imagination. Perhaps that is the reason they are so willing to open their own gates.

Even deeper than their devotion to plants, and many admit to being uncontrolled collectors, they possess a steadfast love of the land. When they speak the word "earth" it seems to resonate from within like a great actress's delivery. The word holds many levels of meaning, from the soil imbedded in the crevices of their fingers to the protection of the planet itself. Truly, these women have earth on their hands.

Starr Ockenga
Livingston, New York

"I learned to build walls by doing it. I never imported any stone.

This rock was a gift from nature."

Eleanor Brinckerhoff Spingarn

The Lure of Stone

ELEANOR BRINCKERHOFF SPINGARN

REDDING, CONNETICUT

In 1951, newly married, Ellie Spingarn and her husband moved into the guest cottage on his family's property. Shortly thereafter, a delivery truck backed into a stone wall by their entrance and knocked it down. When a local mason estimated the repairs at $200, Ellie remembers: "I began thinking, 'I could do that.'"

Over the last 45 years, Ellie has terraced the two-acre property, a north-facing hillside, into a series of interlocking gardens. They are held in place by retaining walls, which range in height from one to eight feet. "I started and just kept on going," she says ruefully, looking around at the more than 600 feet of meticulously fitted walls, linked by stone steps,

that she has built single-handedly. "Remember, I did this over a long period of time. I'm very slow."

From the beginning, Ellie realized she had an opportunity to create unique gardens. She observes, matter-of-factly, "In a different place, I would have made a different garden." The gardens and buildings, strung together into a harmonious enclave of soft browns and grays, crosshatch the property like a game of cat's cradle. A streambed, gouged deep by rushing water, divides the land on a diagonal. Year-round its graceful flow is an ideal counterbalance to the rectilinear lines and angles of the walls. Two simple, flat bridges provide access back and forth between the opposite banks.

Close to the house is a 19- by 34-foot kitchen garden, which Ellie first planted in 1974. It was "made by building an L-shaped six-foot-high retaining wall below it," a project that took a year and required 80 cubic yards of backfill. There she grows tomatoes, various peas and beans, peppers,

PREVIOUS PAGE: Ellie Spingarn's fitted walls not only provide flat terraces for her gardens, but she is able to plant a range of plants such as *Daphne arbuscula, Iberis pygmaea, Arabis × kellereri,* and *Campanula portenschlagiana* in the walls' crevices. THIS PAGE, ABOVE: At the bottom of Ellie Spingarn's sloping property is a woodland, dubbed "The Copse" by a visiting English gardener. "I require a lot of cooperation from my plants in order to keep this place up. As far as maintenance is concerned here, I'm it."

RIGHT: "Any rock garden needs mulch, and stone is ideal. It has been my mulch of choice for many years." *Phlox subulata* varieties, *Veronica rupestris, Aethionema oppositifolium* (formerly *Eunomia oppositifolia*), and *Globularia repens* all grow well in these well-drained, stone-mulched conditions. OPPOSITE: Ellie's in-laws owned a 1950 Farmall Cub; she and the bright red tractor became a team. "I couldn't do all this without the machinery. The Cub is my friend."

cucumbers, and the herbs she uses in the kitchen. "Don't most gardeners love to cook?" she asks.

The hilltop behind the barn is the site of the old vegetable garden, displaced by the advent of the new. Ellie has slowly converted it into a cutting garden that peaks in September, when the rest of the gardens are quiet. Throughout the summer, Ellie makes floral arrangements, changing the combinations as flowers come in and out of bloom. Her favorites are "cottage flowers"—the single-flowered annual and perennial asters, cleome, "small-flowered dahlias in various forms," feverfew, heliopsis, marigolds, *Phlox maculata* and

P. paniculata varieties, Shasta daisies, and zinnias. Bold and bright, she displays them in old crocks or jugs around the garden "in spots that ask for a boost of color."

On a gentle slope near the driveway, Ellie's second husband, Joel Spingarn, whom she married in 1980, has planted "forty-plus" dwarf conifers. His "pets" from a once larger collection, they were the nucleus of the specialty nursery Joel ran on Long Island, New York, for 25 years.

Ellie was determined that the walls that define and outline her various gardens would be permanent, and she developed her own system for building. "Experience was my teacher," she explains. The stone was a given in her landscape. Between the house and the road, she inherited an outcropping of granite "that ranges in color from steel blue to almost yellow. I was fortunate. It's inspiring to have such good-looking stone. And," she laughs, "my back held out as well."

Working a wall, she observes, "is like doing a jigsaw puzzle, where you go along popping things in here and there with ease. Then you reach a point where nothing fits. At that point I quit for a while, and then I come back to it with a fresh look." As she sorts through the stone, she says, "I con-

stantly think: face, paver, cornerstone, clunker, or cap." Square pieces are hard to come by and are especially treasured. To smooth the stone of knobs, she wields a three-pound sledgehammer with a short handle and uses half-inch, one-inch, and two- inch chisels. Leftover scraps of stone often serve as "chinks," thin slices of stone placed to make the wall stones' positions stable. When the stone is too heavy to move by hand, Ellie eases it onto a pair of solid wooden rollers, "tumbles" the stone up a board onto a trailer attached to her tractor, and moves it to the site.

She digs a trench three feet wide and three feet deep, to the frost line in this Zone 5 area of Connecticut. With a three-foot-high wall, as much wall exists underground as aboveground. "Therefore, the wall will never move." The foundation is the place for the "clunkers," stones in odd shapes or with no flat face. Sometimes Ellie has used mortar in the foundation and sometimes not. These days she uses a

ABOVE: Ellie's house, originally just a one-room cottage built in the 1920s, has spread into a long, comfortable home. She turned the granite outcropping at the front of the house to her advantage, planting dwarf flowering shrubs—*Rhododendron indicum* 'Balsaminiflorum', *R.* 'Gumpo', *R. nakaharae, Daphne retusa, D. arbuscula, Deutzia gracilis* 'Nikko', *Genista dalmatica, Rhododendron* 'Yaku Fairy', and *Spiraea alpina.* These she combined with alpines and bulbs that love the rocky conditions. RIGHT: Plants along "The Copse" paths, particularly clumps of the huge lavender faces of *Glaucidium palmatum,* invite pause—and gasps of pleasure.

mixture of sand and pea gravel between the joints, believing that it provides better drainage. She always fits the stone.

Ellie begins the wall, tightly fitted with the flat face outward, four to six inches below grade. As the wall grows in height, she uses a scaffold made of boards laid between cinder block to elevate her to the appropriate working level. "Rock is heavy," she admits. "If you look closely at my walls, you'll see that the bigger rocks are at the bottom."

Ellie knew little about rock gardening when she started. Yet retaining walls and terraces, by their very nature, provide good drainage, which makes an environment hospitable to alpine plants. "In the beginning I used whatever plants I had available." Native phlox (*Phlox subulata*) and daphne (*Daphne cneorum*) grew on the property, a remnant of an attempt at a rock garden by a previous owner. The Dalmatian bellflower (*Campanula portenschlagiana*) was an early standby. "It trails through crevices, its roots finding the good soil several feet back into the terrace. It always makes a good show." To that

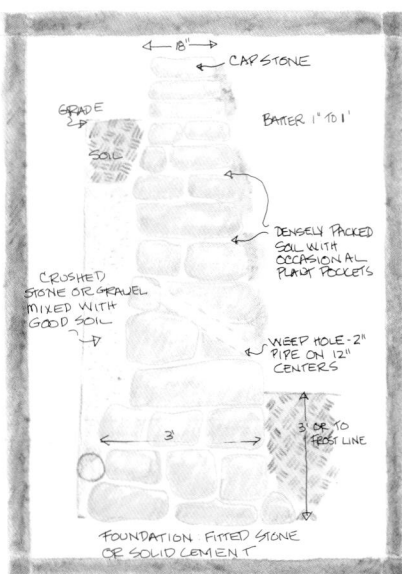

ABOVE: To guide the desired pitch of the wall slightly into the hillside, Ellie places batter boards at the front of both ends of the wall. Using a batter of approximately one inch back for each foot in elevation, she drives nails into each board, in precisely the same configuration, six inches apart from top to bottom. Strings are tightly stretched between the first two levels of nails. She places the stone exactly to the front of the string. She then works each layer of the wall for its entire length before starting the next. When ready for the next, she raises the two lines of string and repeats the entire process. As she works, Ellie backfills the wall to the depth of about one foot. She always adds gravel to ensure good drainage.

RIGHT: Along the banks of the stream, clumps of *Primula polyanthes* and forget-me-nots (*Myosotis alpestris*) have naturalized making a rainbow of color in the spring.

she added other easy-to-grow, diminutive plants: *Astilbe chinensis* 'Pumila', *Geranium dalmaticum*, *Iris cristata*, *Phlox subulata* varieties, *Primula vulgaris*, and *Pulsatilla halleri*.

While the walls that are integral parts of the buildings are built with mortar, most of the retaining walls are laid up dry.

The advantage to the dry-wall method for a gardener is the opportunity to make "planting pockets," small crevices between the fitted stones. "I plant as I build," Ellie says, "laying up each layer of the stone with good soil, which has been through a quarter- to eighth-inch screen." She prepares a mixture of a light-textured loam, peat moss, compost, and bonemeal (to balance her acid soil), testing the mixture's consistency by squeezing it into a ball that barely holds together. "Soil should be solidly packed between the stones. If the roots of a plant reach an air pocket, the plant is not as likely to prosper."

Spring, Ellie says, is the best time to plant a wall, though early fall is also good. It is more difficult to insert plants into a wall than to plant while building. Yet plants, she notes, last only about ten years, and a replacement program is necessary, although some plants self-seed. She prefers to use "starter plants" (seedlings and rooted cuttings), because "they are raring to go. They develop better than a more mature plant." Older plants, which dry out more quickly, are labor intensive. The plants "have their environmental preferences. For example, of the campanulas, *Campanula garganica* lives on and on for me, but *C. cochleariifolia* is not as permanent." If one plant variety goes into decline, another takes over. "They just make room for what does like it here."

In 1963 she discovered the North American Rock Garden Society and immediately joined, placing herself in a network of dedicated and passionate gardeners with similar interests. Ellie became a collector and a connoisseur; she has served as a vice pres-

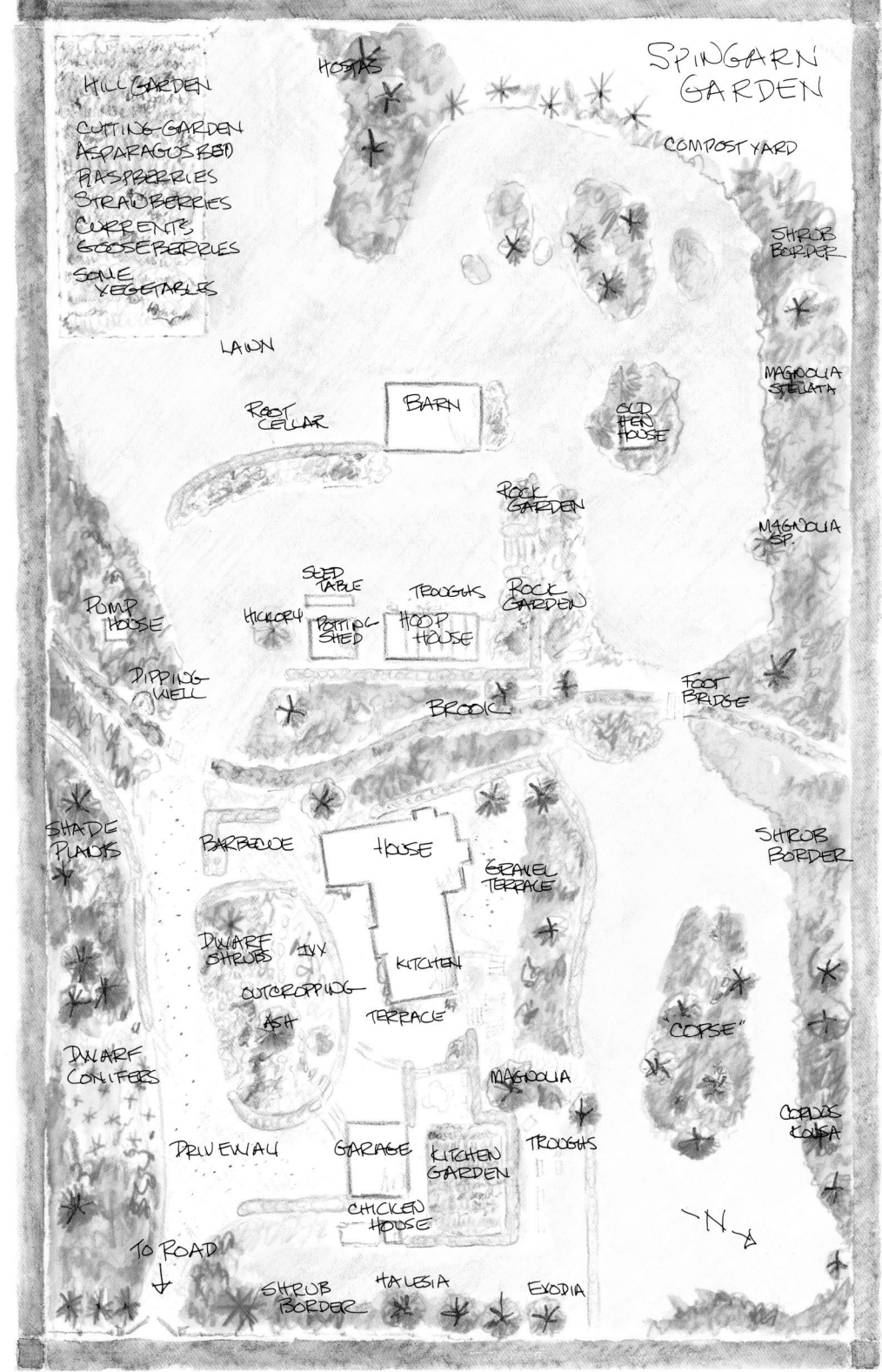

HILL GARDEN

CUTTING GARDEN
ASPARAGUS BED
RASPBERRIES
STRAWBERRIES
CURRENTS
GOOSEBERRIES
SOME VEGETABLES

HOSTAS

SPINGARN GARDEN

COMPOST YARD

SHRUB BORDER

LAWN

ROOT CELLAR

BARN

MAGNOLIA STELLATA

OLD HEN HOUSE

ROCK GARDEN

MAGNOLIA SP.

SEED TABLE

TROUGHS

ROCK GARDEN

PUMP HOUSE

HICKORY

POTTING SHED

HOOP HOUSE

DIPPING WELL

BROOK

FOOT BRIDGE

SHADE PLANTS

BARBEQUE

HOUSE

GRAVEL TERRACE

SHRUB BORDER

DWARF SHRUBS

IVY

KITCHEN

OUTCROPPING

ASH

TERRACE

"COPSE"

DWARF CONIFERS

MAGNOLIA

CORNUS KOUSA

DRIVEWAY

GARAGE

KITCHEN GARDEN

TROUGHS

CHICKEN HOUSE

N

TO ROAD

SHRUB BORDER

HALESIA

EVODIA

ident, continues as a member of the governing board, and has been a recipient of a number of the society's highest awards. As her reputation grew, she was hired to establish and run the rock-garden department of Oliver's Nursery in Fairfield, Connecticut—spreading her gospel further afield.

Ellie grows many of her plants from seed and claims that the North American Rock Garden Society's vast seed list, available to its members,

PREVIOUS PAGES, LEFT: **Most** of the plants in Ellie's walls bloom in spring and early summer, such as the *Aquilegia canadensis.* Yet when plants are not in flower, the tufts of foliage of *Campanula portenschlagiana* or various sedums lend texture and softness to the masses of stone. RIGHT: **The 8-foot-high** retaining wall is 30 feet long. It tapers down to 3 feet at the end. In the middle a door, which leads to a cold cellar, is framed by *Magnolia* 'Ricki' on the left and *Magnolia stellata* on the right.

changed her life. "I have access to a wonderful list, over six thousand different species in 1998." Many on this list, she notes, such as *Campanula piperi* or *Aquilegia scopulorum,* never appear in commerce. Ellie collects and donates seed, about 50 species of both natives and nonnatives in a good year, pointing out that it is this kind of program that pre-

serves plants that are in danger. She is careful to gather seed from American natives, such as *Claytonia virginica, Sanguinaria canadensis, Houstonia caerulea,* and *Aquilegia canadensis,* which are commonly used by other American rock gardeners. Rather than sending the seed to the local society chapter, however, she sends it to other countries, where gardeners are eager for native American plants. As a donor, she can choose 35 different plants from the society's list. Seeds are a minimal fee to members. "These days, I'm trying to taper off. I grow only about two hundred different species—many hundreds of seedlings—per year. What I don't need, I swap or give as gifts, often within the society."

Of course, she cannot resist the lure of stone. More walls? "Well," she admits, "there is one area I never developed," an aesthetic challenge she has grappled with for years, and today a 50-foot-long curved wall—her first—is beginning to take shape. She admits to having almost exhausted her property's rock supply. "I'll be scrounging to get enough stone on these two acres now, but I think I can do it," she says.

"The wall gardens' show here begins in April. Every day something pops into bloom. By mid-May it starts to slow down. By June the rock garden is pretty well finished. Spring is glorious, everything is in bloom. It is a celebration. But I love the garden when it is quieter, more green—all those buns of foliage are beautiful. I can't use a party all the time."

ABOVE: The *Campanula portenschlagiana* that drapes so generously over so many of her walls all came from one plant, purchased from the North American Rock Garden Society in 1964.

ELLIE SPINGARN'S RECOMMENDATIONS FOR WALL PLANTS

BOTANICAL NAME	FLOWER COLOR	BLOOM TIME	HEIGHT AND SPREAD
Aquilegia canadensis	Yellow and red	May–June	10″ by 5″
Arabis alpina	White	April–May	6″ by 12″
Arenaria montana	White	May	4″ by 10″
Armeria caespitosa	Pink	May	2″ by 6″
Asarina procumbens	Creamy white	June–July	3″ by 10″
Asperula gussonii	Flesh pink	May	1″ by 6″
Aubrieta deltoidea and cultivars	Red, pink, purple, lavender	April–May	2″ by 10″
Aurinia saxatilis (formerly *Alyssum saxatile*)	Bright yellow	May	8″ by 12″
Aurinia saxatilis 'Citrina'	Sulphur yellow	May	8″ by 12″
Campanula cochleariifolia	Blue, white	June–July	3″ by 12″
Campanula garganica	Light lavender-blue	June	3″ by 12″
Campanula portenschlagiana	Lavender	June	3″ by 12″
Clematis alpina	Lavender, white	May–June	Vine—plant at top of wall to cascade
Corydalis lutea	Yellow	May–frost	8″ by 12″
Dianthus caesius	Pink	June	6″ by 12″
Dicentra cucullaria	White	April	5″ by 8″
Draba rigida	Yellow	April	2″ by 6″
Edraianthus pumilio	Lavender	May	2″ by 6″
Erinus alpinus	Lavender, white	May	3″ by 3″
Geranium dalmaticum	Pink	June	5″ by 10″
Globularia cordifolia	Light blue	May–June	2″ by 10″
Gypsophila repens 'Rosea'	Pink	June	4″ by 12″
Helianthemum alpestre	Yellow	June	1″ by 8″
Iberis saxatilis	White	April–May	2″ by 10″
Iberis sempervirens 'Little Gem'	White	April–May	4″ by 10″
Lewisia cotyledon	Pink, salmon, white	May	6″ by 6″
Penstemon pinifolius	Orange, red	July	4″ by 8″
Penstemon rupicola	Cherry red	June–July	3″ by 8″
Phlox subulata 'Laura'	Pink	May	3″ by 12″
Phlox subulata 'Schneewitchen'	White	May	3″ by 12″
Primula auricula var. *alpina*	Yellow	April	6″ by 6″
Primula hirsuta	Deep rose	April	3″ by 5″
Primula marginata	Lavender-blue	April	4″ by 12″
Ptilotrichum spinosum	White, pink	May–June	8″ by 10″
Saponaria ocymoides 'Alba'	White	June	6″ by 12″
Saponaria ocymoides 'Rubra Compacta'	Deep pink	June	2″ by 8″
Saxifraga paniculata	White	May	12″ by 8″
Sedum kamtschaticum	Yellow	May–June	4″ by 6″
Sempervivum, all varieties	Various	June-July	Mat
Thymus × *citriodorus* 'Aureus'	Lilac	July	6″ by 12″
Thymus × *citriodorus* 'Silver Queen'	Lilac	July	6″ by 12″
Veronica prostrata (formerly *V. rupestris*)	White, pink, blue shades	May–June	2″ by 8″

A Well-Chosen Path

BIRMINGHAM, ALABAMA

In 1938 young Louise Agee accompanied her parents to see an overgrown piece of land that they were considering buying in Mountain Brook Township on the southeast side of Birmingham. Louise, already a passionate equestrian, had often ridden by the property on route to the local club; she and her friends had dubbed the site "the jungle." She was surprised, but excited, to hear that the jungle would be her future home.

Fifty years later, in 1988, after her parents had passed away, Louise and her husband, John Wrinkle, an attorney, acquired the two-acre property. Over the years, Louise had remained deeply involved in horseback riding, particularly dressage. But, slowly, she had also developed a penchant for gardening. Then, about 15 years ago, "the plant passion took over." She smiles, "I'm a Johnny-come-lately to horticulture."

Once committed, however, she threw herself into gardening wholeheartedly. Today Latin seems to be Louise's second tongue. "I'm not sure-footed on a lot of taxonomy, but I try to keep up," she modestly states. "The more you know, the more you want to know." A class in plant identification at a local college began a discipline of formal and self-imposed study that is typical of Louise's thorough approach to her

interests. She enrolled in other classes, like Propagation and Greenhouse Management, and accumulated a comprehensive reference library, placing the answers to her questions about culture or nomenclature, plant history or new cultivars at her fingertips.

When the Wrinkles moved to Louise's childhood home, the land was a thicket. Other than fine old trees, the bones of the Sunken Garden that her mother had created close to the house in 1950, and a colorful circle of azaleas, Louise had to create a new garden—in her own fashion.

Clearing debris was the first challenge. In the Valley, as Louise calls the steep slopes that lead down to a stream, fallen trees and brambles demanded removal. The streambed required definition; clogged areas needed cleaning.

One of the most striking elements of the garden Louise still refers to as "the yard" is a seemingly endless warren of paths that undulate through the property in pleasant curvilinear patterns. In laying out the paths, Louise enlisted the advice of landscape architect Norman Kent Johnson, who "came and saw with a fresh eye." Different levels are often reached by stone steps, giving the land a terraced effect.

"There is not much open vista in this garden. My goal was to create a sense of privacy and enclosure primarily by natural means. The paths were laid out to lead around bends and turns, which suits me perfectly. I don't like to see the horizon."

Louise Agee Wrinkle

Louise believes in separating or defining areas in the garden. The more formal spaces—the Forecourt and the Sunken Garden—near the house are edged by brick walls; farther from the house many areas are bordered by lines of trees or groups of shrubs. Some are outlined by a combination of constructed wall and living fence. The Sunken Garden is backed on the west side by a line of hickories behind its pierced brick wall, and on the east by a Belgian fence, an espaliered line of charming, native crab apples (*Malus angustifolia*). Planted on a diagonal when they were mere whips, the ten trees form open, diamond shapes. Clumps of white flowers in spring and half-dollar-size red fruit in fall afford seasonal accents.

PREVIOUS PAGES, LEFT: The subtle, soft gray color and incised pattern of the granite millstone fountain are juxtaposed with a background of spring-flowering Oriental azaleas. RIGHT: A meandering stream bisects the section of Louise Wrinkle's garden called the Valley. Its course determined the design of a system of paths on both sides. THIS PAGE, ABOVE: The miniature tree is an extremely slow growing *Acer palmatum* 'Dissectum', which was a gift from Louise's mother at least 25 years ago. Other than removing dead twigs, Louise has never trimmed it. RIGHT: Rather than a sharp incline to climb, intermittent steps in the paths provide more comfortable access to the succeeding grades. In some cases the stone was found on the property. She turned the broad, old stones into a gentle series of steps that lead down to a roadside collection of ilex. OPPOSITE: A storm-casualty tree, left where it fell in Louise's woodland, became a seat, an example of her preference for simple, naturalistic garden ornament.

Openings in gates or shrub hedges hold the promise of different gardens, some of broad view, others of unexpected enclosure. Through an opening at one end of the wall of the Sunken Garden, raised beds of the Cutting Garden can be seen. Its opposite opening leads to a newly refurbished kitchen-and-herb garden, with two raised beds set in diamond-shaped wood forms. Louise repeated the diamond pattern created by the crab apples, but on a different scale and on a horizontal, rather than a vertical, plane.

In designing her garden, besides the repetition of shapes, the understated planting designs, and a smooth flow between gardens, Louise has sought to create a sense of isolation in her increasingly populated, suburban section of Birmingham. Taking a cue from the sound of the stream, she realized that the music of a water feature would help filter out the noise of the ever more traveled road. In the Forecourt she installed a recirculating fountain that runs con-

Besides the access they provide to a range of grades, the paths are laid out with aesthetics in mind. Steep paths on many levels present a washout problem during storms, when heavy rains can instantly produce a destructive torrent of water. Following a number of revisions—wood chips tended to wash downhill and broke down rapidly—Louise has settled on river gravel with a component called Stabilizer mixed in for surfacing the paths. After a few rains, the paths' surfaces have become as "solid as cement." Catch basins have also been built, and miniature stone culverts have been laid across the paths to create breaks in the downward run of the water.

stantly. Elsewhere a newly devised water feature made of a granite millstone is centered in a triangle where three paths converge. It trickles so slowly, so silently, that the water's flow is almost imperceptible, and its location, partially sunk in the ground, is both a surprise and an exercise in restraint.

Ornaments and benches are made from a range of materials and are resolutely discreet. In the Sunken Garden a bench was formed of native Oneonta stone. Louise reports, "It took three tries to get it right." Each time it was made simpler, until it is now "just three flat pieces of stone in the shape of a seat." Above it hangs a cast tortoise shell, the result of a search "for a natural subject." A three-foot-wide clamshell acts as a container for a bromeliad (*Tillandsia*) collection. She notes that a friend recently observed, "Louise, you are nothing but a minimalist."

Because the property was a natural woodland, Louise has kept that spirit in the garden, seeking native plants. Many native azaleas grew on the property, and Louise moves them

ABOVE: In 1967, to celebrate Louise's parents' 40th wedding anniversary, each of their friends presented them with a white or coral azalea, which was planted around a circular terrace. The Circle Garden is a memorial to that romantic event. LEFT: A Belgian fence of native crab apples separates the driveway and courtyard from the Sunken Garden. Acting like a see-through screen, it both defines the boundary of each space and permits open, airy views from either side.

at will, tagging the plants with surveyor's tape to indicate which are the next to march. Then 8 to 12 months ahead of the move, she root-prunes each shrub by spading a circle around its drip line, which stimulates it to make new feeder roots inside the root ball. This technique both makes it easier to dig up the plant and minimizes stress to it.

As Louise became more committed to gardening, she discovered that certain plant families particularly attracted her. She specifically cites the Ranunculaceae, or buttercup family, as a favorite candidate for both study and collecting. She points out the abundance of garden-worthy plants in the family: anemone, cimicifuga, clematis, columbine, delphinium, hellebore, monkshood, thalictrum. "I enjoy studying their relationships, such as comparing the spurs on the flower parts of columbine, delphinium, and monkshood or the leaf shape and color of columbine and thalictrum. This kind of study inspires a close look at plants." She laughs, "Which, of course, means adding new discoveries. I'll run out of room before I run out of ranunculi."

FAR LEFT: **One course of paths leads across the stream via a rustic bridge, with the return over a large, flat, single piece of stone. Scores of native azaleas— the magical, golden apricot–blossomed** Rhododendron austrinum **and the pink-flowered Piedmont azalea (**R. canescens**)—infuse the property with perfume during the month of April. These natives have "graceful growth habits." Here** R. austrinium **is paired with wild blue phlox (**Phlox divaricata**) and Japanese roof iris (**Iris tectorum**).** LEFT: **Stone retaining walls were built to define the stream where needed along the edges. The effect is natural looking, but Louise notes, half jokingly, "While the stones are not man-made, they are man-laid."**

A second family, the ilex or holly family (Aquifoliaceae), has also become a focus of her collecting. Always organized, Louise keeps an up-to-date list of her plants on her computer, where 31 different cultivars of hollies, both evergreen and deciduous, are recorded. One fine example, happily growing in the Forecourt, is *Ilex aquifolium* 'Aureomarginata', which Louise grew from a cutting that had been a gift from a gardening friend. Other choices include *I. cornuta* × *latifolia* 'Emily Brunner', *I. decidua*, *I. pedunculosa*, and many cultivars of *I. verticillata*. While hollies are sited as specimen plants throughout her garden, she has also used them as dividers. One large congregation of primarily evergreen ilex (*I.* × *attenuata* 'Foster #2', *I.* × *a.* 'Savannah', and *I.* × 'Mary Nell') is planted next to the road, forming a dense buffer against traffic. Another group of *I. verticillata* 'Winter Red' and *I.* 'Sparkleberry' slows traffic along the road with its brilliant display of fall fruit.

The native oakleaf hydrangea (*Hydrangea quercifolia*) self-seeds throughout the garden, thrusting its silver-gray foliage in every direction. Louise points to two recent selections, 'Snowflake' and 'Harmony', as having particularly "thick and heavy" blossom heads. "And I am always planting dogwoods." Louise tries to save all dogwood seedlings that are straight species. She observes that they are more graceful than the hybrids, such as 'Cherokee Chief', that are generally available for purchase at nurseries.

The only statue, of Saint Fiacre, the patron saint of gardeners, stands on a stone base against a glossy green background of holly. "On the highest point of the land, he overlooks the garden. He stands there observing everything that goes on." Louise thinks a minute, then continues. "And he is unobtrusive. I like things to be unobtrusive."

Louise's curiosity continues unabated and has led her to investigate topics as diverse as the Asian counterparts to American native perennials, shrubs, and trees. For example, she has experimented with *Illicium anisatum*, the Japanese correlative to the Florida anise tree (*I. floridanum*). She has sought out *Pieris japonica*, as well as growing *P. phyllireifolia*, *Chionanthus retusus*, and *C. virginicus*. She notes that native plants and their Oriental counterparts may flower at different times, like the dainty white bells on the Oriental variegated Solomon's seal, which appear about two weeks earlier than the blooms of the American great Solomon's seal. About rare plants, Louise says, "I'm not too keen on having something that no one else can grow, just for the sake of having it. However, I do like to try new things. Sometimes they surprise me and really work." As she acquires plants, often grown from cuttings or seed, she deposits those that need extra care in her cold frame. The frame, 4 feet deep and 16 feet long, sits above the ground and is topped with a series of aluminum-edged glass shower doors, which are lightweight and easy to move—an innovative alternative to the traditional glass top. Louise does not have a greenhouse. "It's the last thing I need," she claims. "We have such a long growing season here, I need a little rest in December."

Throughout the evolution of her garden, Louise has kept up the ongoing tree-planting program she initiated when she first came to the property. The trees' sculptural shapes echo the gently winding paths. Redbuds have become favorites, and both the purple-leaved *Cercis canadensis* 'Forest Pansy' and the white-flowering *C. reniformis* 'Alba' are recent additions. The variegated *Cornus sericea* 'Green and Gold' stands in an open swath, carved by a storm and dubbed Tornado Alley. The sourwood (*Oxydendron arboreum*), while difficult to transplant, is one of the finest year-round ornamental trees, offering graceful flower panicles in summer and brilliant red color in the fall.

New plants that are just becoming established get a boost from a low-nitrogen fertilizer, sometimes as drastic as 0-14-14. Given no excess nitrogen but plenty of phosphorus and potash, a plant will gain good root structure but not much top

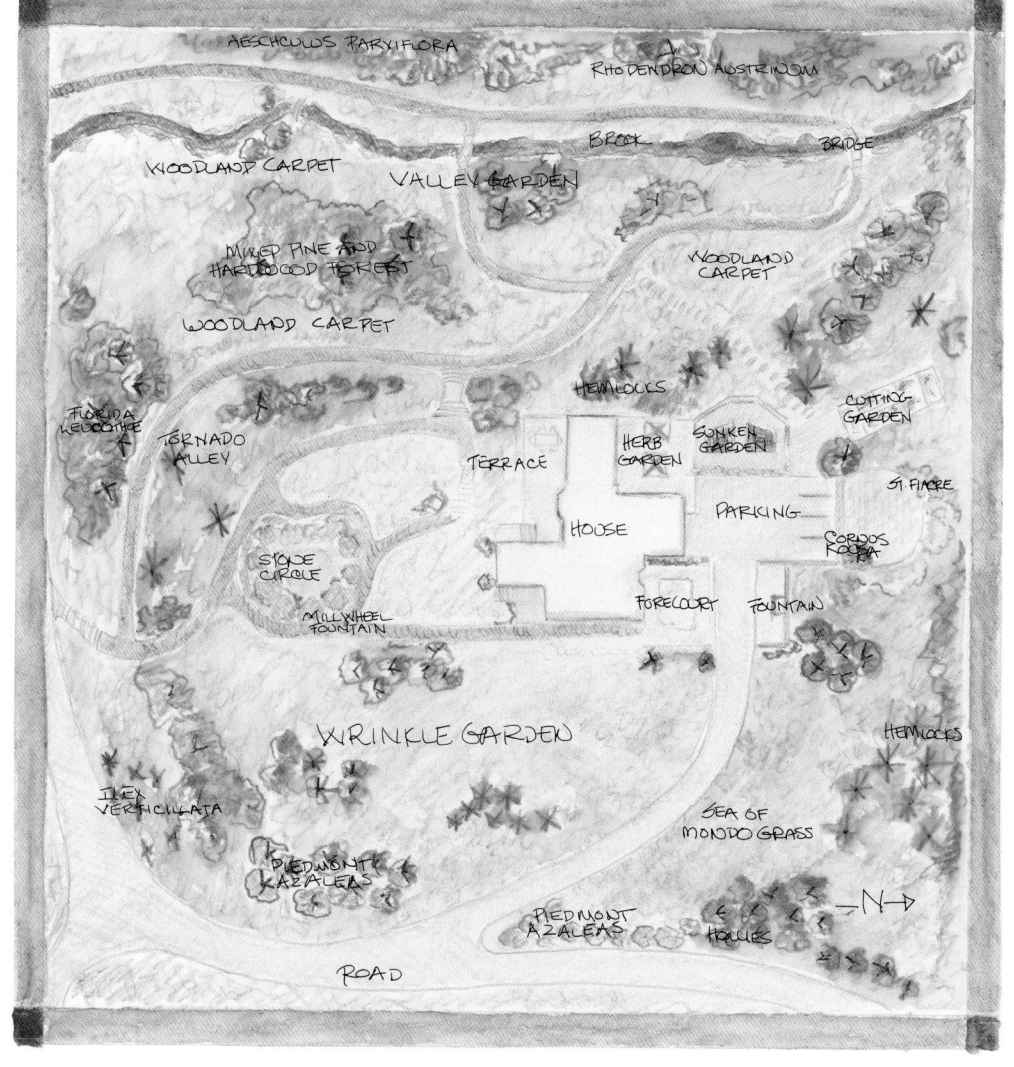

growth for a year or so. Louise recalls a Swiss landscape designer who always made a circle of raw sawdust around the drip line of a new tree. The sawdust ties up nitrogen until it decomposes. Sometimes that causes the leaves to turn yellow, but the roots are hard at work gaining strength that will hold them in good stead for the rest of their lives. "The things you learn from other people, things that have worked for them, those are often the most valuable lessons of all."

While there are a number of single specimens on the property, especially trees, Louise prefers generous plantings. "Don't just dibble and dabble; make a statement," she urges. She points to a large waves of Solomon's seal, amsonia, and native azaleas beside the road that make "a bold statement." She refers to Russell Page, who wryly observed that there are 60-mile-an-hour plants, 40-mile-an-hour plants, and 20-mile-an-hour plants. "Here I need forties," she says.

Storms, heat, and drought can be cruel to gardens in Zone 7b Alabama. A problem in classifying plants according to hardiness zones, Louise notes, is that the USDA and Arnold Arboretum systems are based on cold hardiness, not heat tolerance. "We have so many hot nights and suffer from high humidity. Fortunately, a revised system based on those climatic factors has been newly developed by the American Horticultural Society, which will help gardeners make more educated decisions about choices of plants." To aid her plants through the blistering weather, she installed a 20-zone underground sprinkler system that can be programmed at different increments to compensate for the 100-degree-plus temperatures or lack of rain.

Despite such automated assistance, Louise tends to her garden's needs daily. She generally begins the morning with a walk through the garden to see what tasks need to be done. Along the way, she prunes, picks up fallen branches, and places small colored flags to indicate where a more extensive job is needed or where a new plant will go.

These tasks she balances against the demands of her other horticultural responsibilities, whether they be at the local Birmingham Botanical Garden, serving on the national Publications and Horticulture Committees of the Garden Club of America, judging at horticulture shows, or traveling to attend a board meeting of the Garden Conservancy.

Musing about what her commitment to gardening has given her, Louise says, "It has introduced me to a lot of friends and plants. I don't know which to put first—perhaps I should just equate them."

Over the last ten years, Louise has assembled a broad palette of woodland plants. Growing in clusters and swaths on the slopes of her garden, the plants create a pattern that rivals the most intricate of Persian carpets.
CLOCKWISE, FROM TOP RIGHT: *Narcissus jonquilla 'Simplex'; Trillium cuneatum; Phlox divaricata; Tiarella wherryi; Anemonella thalictroides; Cypripedium calceolus; Helleborus orientalis; Zephranthes atamasco; Asarum arifolium.*

WOODLAND CARPET PLANT LIST
MAXIMUM HEIGHT OF BLOOM 18 INCHES

NATIVE PLANTS

BOTANICAL NAME	COMMON NAME	FLOWER COLOR	HEIGHT
Anemonella thalictroides ***	Rue anemone	White to pale pink	4″
Aquilegia canadensis	American columbine	Red and yellow	Bloom 12–15″, leaves 6″
Arisaema triphyllum ***	Jack-in-the-pulpit	Green and cream (red berry)	18″
Asarum arifolium **	Heartleaf, evergreen wild ginger	Brownish purple	5″
Asarum canadense *	Wild ginger	Brownish purple	4″
Asarum shuttleworthii **	Shuttleworth ginger	Mottled, violet inside	3″
Chrysogonum virginianum	Green and gold, golden star	Yellow	3″
Decumaria barbara	Climbing hydrangea	White	3″; up to 30′ as vine
Dentaria diphylla ****	Toothwort	White	Bloom 5″, leaves 3″
Erythronium americanum ***	Trout lily, common fawn lily	Yellow	9″
Galax urceolata **	Galax, wandflower, coltsfoot	White	Bloom 8″, leaves 4″
Gaultheria procumbens **	Wintergreen	White (red berry)	3″
Hepatica americana **	Round-leaved hepatica, liverleaf	Lavender-blue to white	4″
Heuchera americana	American alumroot	Greenish yellow	12″
Iris cristata ***	Crested iris	Yellow dotted, lilac, blue	4″
Iris cristata 'Alba' ***	White crested iris	White	4″
Mitchella repens **	Partridgeberry	White (red berry)	1″
Pachysandra procumbens	Allegheny spurge	Cream	5″
Phlox divaricata ***	Wild blue phlox	Blue	Bloom 8″, leaves 4″
Phlox divaricata var. 'Fuller's White' ***	Wild phlox, white form	White	Bloom 8″, leaves 4″
Podophyllum peltatum ***	Mayapple	White	12–15″
Polemonium reptans	Jacob's ladder	Lavender-blue	9–12″
Sanguinaria canadensis ***	Bloodroot	White	6″
Shortia galacifolia **	Oconee bells	White	Bloom 6″, leaves 3″
Tiarella cordifolia var. *cellina* ***	Foamflower	White, pinkish	Bloom 9″, leaves 4″
Tradescantia virginiana	Spiderwort	Blue, purple, white	12″
Trillium catesbaei ***	Catesby's trillium	White, fading to pink	8″
Trillium cernuum ***	Nodding trillium	White	12–15″
Trillium cuneatum ***	Whippoorwill flower	Brownish purple	4–18″
Trillium grandiflorum ***	Great white trillium	White, fading to pink	8″
Trillium luteum ***	Yellow trillium	Yellow	10″
Trillium pusillum ***	Least trillium	White-pink	4–8″
Vaccinium crassifolium 'Well's Delight' **	Creeping blueberry	Pink	3″
Vaccinium macrocarpon **	American cranberry	Pink	3″
Zephyranthes atamasco	Atamasco lily	White	8–12″

NONNATIVE PLANTS

BOTANICAL NAME	COMMON NAME	FLOWER COLOR	HEIGHT
Arum italicum ****	Italian arum	Cream (red berry)	8″
Cyclamen hederifolium	Hardy cyclamen	Rose-pink to white	Bloom 4–5″, leaves 2″
Helleborus foetidus **	Bear's foot hellebore	Pale green	15–18″
Helleborus orientalis **	Lenten rose	Cream	12–15″
Helleborus viridis	Deciduous hellebore	Pale green	8″
Iris tectorum 'Alba'	Japanese roof iris	White	6–8″
Vaccinium oxycoccos **	Creeping cranberry	Pink	3″

FERNS

BOTANICAL NAME	COMMON NAME	HEIGHT
Adiantum capillus-veneris	Southern maidenhair fern (native)	6–8″
Adiantum pedatum	Northern maidenhair fern (native)	15–18″
Asplenium platyneuron	Ebony spleenwort (native)	8–12″
Athyrium nipponicum 'Pictum'	Japanese painted fern (nonnative)	6–8″
Polystichum acrostichoides	Christmas fern (native)	15–18″

* May be invasive   ** Evergreen   *** Spring ephemeral; plant disappears in summer   ****Green in winter, dormant in summer

"I like a garden where everything is revealed slowly. As I walk around my garden,

I want to feel enveloped by plants. I like to feel enclosed,

to wander through pathways, and take in a garden plant by plant."

Molly McGuire Grothaus

Microclimate Management

MOLLY McGUIRE GROTHAUS

LAKE OSWEGO, OREGON

Three thousand different plants inhabit Molly Grothaus's garden. Over 40 years, she has collected, propagated, hybridized, and created several discreet gardens: from a woodland to a rock garden, from a perennial shade garden to a scree. "It is amazing the number of microclimates that exist on this small piece of land," she marvels.

The garden covers just one and a half acres, although the Grothauses own an additional acre, which has remained a meadow. On the land's highest point, with a view directly toward Mount Hood—"usually not visible when guests arrive"—Molly and her husband, Louis, a land appraiser for the Transportation Department, built their house. "We built it with our own hands. It was not by choice, it was by eco-nomic necessity. Would anyone choose to do such a thing?"

The couple moved to Portland, Molly's hometown, after spending the first four years of their marriage in California. They'd met when both were students at Stanford. Their first child, a daughter, was born while they lived in California; the second, a son, soon after returning to Portland. (The third, a daughter, now a landscape architect, arrived ten years later.) Renting a "little house" in the southeast section of Portland, the Grothauses began a land hunt. "We looked and looked. On an excursion to nearby Mount Sylvania, we thought we saw a sign, the size of a postage stamp, on this land. The sign had just been put up that day."

Pleased with the lay of the land and its prospects, they

took a six-month option and then finalized the purchase. "We worked on the house every weekend. In a year and a half the only days we took off were Thanksgiving and Christmas. It was really camping out. And I don't recommend it to anyone." In 1952, two years from the time they

broke ground, the Grothauses moved into their home, yet unfinished. "I was dying to have a garden," Molly recalls, noting that the one-floor house had been sited to be at the center of a garden. "We built the greenhouse before we had any living room furniture." Molly's mother was a gardener, so perhaps it was natural that Molly should turn to the earth, but her style is distinctly her own. Eschewing the formality of her mother's generation, Molly decided to make a more informal garden, in which the design would be shaped by catering to plants' specific needs.

The Grothauses joined societies such as the Royal Hor-

PREVIOUS PAGE: **Radiating out on either side of her stone steps, Molly Grothaus has planted shrubs—azaleas,** *Chamaecyparis thyoides* **'Andelyensis',** *C. obtusa* **'Nana',** *Spirea betulifolia* var. *aemiliana,* **and a Japanese maple— which seem to protect smaller plants such as dianthus, geraniums, sempervivens, and saxifrages.** ABOVE: **On the woodland paths, Molly and husband Louis replenish the chipped bark every few years. The seven trunks of an upright** *Pinus mugo* **developed naturally. Molly plants ground** covers, like *Geranium endressii* 'Wargrave Pink', in masses along the paths. RIGHT: *Rhododendron* 'Julia Grothaus' has "an oxblood throat in bud that opens to peach with a ruffled white edge." OPPOSITE: Even on this east-facing bank, there are different microclimates, such as on opposite sides of a nose-shaped rock. "Plants suffer as much as people from windchill. We are in Zone 8, but when the winds roar through the Columbia River Gorge, we get arctic weather from Canada."

ticultural Society, the American Rhododendron Society, the Alpine Garden Society of Great Britain, and the Scottish Rock Garden Club. "I was here in considerable isolation with two little children, and no other adult to talk to all day," she says. "I had to think of something to occupy my mind that wouldn't cost any money. I settled on botany." The membership fees absorbed the couple's spending money. "Well worth every penny," Molly continues. "The societies all had excellent newsletters; I learned a great deal from them. And the seed exchanges are invaluable." Over the years, often through the societies' networks, Molly has also made friends with collectors around the world, exchanging seeds—and plant news. A charter member of the Native Plant Society of Oregon, Molly was one of its first presidents. In 1972 she started the local chapter of the North American Rock Garden Society: the Columbia-Willamette Chapter.

The sloped rock garden, which now measures 10 feet high and 120 feet long, was the first garden to take shape— by necessity. The bank in front of the house was in danger of washing away. First, the Grothauses poured a concrete foun-

dation and then imported rocks to hold it in place. Louis built sandstone steps on a gentle curve leading from the driveway up the bank to a small patch of lawn. "My husband has always had a great eye for shape and form." On this rocky incline with its excellent drainage, Molly began a collection of alpine plants that, over the years, has grown to include the present inhabitants: *Penstemon hirsutus, Scutellaria alpina* 'Alba', and *Geranium cinereum* var. *subcaulescens.* Always celebrating diversity, Molly says, "Rock garden plants are wonderful; they cover the whole range of plants. So many can be grown in a small space." Giving the garden a unique character of shape and texture, Molly integrated numerous small shrubs, including azaleas and rhododendrons.

Flowering shrubs—and trees—are the cornerstones of the Grothaus garden. Molly points out that the Pacific Northwest is Rhododendron Country. "They love it here. Most gardeners end up specializing in what likes them." A collec-

tion of rhododendrons—the Grothauses have over 400 varieties, many of them species plants—can be planned so a garden can have almost year-round bloom, from October to August, Molly says. "I guess that just leaves out September. Well, there are some slow periods in July, too, until the species *auriculatum* blooms in August."

Both Molly and Louis have been collectors of rhododendrons and azaleas almost from the beginning. Many have been grown from seed collected from sources around the world, especially the Himalaya, "the epicenter" for rhododendrons. "They have been a passions of ours, particularly species." Both have been active in the American Rhododendron Society, with Molly acting as editor of its newsletter for six years, and the Rhododendron Species Foundation. For 13 years Louis was the volunteer chairman of the Chrystal Spring Rhododendron Garden in Portland. To honor the Grothauses' achievements, H. H. Davidian, the now-retired taxonomist of the Edinburgh Botanic Garden, named *Rhododendron grothausii* for them. "I guess it was a thank-you on behalf of rhododendrons," Molly says with a smile.

Both have worked at hybridizing, which Molly says is almost too easy. About 30 of the hundreds of rhododendrons she has hybridized still grace her garden; most are unnamed and unregistered, with the exception of one bred for flat-shaped flowers, a plant habit appropriate for small gardens, and apricot flowers—her favorite color. The result, a distinctive, graceful plant answering her criteria, was named 'Julia Grothaus' for her younger daughter and won an Award of Excellence from the American Rhododendron Society in 1988. "Registering rhododendrons means plugging them," Molly remarks. "It's a little like promoting champion dogs, and we've simply never been interested in that."

LEFT: Two of Molly's unnamed but carefully numbered rhododendron hybrids form a bower of bloom in the lower garden. RIGHT: An apricot-colored bearded iris bred by Molly accents one of the perennial borders. "It remains unnamed, but I keep it for sentimental reasons."

When it comes to plants, however, Molly admits to having a fair amount of patience—and sentiment, too. "Many plants have stories." As a little girl, she played in a neighbor's birch grove, which was underplanted with daffodils. "I knew I wanted to duplicate that feeling here." One of her first projects was to install a cluster of five birch trees just to the north of the house. "I spent a good deal of time placing them, so their relationship changes as I move around them." The native birches' diameter now measure 18 inches. She

also brought favorite plants from her mother's garden to her own, including root cuttings from herbaceous peonies. Molly's mother had planted the peonies in the 1920s, and Molly has been able to identify them by going through her mother's old purchase records. "I also rescued little prunings of snowball bush [*Viburnum opulus* 'Snowball'] that were growing on Mother's compost pile and started them here.

"You have to get to know a plant to know where to put it. You have to listen to what a plant wants done," she says, then adds philosophically, "I try to provide the best habitat that I possibly can. On a summer day there can easily be a thirty-degree difference between the rock garden and the shady side of the house. In winter, the lower garden may be twenty degrees colder than the more protected back garden." These differences are always a consideration when selecting a plant's home. "I will try a plant in two or three

A yellow-and-orange-themed perennial bed in the lower garden is surrounded by rhododendrons, creating a lavish background for the smaller geums, irises, daylilies, salvias, and grasses. Molly credits the rhododendrons' prolific bloom to "humus, humus, humus, and sand. They like rich food and a well-drained location."

different locations. We've moved big rhododendrons around as though they were born on wheels. If you move them at the right time of the year—early spring—it's easy." To accommodate a growing number of woody plants, the Grothauses expanded toward their meadow. The "lower garden" covers only three quarters of an acre, but the warren of maze-like paths belies its size.

Rhododendrons and azaleas dominate the densely planted population of the lower garden, but often they are set off by other choice specimens, a dove tree (*Davidia involucrata*) and *Pieris japonica* 'Valentine Valley'. "The *Stewartia malacodendron*—it has yellow flowers with a purple center, with purple bleeding into the petals—is just about my favorite. However," Molly adds, "it is pretty hard to beat the bark on a *Stewartia pseudocamellia*." An enkianthus (*Enkianthus campanulatus*), grown from seed she ordered from

India that she saw in the journal of the Royal Horticultural Society, is now 40 years old.

Partial to plants with year-round interest, Molly points to a 25-year-old, 15-foot-high *Viburnum plicatum* var. *tomentosum* 'Pink Beauty'. "It blooms in the spring and then again in the fall; its berries are red." *Viburnum hartwiggeii*, grown from seed from the RHS seed exchange many years ago, "is a glorious red in the fall and produces huge clusters of berries, which the birds leave alone. It is extremely decorative, and I have never seen its name printed anywhere since." Harry Lauder's walking stick (*Corylus avellana* 'Contorta') drips showy, yellow catkins, from twisted branches, while other plants are resting. "And years ago, a nurseryman gave us half a dozen unnamed Japanese maples, which we have placed around the garden. The one at the fence opening turns a beautiful apricot color in the fall." In the spring the foliage is a russet, so full and rounded it might be the velvet cape worn by a magician.

The plants, now in maturity, form high, dense walls, gently curving like those of an old castle. Often, when the breezes blow the leaves in the upper gardens, the occupants here stand perfectly still.

Gradually, Molly has integrated perennial borders with specific color themes into the lower garden. More open to the sky, they provide visual relief from the otherwise dense planting. A peach-and-apricot bed includes *Astilbe* × *arendsii* 'Salmon Queen', apricot-colored *Hemerocallis* 'Ruffled Apricot', *H.* 'Little Bee', and *H.* 'Mary Molevan'. A yellow-and-orange border contains anthemis, *Carex stricta* 'Bowles' Golden', *Geum elatum* 'Fire Opal', and *Coreopsis verticillata* 'Grandiflora'. A pink-and-purple border has *Malva moschata* and "nice small hemerocallis" 'Pink Prelude', 'Little Missy', and 'Little Lassie'. Within each border, Molly uses blues and lavenders—'Johnson's Blue' geranium, aquilegias, *Aster novibelgii* 'Blue Carpet', and Siberian irises—to "provide accents." Bearded irises bloom in most of the borders, remnants of another of her passions.

Many of Molly's plants have been started from seed in her

The design of pathways is crucial to the way Molly wants her garden to be experienced. Different areas are linked by winding paths, revealing only portions of the garden at a time. Often the path will lead straight to a specimen plant, then divide to skirt the plant, allowing it to be seen from all sides. Steps of stone or concrete lead up and down the steeper inclines, such as these through an azalea garden next to the house. In the foreground satsuki hybrid azaleas 'Amagasa' and 'Higasa' mingle at the path's edge. The tightly formed *Abies balsamea* 'Nana' provides an intense green accent on the right and invites inspection. Molly thinks that curved paths suggest that the viewer pause and look closely at plants. Wide paths, such as those dividing two perennial borders on the other side of the house, may be made of turf, which is soft underfoot.

world is to walk into a greenhouse and inhale plant breath—it's a wonderful smell." In recent years the greenhouse has become primarily a small bulb house. During the first six months of the year "something is happening every day."

For bulbs, proper watering is a crucial part of their schedule. "You need to watch them. When they are coming up, you must give them water; when they're going dormant, gradually dry them off." Molly also says that growing small plants, such as a congregation of 14 different species of cyclamen, at bench height allows her to really appreciate their beauty—and the variety within one genus.

In front of the greenhouse, the scree was formed 15 years ago when Molly ordered a truckload of gravel and had it dumped in the middle of the open space. She installs plants into the scree complete with the soil from their pots, but the mound of gravel, spread out a little, remains essentially the way it was deposited. It is home to rock garden plants such as *Globularia repens*, with its blue pincushion head; saxifrages; *Daphne cneorum*; and *Kalmiopsis leachiana*, a low, evergreen shrub with clear pink flowers. Gathered, too, are the "hard-to-grow triumphs": *Petrophytum caespitosum*, *P. cinerascens*, and *P. hendersonii*, all of which have little bottlebrush flowers and are native to the western mountains. These plants appreciate rapid and complete drainage. The scree is another microclimate, Molly explains. Even in that small area, the snow melts three days faster on the south "slope"—which is only six feet away—than on the north.

Molly has repeatedly propped an old wisteria, which no longer has a middle. "It is tied to a pipe, which holds it against falling over. I like the way it seems to be sitting on its knees," she remarks.

"This is a real hands-on garden. We have done it ourselves. Well," she concedes, "twice recently, we had a man

greenhouse and nurtured in nursery beds on the western border of the property. The area is divided from the main house and garden by a living wall, which is not planted so densely that an intriguing view of the greenhouse cannot be seen through the foliage. The work area also includes a lath house, tiers of flue tiles planted with bulbs and alpines, a vegetable and berry garden, a scree, and a peat bed.

The 12- by 18-foot greenhouse has progressed through a number of incarnations from alpine house to cactus habitat, but it has always housed seedlings. "I usually have about a hundred and fifty going at a time." The greenhouse is her first stop each morning as she examines new blooms and checks the seedlings. "I think one of the nicest things in the come in and mow the grass. And on occasion, when we were away, we had a high school student water the greenhouse. But that's it for hired help—we've done the rest." She thinks a moment. "I guess I was blessed with energy."

Molly keeps track of her plants and their sources on a computer. Whenever a new plant comes into the garden, she makes a note and leaves it beside the computer, reminding her to enter pertinent information, including the plant's location, the next time she "fires the machine up." Now an inch thick in printout, the record is an invaluable resource—a history of the plants in her garden.

The diversity of expertise that is a hallmark of Molly's gardening, plus her commitment to horticultural preservation, has thrust her into a leadership role in local gardening circles. With a group of other dedicated gardeners, Molly was instrumental in the organization of the Berry Botanic Garden in 1978, a species garden of shrubs, trees, and perennials, and has served as both its president and and member of its board. Begun in 1938, it is the site of a collection assembled by Rae Selling Berry, who was dedicated to protecting species plants, particularly primulas, alpine plants, rhododendrons, lilies, and other natives. Species plants, Molly says, "have a provenance, an identity. You can go someplace in the world and see them growing in their natural habitats."

The Berry Botanic Garden is now the home of the Seed Bank for Rare and Endangered Species of the Pacific Northwest, established in 1983 with more than 2,500 accessions. Besides collaborating with other botanical gardens and arboretums, the bank works in conjunction with the United States Forest Service and the United States Bureau of Land Management. The seeds are dehydrated, to reduce the water content, and then frozen. "No one really knows the length of time seeds will be viable in storage, because it just hasn't been done before. But it is an effort toward the saving of plants; keeping them from going extinct." The first of its kind in the region, the seed bank was Molly's idea.

Completing a circuit of her garden, Molly passes through a narrow opening between two rhododendrons, poised like columns of flowers decorating the sides of a doorway. Both, in complementary shades of peach and pink, are her own hybrids. "I planned this garden to have points of interest along the way, like lures to pull you around a corner. Then, unexpectedly you see the next point of interest. It is cozy that way. Seeing it little by little, I can always enjoy the surprises."

CLOCKWISE, FROM TOP RIGHT:
Tulipa batalinii 'Bright Gem'; *Phlox bifida*, *Veronica orientalis* ssp. *orientalis*, *Gentiana acaulis*; *Fritillaria acmopetala*; *Sternbergia lutea*; *Tulipa urumiensis*; *Tulipa vvedenskyi*; *Dianthus* 'La Bour Boule'.

MOLLY GROTHAUS'S FLUE TILE GARDEN

were submerged in the ground. In a "terrible winter" Molly unrolls black plastic over the tiles, like a blanket, holding it down with 2x4s to keep it from blowing away. Trying to leave it as cover for only two weeks at a time, she removes the plastic as soon as the weather moderates.

TULIPS IN FLUE TILE GARDEN

Tulipa altaica
Tulipa batalinii
Tulipa biflora
Tulipa cretica
Tulipa hageri 'Splendens'
Tulipa humulis
Tulipa kolpakowskiana
Tulipa maximowiczii
Tulipa mogoltavica
Tulipa montana
Tulipa orphanidea
Tulipa persica
Tulipa pulchella 'Odalisque'
Tulipa sosnowskii
Tulipa systola
Tulipa tarda
Tulipa turkestanica
Tulipa undulatifolia
Tulipa vvedenskyi

FRITILLARIAS IN FLUE TILE GARDEN

Fritillaria acmopetala
Fritillaria biflora
Fritillaria corsicus
Fritillaria davisii
Fritillaria graeca ssp. *ionica*
Fritillaria graeca ssp. *thessala*
Fritillaria hispanica
Fritillaria involucrata
Fritillaria messanensis ssp. *gracilis*
Fritillaria montana
Fritillaria pallidiflora
Fritillaria pluriflora
Fritillaria pyrenaica
Fritillaria ruthenica
Fritillaria tenella
Fritillaria tubaeformis

One day Molly's husband came home with a flue tile, "a second," wondering if Molly might find a use for it. "The tiles were a bargain," she says, and she bought 114 of them, which she lined up in seven tiers just outside the greenhouse.

The tiles, used in the construction industry for lining chimneys, measure 16 by 12 inches by 12 inches in height. Molly filled each with at least three inches of gravel. "The beauty of the system is that you can vary the planting medium in each tile." Some were placed in filtered shade, some in full sun.

Generally, Molly clusters plants in groups, designating certain sections for particular types of plants. For example, she duplicates the dry, hot conditions of Southeast Asia for 19 different species tulips and over 16 small species fritillarias. Each is planted in a group of 5 to 20 bulbs of the same species. Small lilies, such as *Lilium oxypetalum* var. *insigne* or *L. sherriffiae,* which require more humus and watering on a year-round basis, are at home in another section.

The front row of tiles is deliberately planted with alpine plants: *Veronica orientalis* ssp. *orientalis, Genista pilosa* 'Vancouver Gold', *Phlox bifida* 'Betty Blake', *P.* 'Crackerjack', and *Gentiana angustifolia.* Most are evergreen, to ensure ongoing interest and to camouflage against ripening bulb foliage. "Bulbs going dormant," Molly warns, "are not pretty."

Other bulbs growing in the tiles are *Chionodoxa siehei, Colchicum kesselringii, C. corsicum, Crocus medius, C. pulchellus, C. serotinus* ssp. *clusii, Muscari aucheri, M. comosum, M. latifolium, M. leucostemon,* and *Sternbergia lutea.* Many of the bulbs were "explorer seed collected."

The flue tile system, which gains a patina like terra-cotta over time, can be adapted to a range of plants. It is particularly good for plants that like rapid drainage, which is why Molly's concentration is bulbs and alpines. "It's like a great big collection of pots, but not as exposed." The "down side" of the system is that the raised nature of the tiles exposes plants to more cold than if they

A Process of Selection

POLLY HILL

NORTH TISBURY, MARTHA'S VINEYARD, MASSACHUSETTS

"My daughter, Louisa—she's a crab apple and an azalea," Polly Hill smiles, referring to plant introductions that she has named after her daughter. Her sons, husband, and grandchildren are immortalized in the plant world as well. Over the 40 years since Polly began growing and selecting ornamental trees and shrubs in the extraordinary arboretum she has created at Barnard's Inn Farm, she has registered more than 75 plants, many of which have been introduced into the nursery trade. Quite a record for a woman who has never run a commercial enterprise. In fact, she has never sold a plant.

Polly Hill's parents, Margaret Keen and Howard Butcher, Jr., bought the flat, 47-acre parcel in the middle of Martha's Vineyard in 1927 as the family's summer retreat. Over time, Polly's mother restored the "derelict" buildings, turning the knot of weathered buildings into a classic, understated Vineyard farm. Polly's parents instilled in their six children a love of their land and of the tiny island. Traditions, set by farmers and seafarers, give the Vineyard its timeless, natural character. Residents adhere to unspoken rules with religious fervor. Woe to the interloper who does not respect the code. "The land," Polly observes, "should stay the way it is."

"Mother was a natural architect. And she was a collector. She loved antiques." Polly remembers, "She was a wonderful housekeeper, and she made the place comfortable for us." But she was not a gardener. In fact, she really did not want Polly to begin a garden, fearing it would demand extensive care and recognizing limits to what can be accomplished in the Northeast's brief summer months. Little could she know what her daughter would later be able to achieve in the "summer," a season that Polly now prolongs from April to November. Polly's father, however, was always interested in trees. Not as a grower, more as an appreciator. "My father only knew trees' common names, but he loved them," she recalls.

Polly took over the maintenance of the farm after her mother's death in 1957, but she viewed her role as caretaker for her father until he remarked one day, "Have you any idea how lucky you are to have this beautiful land?" From that point on, the place of carefree childhood summers and languid adult vacations became the locus of Polly's passion—and her avocation, as she realized that her fortune was a piece of earth. And, in its "impoverished" soil, her future fame took root. At 50 years of age she undertook an ambitious program

"Time does things. It is part of your outfit. You can't control it,

so you ignore it when you do things on this scale. With plants, you watch and you wait."

Polly Hill

PREVIOUS PAGE: A grassy road divides the *Stewartia koreana* "forest" on the left from a rhododendron bed, which features several Exburys, the lively pink *Rhododendron* 'Cecile', and the more delicate *R.* 'Sugared Almond'. THIS PAGE, ABOVE: Polly Hill created an elegant pleached European hornbeam arbor from 16 *Carpinus betulus* 'Columnaris', a process that took 20 years. Giving the arbor its annual haircut takes a full two weeks. ABOVE RIGHT: The Hill house is a converted cow-and-pig barn transformed by Polly's mother in the 1930s. BELOW RIGHT: On Martha's Vineyard, stone walls are built only one rock deep. Each stone is carefully balanced and secured by another; the effect is sculptural and "lacy," with light falling through the crevices. OPPOSITE: A bower of locust formed into an arch faces a stone wall and the Pine Grove. It provides an inviting, shaded seat. Covered with rich purple clematis—"this wonderful thing is 'Lasurstern',"—it offers shade in the middle of the day.

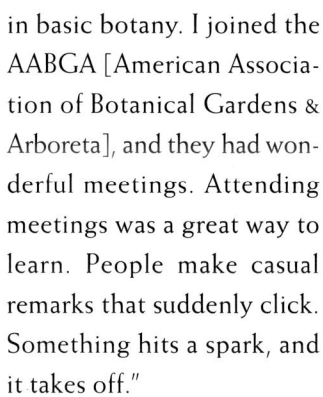

had to come out." However, the pine trial quickly "led to a broader interest in conifers."

Undaunted, Polly continued conducting her experiments, quietly and steadily, in every corner of the property. It was slow work, particularly since most of what Polly grows is started from seed. "From a cutting," she admits, "it is much faster." Polly and her husband, Julian, a research chemist, and children wintered near Wilmington, Delaware—a center of horticultural activity. Polly quickly began to augment her experimentation with plants with more formal study. Living near both Winterthur and Longwood Gardens, Polly became interested in learning "what made those institutions tick. I took course after course, particularly at Longwood. And then I went to the University of Delaware and took courses in basic botany. I joined the AABGA [American Association of Botanical Gardens & Arboreta], and they had wonderful meetings. Attending meetings was a great way to learn. People make casual remarks that suddenly click. Something hits a spark, and it takes off."

One such offhand remark ultimately led to a longtime relationship that was an important influence on Polly's professional growth. Preparing to leave for a trip to Japan in 1956, Polly asked Russell Siebert, the director of Longwood, if he wished her to bring anything back. At first he said no. But he quickly changed his mind and arranged an introduction to Dr. Tsuneshige Rokujo "'because he has some psilotums.' I said, 'What are psilotums?' Which I soon found out are a fern ally, *Psilotum nudum.*" A correspondence between the two plant enthusiasts matured into a horticultural collaboration. "Rhododendrons were Dr. Rokujo's specialty. He was a hybridizer and he had the nakaharae [dwarf azalea], which was unknown in the

of selecting, nurturing, and introducing new tree and shrub species and cultivars whose seeds had come from around the country—even the world.

Polly set goals, and one of the first was to work with pines, believing that Vineyard residents needed sturdy trees to act as windbreaks. Her first undertaking was planting a pine grove on the northern boundary of the land. "I planted about eighty-five limber pines on our northern boundary. It took them only twelve years to die. They grew very big and began to die from the bottom up from some disease. They were a poor choice, or a poor seed lot, I found out. They all

West, in his garden." Polly set her mind on developing an evergreen, prostrate azalea strain that could be used as a ground cover in American gardens. Over the years, Dr. Rokujo sent a variety of seeds for Polly to assess.

Barnard's Inn Farm has become not only Polly's testing ground for plants but an arboretum tuned with a fine eye to aesthetics. Along the edges of the well-maintained fields, trees are clustered as though standing in intimate conversational groups, adhering to the local adage "Keep the centers of the fields open and the old walls visible." Polly has retained the rectilinear configuration of the fields, and the old stone walls, originally laid out to contain sheep, act as divisions between named fields and subtle displays of plant families in various stages of growth and performance. Trees and shrubs are given ample spacing, with room to stretch their branches to the limit. Most stand in circular beds of mulch.

The walls, many of them four feet high, have all been restored. Polly also made use of large stones, majestic hunks of

ABOVE: Polly located the Playpen, enclosed within 10-foot-high fences, at the southern edge of the property, "so it would not be in anybody's view." Though the occasional baby rabbit is able to penetrate the compound, the structure has altered the deer's lifelong trail habits, enabling Polly to cultivate an array of azaleas, camellias, rhododendrons, and other plants attractive to animals. LEFT: In an area designated for a congregation of conifers, *Tsuga canadensis* 'Pendula', *Cephalotaxus harringtonia* 'Fastigiata', and *Juniperus chinensis pfitzeriana* 'Mathers Blue' form a tapestry of greens and grays.

granite found on a rock pile that had been discarded by farmers who could not use them as posts, steps, or parts of walls. Some have become monoliths, like palace guards watching over the perimeter of the property, their feet hidden in foliage. Others, lying on their backs, are benches to entice contemplation of the views. Paths laid out with a designer's hand gently curve to expedite efficient plant overseeing—and pleasant strolling. Flowers such as white Siberian iris are naturalized in the meadows. An accomplished photographer, Polly notes, "The evening light and the morning light are very lovely."

Named areas of the property harbor plantings that reflect the range of Polly's interests in growing trees and shrubs from a number of plant families, both deciduous and evergreen. Conifers are concentrated at the edge of the West Field and in the Arboretum. Her favorites "come from all corners of the world." They include the incense cedar, *Calocedrus decurrens*, "a massive, handsome tree with splendid bark"; and the Nordmann fir, *Abies nordmanniana*, "with elegant branching, fat-needled twigs, and lower branches that sweep the ground." She particularly fancies the spruce *Picea orientalis* because "the short needles are closely set and the whole tree is a rich dark green." But she also delights in cryptomeria, sciadopitys, selected chamaecyparis, and abies and favors dwarfs, weepers, and oddities, such as *Araucaria araucana*, the monkey puzzle, with its dripping branches and trunk resembling an elephant's foot.

Polly now owns more than 65 acres, about 20 of which are cultivated; the rest remain woodland. She patrols the property in a Kodak-yellow electric cart, a traveling hospital of sorts. The cart's large, flat bed holds tools, labels, fertilizer, pots, stakes, and two drums of water. Plants such as *Chamaecyparis pisifera* 'Aurea' (LEFT) and *Picea abies* 'Inversa Pendula' (ABOVE RIGHT) receive her attention and care.

Northwest of the Pine Grove, the wall opens into Holly Park, the site of Polly's work with *Ilex opaca*. Other hollies are grown in the nearby Holly Triangle and North Field, where Polly has developed eight *I. verticillata* cultivars, selected for fruit color that varies from crimson to orange, height, times of fruiting, hardiness, and drought tolerance.

To the south, a grove of stewartias glows golden in the late-day sun. "I think," Polly says, "stewartias are the plant of the future. They don't take a lot of fussing. They are naturally espaliered. They don't need much shaping, just a little when they are young; they have a lovely habit. They bear shapely flowers that come late, when everything else is finished, and you are glad to have them. They seem awfully healthy, and they have beautiful bark in winter." Polly has introduced nine different stewartia cultivars, all of which she began from seed: "koreanas, ovatas, and one I thought was a koreana, but it turned out to be a hybrid, a natural hybrid." She believes that the currently popular pseudocamellia species is less desirable than the koreana; the koreana's flower is less cupped and therefore showier. Along Dogwood Allée, a dramatic straight-as-an-arrow path, 30 Kousas parade in double file. Many, with lively names like 'Steeple', 'Square Dance', and 'Snowbird', are Polly's introductions.

One of the richest areas, dubbed the Playpen by Polly's husband, Julian, began as a utilitarian idea to keep the deer at bay, but now, as Polly says, "It's the best." The 300-foot-long, 35-foot-wide enclosure is a gallery with transparent walls.

The plants flourishing within this safe haven range in height from the stately *Magnolia hypoleuca* 'Lydia', honoring Polly's enthusiastic gardening granddaughter and an arching leatherleaf, many-trunked *Rhododendron metternichii* to a carpet of dwarf azaleas. Many of the azaleas are of Polly's acclaimed 'North Tisbury' group. There, too, live the camellias. "I haven't introduced any camellias, but they were one of my original objectives." Spring color within the fencing is a dazzling confection of white, cream, pink, and red. Divided by a broad grass path, plants preen and bloom in communal security.

While Barnard's Inn Farm is in Zone 6, the Playpen was built in a frost pocket, and it can be even colder. "It's kind of a low point. So it's a good test place." The soil is amended each time a plant is moved, and a container of compost is always at hand. Made from aged wood chips, kitchen scraps, manure, and "endless leaves, chopped or unchopped," the compost has changed the quality of the soil to rich, black earth. But, Polly adds, "We have always had good drainage, and that is crucial to plants."

In the early days, Polly's nephew carved out a nursery, discreetly located near the southern perimeter, where it sits today, three 60-foot-long, 4-foot-wide rows, divided by 2-foot-wide paths and fenced with wire to keep the little animals out. "It runs north and south, so it receives the light moving around all day." If plant volunteers arrive unannounced, they are welcomed. "All kinds of trees volunteer here. The nursery's soft and ready, and it gets more watering."

Polly points out, lest anyone think these plants are pampered, that theirs is New England living. Her plants are taught to fend. She has no greenhouse, no cold frame. While she does use the nursery, many plants are planted out when they are very young. "I put them out very small because I have to be able to handle them. Many aren't as tall as grass and you can't really see them. Sometimes they tend to be run over. Or trampled by deer. However," she continues, "for the first two years, we do try to treat them right." With young plants, her advice is "Mulch, mulch, mulch, water, water, water." The plants teach her what they like and she gives it to them. "Then they go their way. Some just up and die. And you have no idea why. Others live despite everything." These are Yankee plants. Tough, strong, independent. And beautifully pruned and shaped.

"I think you should give a plant room and care if you want to have it be beautiful. And I don't want something ugly around. If it's ugly, I take it out. Last year and this year I've had a big policy: If I've given a plant twelve or fifteen years and it's still ugly, out with it."

Polly has sought seeds from a variety of sources. Besides her Japanese suppliers, she has exchanged seeds with the American Horticultural Society, the Arnold Arboretum in Boston, the Morris Arboretum in Philadelphia, Longwood Gardens, Chollipo Arboretum in Korea, other horticultural societies, and private growers. Many of Polly's introductions still live only in botanical gardens, as it takes years for nurseries to build up enough stock to bring plants to the public. On the other hand, the popular weeping 'Louisa' crab apple already "sells thousands each year." And for aficionados, 'Milk & Honey' has come to be *the* stewartia.

Often the histories of Polly's plants rank with the adven-

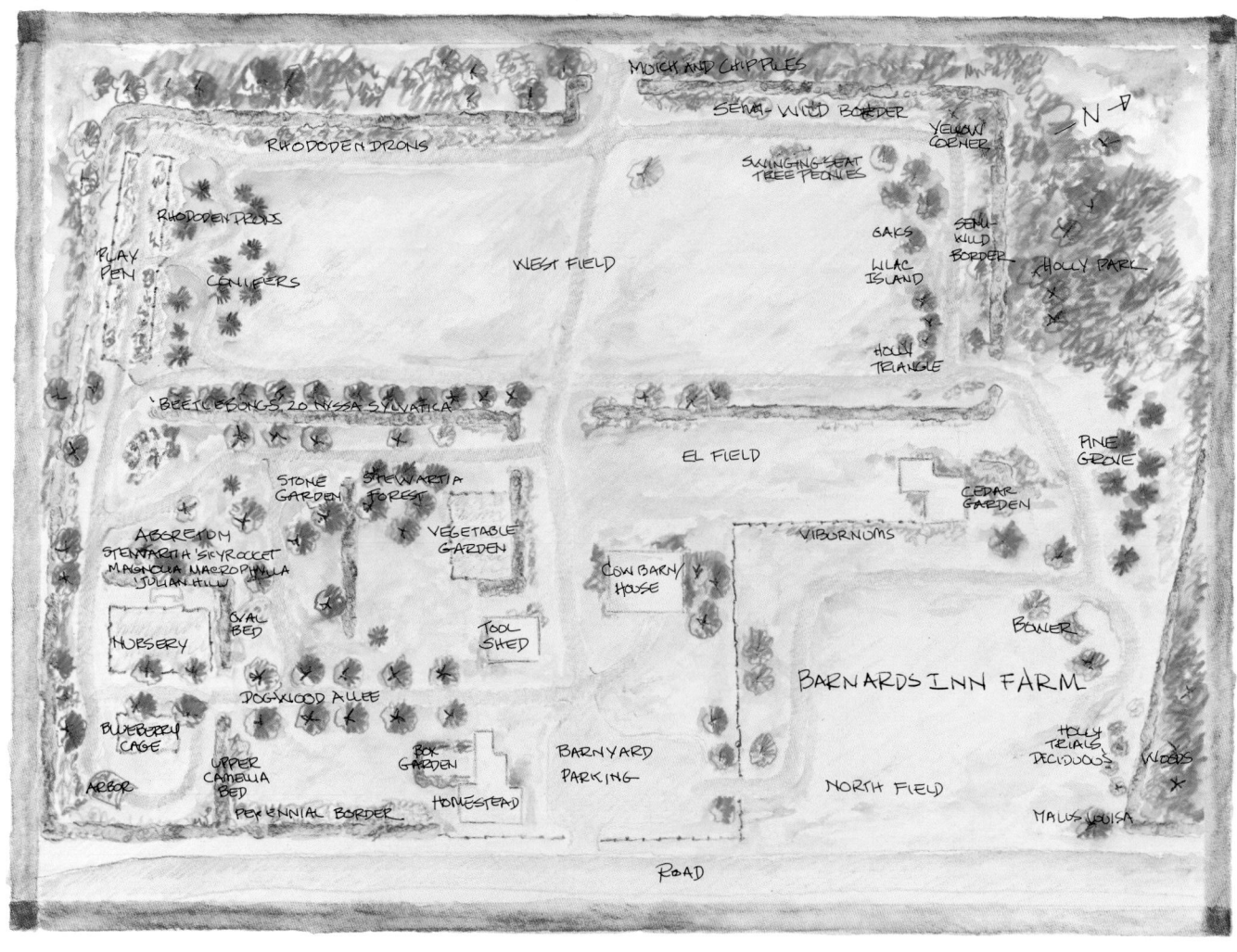

REGISTERED INTRODUCTIONS AT POLLY HILL ARBORETUM

Abies lasiocarpa 'Martha's Vineyard'
Chamaecyparis thyoides 'Qiana'
Clematis 'Gabrielle' (hybrid)
Clematis 'Starfish' (hybrid)
Cornus kousa 'Big Apple'
Cornus kousa 'Blue Shadow'
Cornus kousa 'Gay Head'
Cornus kousa 'Julian' *
Cornus kousa 'Pollywood'
Cornus kousa 'Snowbird'
Cornus kousa 'Square Dance'
Cornus kousa 'Steeple'
Ilex crenata 'Muffin' (male)
Ilex opaca 'Barnard Luce'
Ilex opaca 'Martha's Vineyard'
Ilex opaca 'Nelson West' (male)
Ilex opaca 'Villanova'
Ilex verticillata 'Aquinnah'
Ilex verticillata 'Bright Horizon'
Ilex verticillata 'Chickammoo'
Ilex verticillata 'Earlibright'
Ilex verticillata 'Quansoo' (male)
Ilex verticillata 'Quitsa'

Ilex verticillata 'Shortcake'
Ilex verticillata 'Tiasquam'
Ilex 'Pernella' (hybrid)
Juniperus virginiana 'Essex Weeping'
Juniperus virginiana 'Martha's Vineyard' (dwarf)
Magnolia hypoleuca 'Lydia'
Magnolia macrophylla 'Julian Hill'
Magnolia officinalis 'David' (hybrid)
Malus hupehensis 'Garlands'
Malus hupehensis 'Wayne Douglas'
Malus 'Louisa' (hybrid)
Oxydendrum arboreum 'Chameleon'
Rhododendron atlanticum 'Marydel'
Rhododendron cumberlandense 'Chalif'
Rhododendron cumberlandense 'Sizzler'
Rhododendron cumberlandense 'Sunlight'
Rhododendron kaempferi var. *leucanthum* 'Corinna Borden'
Rhododendron kaempferi var. *leucanthum* 'Libby'
Rhododendron macrosepalum 'Lady Locks'
Rhododendron makinoi 'Lydia Richards'

Rhododendron makinoi 'Temple Flutes' *
Rhododendron nakaharae 'Fuzzy'
Rhododendron nakaharae 'Mount Seven Star'
Rhododendron nakaharae 'Nakami'
Rhododendron sanctum 'Zeke'
Rhododendron viscosum f. *glaucum* 'Delaware Blue'
Rhododendron yakushimanum 'Wild Wealth'
Rhododendron 'Alexander' (hybrid)
Rhododendron 'Andante' (hybrid)
Rhododendron 'Bartlett' (hybrid)
Rhododendron 'Big Yak' (hybrid)
Rhododendron 'Eiko San' (syn. 'Balsaminaeflora') (hybrid)
Rhododendron 'Gabrielle Hill' (hybrid)
Rhododendron 'Hot Line' (hybrid)
Rhododendron 'Jeff Hill' (hybrid)
Rhododendron 'Joseph Hill' (hybrid)
Rhododendron 'Late Love' (hybrid)
Rhododendron 'Louisa' (hybrid)
Rhododendron 'Marilee' (hybrid)
Rhododendron 'Matsuyo' (hybrid)
Rhododendron 'Michael Hill' (hybrid)
Rhododendron 'Midori' (hybrid)
Rhododendron 'Pink Pancake' (hybrid)
Rhododendron 'Red Fountain' (hybrid)
Rhododendron 'Samisen' (BIF #1) (hybrid)
Rhododendron 'Susannah Hill' (hybrid)
Rhododendron 'Trill' (hybrid)
Rhododendron 'Tsuneshige Rokujo' (syn. 'Shigi') (hybrid)
Rhododendron 'Wintergreen' (hybrid)
Rhododendron 'Yaye' (hybrid)
Rhododendron 'Yuka' (hybrid)
Stewartia koreana 'Ballet'
Stewartia koreana 'Milk & Honey'
Stewartia koreana 'Mint Frills'
Stewartia malacodendron 'Delmarva'
Stewartia ovata 'Red Rose'
Stewartia ovata 'Royal Purple'
Stewartia ovata 'White Satin'
Stewartia sinensis 'Mei-Li Shu' *
Stewartia 'Skyrocket' (hybrid)

* Not registered

ture stories of the nineteenth-century plant hunters. The seeds for her celebrated 'Mount Seven Star' azalea (*Rhododendron nakaharae* 'Mount Seven Star'), for example, required the efforts of friends who traveled to Taiwan in search of the elusive species. "I got a little pinch of dust in a bag and planted it. And two came up. And one lived. And that's 'Mount Seven Star'. And it's a honey, a real beauty." The blossom is "cadmium red." The nakaharae, Polly believes, are outstanding because "they are the latest to bloom, the lowest, the twiggiest—and they are surprisingly hardy, considering that the species comes from Taiwan."

She reminds, "You can have the same species with a lot of variation in the wild. And you never know what's gotten into it somewhere else." As with many plants, Polly says, "I favor the species, because you get a balance between flower and foliage and habit that time alone can produce." She cautions

that in the process of hybridizing, fragrance is usually the first feature that is sacrificed. She touts the atlanticum azalea as "a very fragrant species." Hers, of course, has a story: Julian, a birder, discovered it while out on a birding trip in Delaware, near the Choptank River.

Polly often names plants for the location where their seeds were collected. Other names are purely descriptive, like the stewartia hybrid 'Skyrocket', which Polly says has "just gone shooting up." And, of course, there are those christened for family or friends, such as *Magnolia macrophylla* 'Julian Hill' and *Cornus kousa* 'Julian', both named for her husband. Polly has registered more than 30 different azaleas alone, and her Barnard's Inn Farm cultivars of other plants span the alphabet from abies to stewartia.

Of her numerous experiments and introductions, she recalls, "I'd grow them. Different cultivars would occur. I would evaluate them.

In this view directly through the north gate of the Playpen, the sculptural, arching trunks of a *Rhododendron yakushimanum* hybrid catch the evening light. A path beckons between the crisp foliage of *Ledum groenlandicum* on the left and the feathery, red leaves of *Acer palmatum* 'Dissectum' on the right.

Then other people would evaluate them and see what they were worth." In defense of her painstaking process, she explains, "If you grow from seed, you pick the best of that seed run. If you have three children, you aren't going to get three alike, are you?" Growing from seed allows her to monitor each plant's progress, its adaptability, its habit, and its hardiness. She has proven that a previously designated zone of hardiness can often be extended, if the plant is grown from seed.

Polly makes it clear that she is not a hybridizer. "If I were a hybridizer, I would take pollen from plant A and put it on plant B. I do not do that." Rather, she prefers to locate seeds, and through growing and selecting, she time-tests plants and, in some cases, challenges established wisdom on hardiness. With azaleas it takes about 20 years to make an introduction. For a choice stewartia, "I had seven or eight seeds, planted two out; one died, but one lived for twenty-nine years and then it bloomed. It was a plant I was determined to grow. It isn't supposed to be hardy here. I still have it; it's a lovely tree

I call 'Delmarva' [*Stewartia malacodendron* 'Delmarva'], named for the peninsula that incorporates Delaware and parts of Maryland and Virginia where the seed came from."

Polly gives generously of plants, cuttings, and seeds to friends, to institutions, and to interested nursery growers. Her record keeping is simple: it is focused on the ongoing history of her plants. She prepares no catalogs. She does not advertise. She just does what she loves to do—grow plants. "I believe in public horticulture," she says. In accordance with her wishes, Barnard's Hill Farm has recently been purchased and established as a foundation, the Polly Hill Arboretum, dedicated to conservation, experimentation, and education.

Wander, "but not touch." Except to look at the labels, which are always on the north side of the plant. Each tells the date of planting, its number in Polly's record system, and its full name. There is no charge to visit, just a gracious, open-gate policy, an invitation to enjoy and to learn.

"Preservation of our heritage

is so important. And if we don't care for that heritage, who will?"

Anne C. Carr

In Praise of Tradition

ANNE C. CARR

ATLANTA, GEORGIA

"It's all in the details, isn't it?" muses Anne Carr. She looks around her walled entrance garden, silently assessing it. A white garden, it is pure and elegant. The choice of plants and a single ornament, a statue depicting Spring, create a harmony that belies the deliberation behind every aesthetic decision. Anne modestly credits the garden's heritage: a premier architect, original owners who loved gardening, and advice from Atlanta's garden guru, Ryan Gainey. In reality, however, the garden reflects Anne's singular style as clearly as a mirror on her wall. "I guess," she says, "I like understatement."

Thirty years ago Anne and her husband, Julian, purchased their yellow-and-white house on five acres in Atlanta's parklike Buckhead district. Built in 1938, it was de-

signed by Philip Trammell Shutze with references to vernacular eighteenth-century American farmhouses. Increasingly sophisticated additions, appropriate to their historic periods, have been added over the intervening years. But the house carries a patina that suggests it has survived centuries, giving it a demeanor of timeless dignity.

The transition from indoors to out is easy and graceful. French doors open onto verandas, which lead to the gardens. Anne notes with pleasure that "every room opens into a garden; every window has a garden vista." It is a home for outdoor living, a haven for a gardener.

Anne became a gardener in her early twenties. She had grown up in Atlanta, but her father, a candy manufacturer, moved his plant and his family to New Jersey in the 1920s. Returning to Atlanta in her late teens, Anne made her debut, and during that year of social activity, she met and fell in love with Julian Carr. They married, and after living in Boston for a short time while Julian completed law school, the young couple settled in Atlanta for good.

PREVIOUS PAGE: An allée of 12 double-flowered Kwanzan cherry trees (*Prunus serrulata* 'Kwanzan') runs parallel to the white fences that line Anne Carr's driveway. In mid-April their powder puffs of pink blossoms herald spring in spectacular style; the white fences, Anne feels, provide a good foil for the intense pink of the blooms, which might be too strong without it. THIS PAGE, ABOVE: A pattern built into the brick wall of a secondary walled

garden is a reverse arc, and the gate continues the flow of the curve. RIGHT: In developing the elements of the White Garden, Anne studied 18th-century formal garden patterns and adapted them to her planting scheme. OPPOSITE: A carved stone season, the cherub Winter, stands in a bed of caladiums and impatiens in the prevailing white-and-green palette of Anne's garden. "I believe in angels," Anne says with a smile.

Almost immediately, Anne joined the Cherokee Garden Club, which has been her gardening home for the last 60 years. As a young woman she found it to be rich in accomplished, generous gardeners who took her under their gardening wings and invited her to their gardens. "I could not believe how many beautiful gardens there were in Atlanta in those days. I learned so much just by looking," she remembers. "Just by looking" could almost be the motto of this thoughtful gardener, who relies on her visual instincts, cocking her head and looking carefully even when she is doing simple tasks, like adding a plant or pruning a rose.

When the Carrs bought their house, the structure of the

gardens was in place. Two of the gardens are fully enclosed by walls; most of the others, from single borders that outline a veranda to beds that follow the contours and angles of the house, were part of the original architectural plan. Anne still refers to those drawings regularly, studying the ways a scale rendering can instruct her decision-making processes.

Anne did not make changes immediately and is quick to point out that the traditions, the contributions of other gardeners, are all part of this garden's character. Two of the first Kousa dogwoods (*Cornus kousa* var. *chinensis*) in Atlanta, planted in 1939 or 1940, were growing in the garden; they are still there, as are mature specimens of English boxwood planted by the first owners.

Slowly, after living with the garden for a number of years, Anne began to give it her own signature. She never feels she has to make alterations just for the sake of change. She respects the history of a place, even if it is only measured in decades. The 50- by 35-foot entrance garden, originally sectioned into parterres, was filled with roses. "They looked awful in the winter," she recalls. "I wanted a garden that looked beautiful in all seasons, and I wanted more space for sitting to the side and enjoying it. The garden should not be something just to look upon, but to live in."

Nature nudged Anne into her renewal program. A large live oak that shaded the corner of the garden died, allowing much more light into the area. Anne removed the roses and opened up the central area, which is now where the "little ones"— eight grandchildren and one great-grandchild—play.

"I love white flowers, and this seemed the place to make a White Garden. White and shades of green." The narrow color palette would be cool in the summer, but she also knew that a careful choice of plants could offer more distinct architectural interest all winter. Shapes of trees and shrubs, textures of leaves and bark would all be integral to the design.

Today the parterres are gone. The central area is lawn; along the sides, the beds are edged with box and accented with box balls. The walls host espaliered, fall-blooming sasanqua camellias. A trio of *Hydrangea paniculata*, grouped like the *Three Graces*, are tightly pruned to display their

gnarled trunks and rounded heads. Three crape myrtles, also pruned high to show off their seemingly polished bark, stand in a bed of white vinca and bleeding heart. The variety 'Natchez', Anne says, has held up well; it does not die back in severe winters, as do many other crape myrtles.

Anne seeks varying shades of green in foliage, adding subtle color range to the design. The leaves on a variegated cotoneaster, for example, are tinged with white. She warns, "Cold can damage them, turning the leaves brown. I always pick up backup plants when I see them at nurseries." The native oakleaf hydrangea, closely pruned, provides a soft gray-green curtain, particularly in the spring; its large, velvety leaves contrast with the feathery foliage of the golden spirea. The yellow berberis, highlighting spring's elevated position, is really, Anne concedes, too big a plant for the location. "I have to cut at it all year, but I just love the color and texture, so I put up with its rapid growth habits." Behind the wall a line of sophora trees (*Sophora japonica*) drip char-

ABOVE: The central area of Anne's White Garden was turned into a grassy carpet surrounded by a brick walkway; its corners are punctuated in fans of brick. The beds are outlined by one course of brick and raised slightly above the level of the paths. A wide terrace along one side affords room for a white iron Victorian table and chairs.

LEFT: The walls of the White Garden are painted the yellow of the house both inside and out. Though large, the house is built on a comfortable scale. Rounded balls of English boxwood, planted by the original owners, are clustered around the property.

treuse tassels in the spring, like a theatrical backdrop staged to enhance the other woody plants' performances.

A garden of such subtlety takes constant maintenance, requiring that Anne replace and synchronize plants through the seasons, with some plants held in the wings, like understudies, ready to take over for an ailing actor. For example, four cone-shaped yews (*Taxus cuspidata* 'Capitata') "make a good contrast to the box. I like them so much bet-

While the tulips in this garden are all of one variety—'White Triumphator'—Anne plants the bulbs at different depths, from four to eight inches, which affects their stem length, thereby making the tulips grow to varying heights. "I didn't want to see all the tulip heads at one level." White pansies fill all the crevices in abundance.

ter than other conifers that look like Christmas trees. But the yews don't last through the heat of the South for long. I have to replace them about every four years."

The stars of spring are the white tulips, which Anne plants by the dozens. They fill pots, large and small, and are planted in the ground as well, all around the garden. When the tulip bulbs have been pulled out and discarded, other white flowers take over: astilbes, foxgloves, geraniums, irises, cosmos, and roses, both climbing and tea. Several clematis "sprawl across" the shrubs, besides making their way over the walls. Anne even risks vigorous growers such as white-tinged ivy and strawberry begonia (*Saxifraga stolonifera*) because she values their variegated foliage and their evergreen, winter presence. If they misbehave, like Lady Macbeth, she cries, "Out," and they are banished or given to friends.

The other walled enclosure, called the Fountain Garden, rather than being a rectangle like the entrance garden, terminates in a half-moon brick wall; as a contrast, the walls of this courtyard are left the natural rose hue of brick. The shapes of the beds follow the curve of the wall. The shaded garden is guarded by a grand crab apple, "a 'Professor Sargent', I think," says Anne, "although it's so old, we really don't know its name." The English daisies (*Bellis perennis*), *Erysium* 'Bowles Mauve', forget-me-nots, hellebores, hostas, muscari, thalictrums, tulips, and *Veronica prostrata* (particularly any of the varieties with gold-tinged leaves) bear flowers in shades of blue and yellow. "While I love white flowers, I love color too. Oh, I just love it all, don't you?"

Elsewhere around her house, Anne has added new beds and borders where none existed

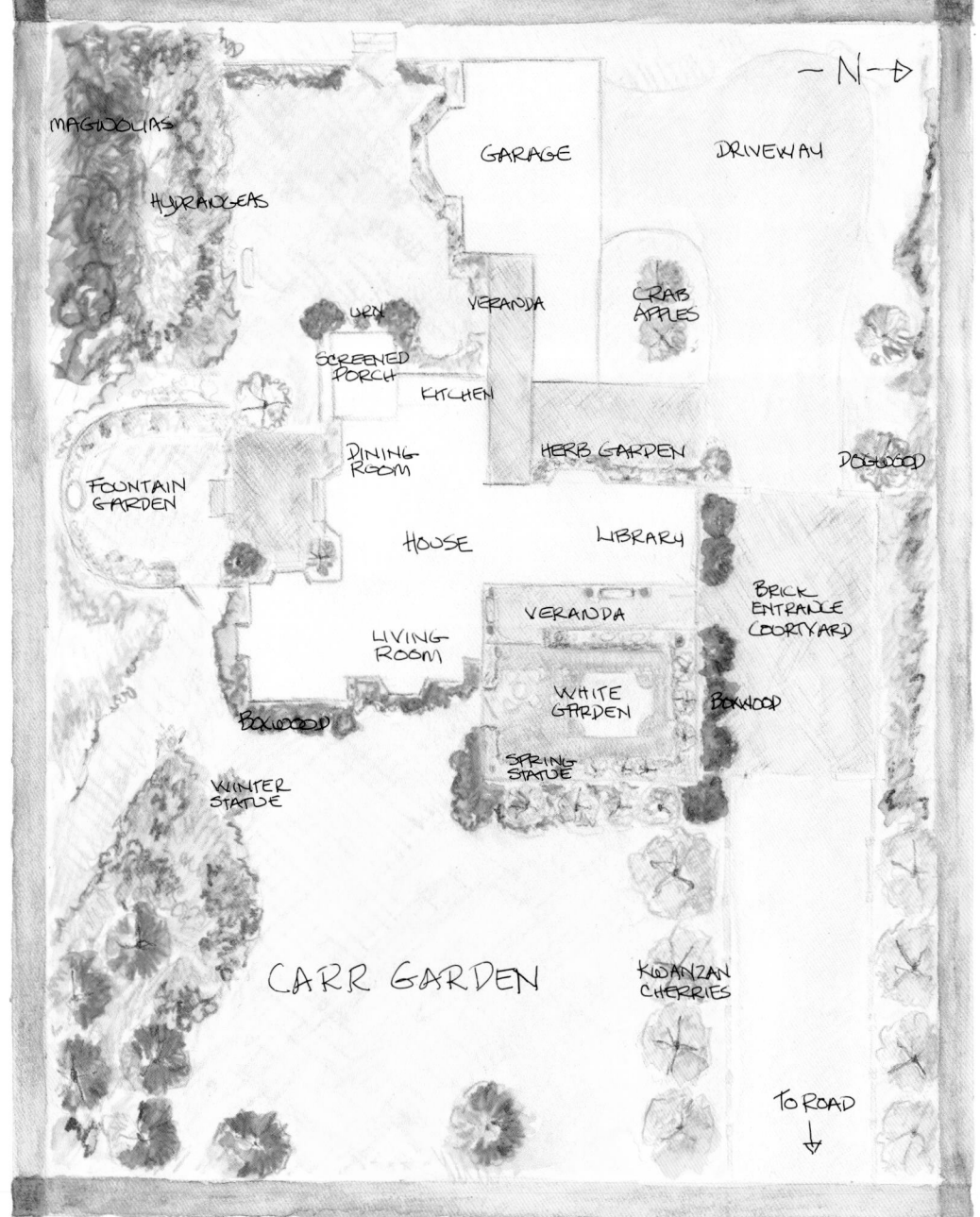

ANNE CARR'S WHITE GARDEN PLANT LIST

PERENNIALS

Astilbe × arendsii 'Bridal Veil'
Boltonia asteroides 'Snowbank'
Convallaria majalis
Dicentra spectabilis 'Alba'
Digitalis purpurea 'Alba'
Digitalis purpurea 'Excelsior'
Ficus pumila
Hedera helix 'Goldchild'
Iberis sempervirens 'Snowflake'
Kalimeris mongolica
Lamium maculatum 'Beacon Silver'
Liriope muscari 'Monroe's White'
Phlomis fruticosa
Phlox divaricata 'Fuller's White'
Saxifraga × *arendsii* 'Snow Carpet'
Saxifraga stolonifera
Stachys byzantina 'Helene von Stein'
Stachys byzantina 'Silver Carpet'
Vinca minor 'Alba'
Viola × *wittrockiana* 'Crystal Bowl White'

ANNUALS AND TENDER PERENNIALS TREATED AS ANNUALS

Bacopa × 'Snowflake'
Caladium × *hortulanum* 'Candidum'
Cosmos bipinnatus 'Sonata'
Cosmos bipinnatus 'Tall White'
Dracaena indivisa 'Spikes'

BULBS

Crocus cartwrightianus 'Albus'
Crocus vernus ssp. *albiflorus* 'Snowstorm'
Endymion hispanicus 'Alba'
Scilla hispanica (now *Hyacinthoides hispanica*)
Tulipa 'White Triumphator'

List prepared by Gail Griffin.

SHRUBS

Berberis thunbergii 'Aurea'
Buxus microphylla 'Winter Gem'
Buxus sempervirens
Camellia sasanqua
Cotoneaster horizontalis 'Variegatus'
Eucalyptus cinerea
Euonymus japonicus 'Microphyllus Variegatus'
Hydrangea macrophylla 'Mariesii'
Hydrangea paniculata 'Grandiflora'
Hydrangea quercifolia
Spiraea × *bumalda* 'Goldflame'
Spiraea catoniensis 'Lanceolata'
Taxus cuspidata 'Capitata'

TREES

Lagerstroemia indica 'Natchez'
Sophora japonica 'Regent'

---

before. Along the screened porch a collection of pulmonaria, camellias, and 'Casablanca' lilies brings bloom to the feet of those enjoying Anne's iced tea. A new herb garden has recently taken shape along the side of the kitchen courtyard. Two pear trees are espaliered against the wall. Shades of purple and lavender dominate. Topiaries of scented geraniums stand in pots, their feet blanketed in purple-leaved mustard. Rosemary, different varieties and colors of basil, parsley, and thyme form decorative shapes in the beds. A single bay, *Laurus nobilis*, seemingly puffed with self-importance, stands in the center. Nasturtiums and violas—"You almost have to fight them as the summer progresses, but they are so charming"—are grown for color and for salads.

Caring for her garden takes constant work. "Julian takes exercise; I garden. I can't imagine spending time running when you can work in the garden instead." And, she says, the work keeps her in good shape. A small pillow sits with her tools outside the kitchen door; on it is stenciled "Gentlewomen . . . may doe themselves much good by kneeling upon a cushion and weeding. William Coles 1657."

"Four mornings a week, a Baptist minister who is a gardener, and who worked in the garden before I came, meets

Anne completes her gardens' picture by relating views through their gates or doorways. Often a few steps, slight grade changes, give further definition to the different garden spaces.

me in my kitchen at seven o'clock. We go over what needs to be done that day. Then we each do our own tasks, often working side by side. We've been together for thirty years." An Atlanta horticulturist and friend, Gail Griffin, also helps in the garden when Anne needs her.

Gardening runs in the Carr family. "My father was a hobbyist gardener. He loved to plant azaleas. And Mother gardened also." The Four Seasons statues, which are placed around Anne's garden, were inherited from her mother. "Julian's mother, too, was a wonderful gardener. She built a summer house, a Swiss chalet, in Highlands, North Carolina, where she made a rock garden, planted with mountain natives. We often visited and drove all over the mountains identifying plants."

Part of Anne's discipline is keeping records, including bills of all plant purchases, in files. She also clips articles that pertain to her plants. All are organized for quick reference. In the garden, unusual plants have quiet labels, reinforcing her philosophy: "Everything is better plain."

Studying and reading about plants and gardening history, and applying this learning to her own garden, has led to a passion for gardening books, particularly old volumes. After a 1973 trip to the Cheekwood Botanical Garden and

Museum in Nashville, Tennessee, introduced her to the institution's botanical library, she found a way to infuse her passion into Atlanta's horticultural community. She proposed to the Cherokee Garden Club that it start a similar library in Atlanta. The members immediately responded, and the Cherokee Garden Library, named, like the club, for Georgia's state flower, the Cherokee rose, opened in 1975.

"We determined that the library would be primarily American, with a concentration on southern agriculture and gardening. We, of course, have also added representative material from Europe, to round out the scope of the library," Anne reports. "We had great fortune in finding Elizabeth Woodburn in 1977, and she became our adviser." Elizabeth Woodburn, one of the first antiquarian booksellers to concentrate on books about American agriculture and horticulture, was the doyen of the field until her death in 1985.

A stream of water at the center of the Fountain Garden flows into an oval bowl. Decorated with motifs that harken back to ancient Egypt, the vessel is a reference to the past that pleases Anne, who delights in studying garden history.

When Elizabeth Woodburn was ready to sell her own collection, she was approached by institutions, including the Smithsonian. Observing the commitment and enthusiasm of these women in Atlanta, however, she believed that the newly established Cherokee Garden Library would be the place where her collection would do the most good. Housed in the Archives building of the Atlanta History Center, the books would be readily accessible to those doing research.

With Anne leading the campaign, the women of the club raised $25,000 in six months to buy Elizabeth Woodburn's collection of more than 200 books of rare vintage, tracing the history of American horticulture from 1634 to 1900. Later acquisitions include the 400-book library of Elizabeth Lawrence, beloved author of *A Southern Garden* and *The Little Bulbs*, and the Anne Chapman Pomaria Collection from the Pomaria (South Carolina) Nursery, which operated from 1840 to 1878 and specialized in native southern and exotic imported plants. The library now numbers over 5,000 volumes—and is still growing.

Anne enjoys listing the library's range of assets and invites gardeners everywhere to come visit. She hopes that the library will inspire other garden clubs to undertake similar ventures. "Discovering the plants that were used in seventeenth- and eighteenth-century gardens is like solving a mystery," she smiles. "Only better."

A CONVERSATION BETWEEN LIFETIME FRIENDS AND GARDENERS

LOUISE RICHARDSON ALLEN AND ANNE C. CARR

ANNE: Remembering our friendship together is such a pleasure. I have always admired you. I remember that you and I both went to the Presbyterian Sunday School, and one Sunday you invited me to come back to your house. We were about six or seven.

LOUISE: Your memory goes back a lot longer than mine, so you'd better continue.

ANNE: I came out to your wonderful house on the hill, and it had a ballroom, maybe the only private ballroom in Atlanta. And we played in the ballroom that afternoon.

LOUISE: We must have slid up and down. Great fun.

ANNE: And you had chairs, little chairs, and we played under them. Games that little girls play. We must have done that several times. And then you went off to school.

LOUISE: I did go off to school quite young, to Virginia, where we had to speak French. I was devastated. Even mathematics, we had to do in French. Well, you know that is absurd. And I didn't want to leave Atlanta.

ANNE: There was a long time we didn't see each other. My father's business moved up north. And I met Julian when I came back here to make my debut. Then I married, and when we came back to Atlanta, you were wonderful to me. We rented your little house, a house on your family's property that you and Ivan had lived in when you were first married. So we renewed our friendship so quickly. You and I worked on Junior League projects together. Like "Song of the South."

LOUISE: And we were together a lot. We began a life of working on projects together. That was the beginning of being involved in community projects.

ANNE: Because I think you were the president of the Junior League at that time.

LOUISE: And it was wartime, too.

ANNE: It was World War II. We'd better say that, or people will think it was the Civil War. We both believed in community service. And that's when we started gardening, but not to the extent we do now. I joined the Cherokee Garden Club when I was about twenty-two. And the women in the club were wonderful women, and that started me. That's what turned me on to gardening: the wonderful gardens I saw.

LOUISE: Well, Anne, I don't think I gardened nearly as much as you at that time. Ivan had the wanderlust. We moved about seven different times. He loved to buy a house, and then he loved to sell it. So I didn't have many flowers by the front door. Just some foundation plantings. But I got tired of that, and when we built this house, I said, "You're going to have to drag me out of this one." And I started gardening here. We started with just a little planting around the house about forty years ago.

ANNE: Then one day, when we were playing golf, you told me that the house next door to you was for sale. You said, "It has a marvelous garden." And I saw it and liked it very much.

LOUISE: It was perfect for you.

ANNE: And then, Louise, you got me interested in the grounds of the Atlanta Historical Society. We both gardened together on those projects. You had interested thirty-two garden clubs in maintaining the gardens. So I worked with you on the advisory committee for the grounds. That's when you and I really became involved in gardening together.

LOUISE: We still talk to each other every morning about eight-fifteen. We have so many projects to organize and that's when we do it.

ANNE: Some people are more involved in their social lives and having luncheons or playing bridge, but we'd rather do something more productive.

LOUISE: When we talk, we confide, and we solve problems having to do with organizations we're involved in. We work on the overall picture of what needs to be done.

ANNE: We don't really give advice about gardening. But we share the mechanics, like you'll tell me about a tree man you have, or we'll recommend someone who can supply plants. It's a big help.

LOUISE: I don't consider myself a real gardener, but so far the things we've put in the ground have worked. I give things room. I rarely have to pull things out because they're in the wrong place.

ANNE: You are so interested in plants. Wherever you go, you take flowers.

LOUISE: I love to go to your garden.

ANNE: And I love your view. I admire what you do, mostly because it is different from what I do.

LOUISE: One thing that has always helped us over the years was going to look at plants. I see a plant and think it would look good in my garden, and so I write it down and then hunt it down.

ANNE: We've both gone to see gardens, here in Georgia and in other countries, and that's helped. And books are so important. Learning about the history of plants and gardens.

LOUISE: We've also been fortunate to have wonderful speakers on gardens. The garden clubs bring them. It's valuable, inspirational. Even that old grump from England.

ANNE: Yes, when I drove him back to the airport, he observed, "There must not have been very much in Atlanta to burn."

LOUISE: Anne, we do give each other advice. Yesterday, for example, you said that the white rabbit [an iron ornament] didn't go there. You were right. It was an eyesore. I moved it. Some people like showy things. We have the same way of thinking. Quieter, I guess.

ANNE: Yes, some say I should have more color in my garden. It ought to be more spectacular.

LOUISE: I love seeing your garden, but quite frankly, it wouldn't suit me. I'd worry about it too much. Yours is meticulous, and you take very good care of it yourself.

ANNE: We respect each other's vision. While our gardens are very different, they are both simple, maybe understated. You know, we must have something of the same demeanor, because sometimes when I go out, people think I'm you. They ask me how your son is, and I say, "Oh, just fine." I don't know, maybe it's honesty, Louise.

LOUISE: Well, there's not meant to be any pretense. With us. Or with our gardens. They do mistake us for one another. Maybe we look alike.

ANNE: I think it's more than that. I can be really honest with you. I don't flatter you. Julian says to me, "Have you been with Louise today? I can always tell when you've been with Louise, because you feel better."

LOUISE: That's so good. We've had good times: working, gardening, talking.

ANNE: We're like sisters—without the fussing.

A Gracious Way

LOUISE RICHARDSON ALLEN
ATLANTA, GEORGIA

"My garden," says Louise Allen, "is not really a garden in the way people think about gardens. I have very few flowers. But I do love trees, and always have." Louise strolls along a path, curved as though by the sweep of a calligrapher's pen. She runs her hands over branches that seem to reach out to her: a native dogwood, an aesculus, a magnolia. Pausing before a dense wall of mahonia, displaying its blue-green berries, she observes, "I don't believe I ever planted a mahonia. They have all just appeared over the years—and in the nicest arrangements. If I had planted them with deliberation, I could not have made them look better."

Volunteerism has to a large degree determined the course of Louise's life as well as that of her garden, and her efforts on behalf of various civic organizations and garden clubs in and around Atlanta are legendary. Perhaps because Louise presided during Atlanta's twentieth-century trial by fire in the 1960s—when her husband, Ivan Allen, Jr., served two terms as mayor of Atlanta—and helped bring it through victorious, she remains a First Lady in Atlanta's heart. When a new civic project needs a leader, Louise's phone rings. "We, the people of Atlanta and I, well, we just love each other."

The Allens' natural-looking landscape surrounds an H-shaped house that Louise and Ivan built in 1952 on 12 acres that once belonged to Louise's parents, Josephine and Hugh Richardson. It is land where Louise played as a child. The Richardson house, called Broadlands, was built in 1924. It was sited on the highest prospect of 250 acres of forest and farmland in the then undeveloped district of Atlanta now known as Buckhead.

As a young girl, Louise attended boarding school in Virginia. She missed her home, but, she says, "the experience broadened my view." After high school, she went north to Vassar College for two years: "It was just too cold up there; I nearly froze to death." So she returned to her beloved Atlanta. She spent the following summer in Europe as part of her education. That trip whetted her appetite for seeing the world, which she claims has always influenced her attitudes toward gardening. She points to a paperbark maple (*Acer griseum*), delighting in its copper-colored bark, which she first saw at Stourhead in Wiltshire, England. After her trip, she recalls she sought specimens for her own garden "with much effort. Frank A. Smith, a great nurseryman here in Atlanta, had two stuck in

"For me, it's the volunteers that make it all work—in both plants and people."

Louise Richardson Allen

them to my own garden. The first time I saw the climbing hydrangea [*Hydrangea anomala* ssp. *petiolaris*], it was on gray walls in Scotland. I thought, 'Why not in Atlanta, too?'" On a 1963 safari trip to Africa, the Allens visited Capetown and were so enamored with the Dutch step-gabled architecture that they came home armed with photographs and immediately adapted facades of their own ranch-style house to resemble what they had seen.

A few years later, inspired by a journal her mother kept on her wedding trip around the world, Louise and a friend went to Japan. She particularly wanted to experience Japanese gardens first hand and remarks on how she determined to bring their spirit of serenity to her own plot of land. The only class that Louise has ever taken was in England. With four Atlanta gardening friends, she attended one of John Brookes's week-

long seminars at his School of Garden Design at Denmans in West Sussex. "What I remember most strongly about that class was Mr. Brookes's discussions about natural planting. From England, to the Orient, to South Africa, I've always tried to collect good ideas and bring them home."

While Louise has often traveled, "and loved every

PREVIOUS PAGE: Below a terrace that overlooks fields, a pierced brickwork wall encloses Louise Allen's only flower garden. THIS PAGE, ABOVE: Among the non-native plants Louise has introduced into the landscape are her prized maples, including *Acer palmatum* var. *dissectum* 'Atropurpureum'. RIGHT: A baby *Magnolia grandiflora* volunteer, just 24 inches high, grows within the protective umbrella of a Japanese maple. OPPOSITE: Part of Louise's skill as a gardener is her seemingly casual mixing of indigenous plants with exotics. All flow into a harmonious setting that appears natural, though, as Louise is quick to note, "it *has* taken forty years."

barrels down by his creek." She laughs, "Nobody wanted them, because their bark was peeling. I told him I did."

Louise recalls that Frederick Law Olmsted went to England in 1850 and was deeply influenced by a visit to Birkenhead Park, near Manchester, which is considered to be the first public park. She says, "He was interested in naturalness in parks, as championed by the English Romantics." Noting that a number of parks in Atlanta, such as Inman Park and Ansley Park, are patterned on his principles, she says, "Perhaps, a hundred years later, on a more modest scale, I had the same experience. It is the natural landscape, tamed, of course, as humans do, that I respond to most deeply."

Learning by traveling has been a significant part of Louise's gardening education. "I see things unfamiliar to the Georgia landscape, write them down, and when I return try to adapt

moment of it," her attachment for the land where she grew up and the city where she was born is so powerful that she never wanted to settle in any other place. Louise and Ivan married on New Year's Day in 1936. They lived in a succession of houses, often building them on parcels of Louise's parents' land. But moving from house to house did not encourage the permanence Louise needed to really begin gardening. "A few flowers by the front door is not a garden," she observes. "When we finally built this house, I dug my heels in and said, 'No more moving.'"

Settled in the home where she determined to spend the rest of her life, Louise could finally give her gardening instincts free rein. She credits her mother for establishing her own gar-

dening roots. "My mother was a great gardener, although her gardens were certainly different from mine. But," she says, reflecting on the grandeur of 1920s gardens, "it was a different age." Though her gardens were formal, Josephine Richardson had a love for trees, and she passed it on to her daughter.

While her friends made flower gardens, which she hastens to say she "enjoys and admires," Louise planted trees and shrubs, allowing their progeny to proliferate. Most are natives—hickories, beech, hawthorns, tulip poplars, viburnums, buckeye, oakleaf hydrangeas, quince, rhododendrons, and azaleas. "I've always believed in encouraging what will be the happiest in a garden." A primary consideration is the selection of plants that are drought- and heat-resistant, "as

Louise designed her walled garden to contain a small pool as a focal point. "Water," she says, "no matter how small the amount, provides a restful, calming element in any garden. I enjoy the changing colors of the reflections throughout the day—and in all weather."

summers can be brutal." A pump house marks the spot where a well was dug as a supplemental water supply, a crucial aid to survival for many of her plants.

Though her primary interest these days is native plants, she does not claim to be a purist. "I have a love for Japanese maples and have planted a number," she says. "Wherever they are planted, they bring life into the landscape. I relish their splashes of red amongst the dogwoods. And if I'm going to quickly dress up my living room, one branch in a simple vase is all I need." The Japanese maples, she continues, "seem to like it here as well as the natives. I really do not do anything special for them. Once a year I hire a professional to prune them. He lies on his back for a day clipping from

underneath to help them maintain their sculptural shapes."

To these she has added other fine nonnative specimens: a European beech (*Fagus sylvatica*), a Persian parrotia (*Parrotia persica*), and a Chinese pistachio (*Pistacia chinensis*). Both nandina (*Nandina domestica*), with its bright red fruit that ripens in the fall and persists through the winter, and loropetalum (*Loropetalum chinense*), which offers a fleecy cloud of creamy flowers in spring, she believes, are underrated plants and should find their way into more gardens.

With its organic forms and shapes, and textures and colors that play off each other, Louise's garden is sculptural in effect. However, Louise did not set out to make that kind of a garden. "My garden just evolved over the years," she says. "I don't remember having any organized plan. I saw a shrub I liked, I looked around for a proper place for it, and I

planted it. And I have rarely moved anything I planted. I gave each plenty of room and the best conditions I could, including soil preparation."

In the early days, she practiced double digging. The technique involves removing the topsoil to the depth of approximately one foot and setting it aside. The subsoil is then loosened and amended with organic matter, aged manure, and sand. The topsoil, also enriched with the same improvements, is then replaced. "It's important to upgrade the earth."

The only formal design that Louise "imposed" on the landscape is a garden directly below the house's broad terrace. A walled garden of pierced brickwork that terminates in a half circle, it has as its focal point a water nymph kneeling at the edge of a goldfish pond. The nymph is cloaked in a cut-leaf Japanese maple. "It is the only enclosure I have ever made.

Sometimes I'm not sure about it. I always like to be able to look out in every direction. But I *can* see through the brick wall.

"Design in my garden, if it can be called that here, is often based on necessity. The quiet road we live on became not so quiet. So we have encouraged a woodland to grow between us and the road. The grade from the road slants downhill, so we fitted stones into the bank and planted around them. Solu-

tions are practical." As much as Louise loves the dogwoods, she reflects on their decline through disease, primarily the leaf and stem anthracnose, *Discula,* and the necessity for planting alternative trees. She recommends those with multiseason interest. She points to the Japanese stewartia (*Stewartia pseudo-camellia*), newly placed in the woodland, and also cites some native possibilities with similar growth habits and deli-

cate flowers: the fringe tree (*Chionanthus virginicus*), the Carolina silverbell (*Halesia carolina*), the redbud (*Cercis canadensis*), and the sourwood (*Oxydendrum arboreum*).

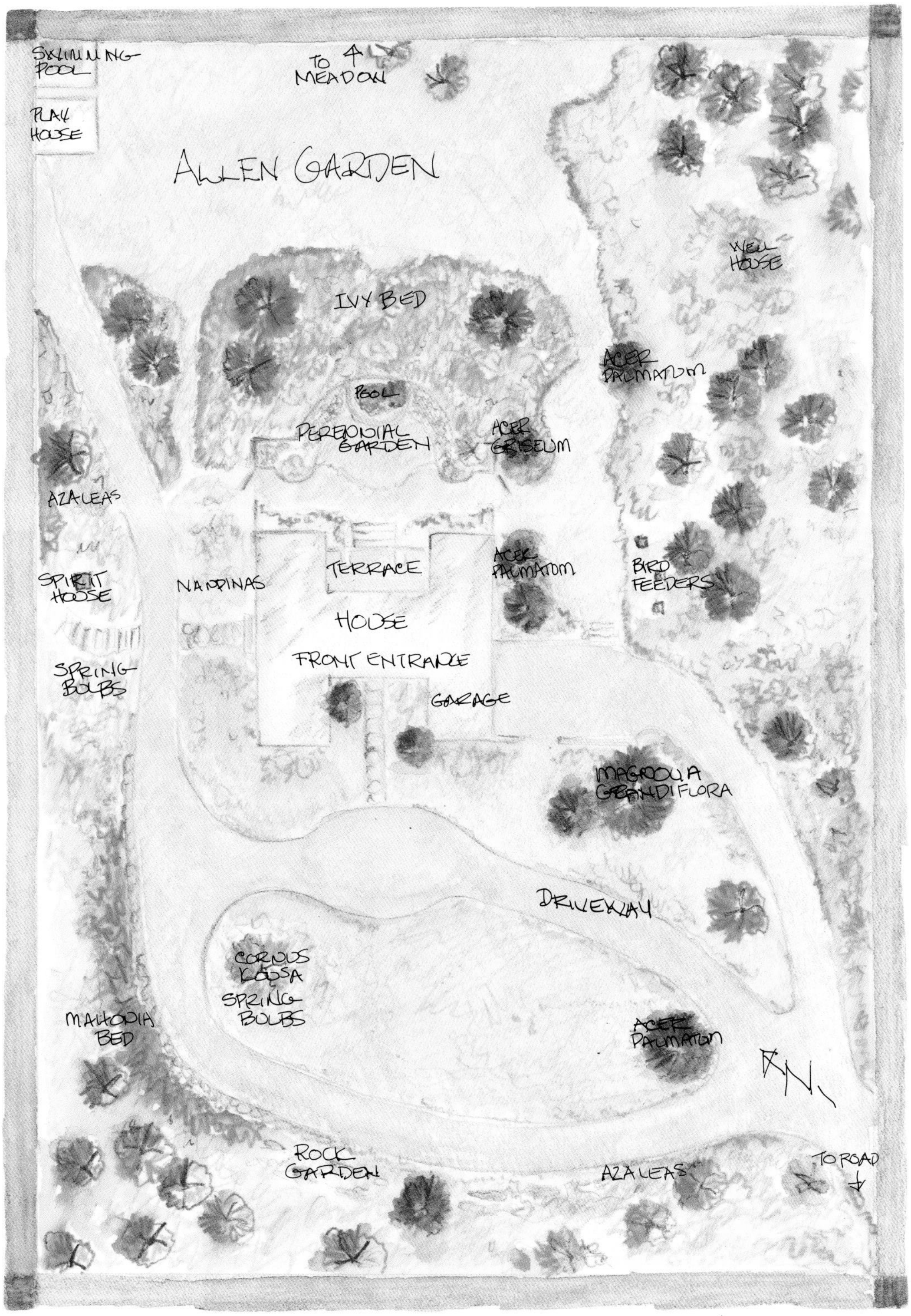

Other areas such as the meadow at the foot of the garden have changed little over the years. Lying in a floodplain, with creeks on two sides, the meadow is occasionally under water. Louise is thankful for the expanse of open land, which, in this day and age, she says, could probably not remain untouched if it were more suitable for development. Yet, while the area around her grows with houses under construction on every available lot, this nine-acre meadow prevails. Forty years ago the Allens planted water oaks (*Quercus nigra*), grand, primal trees, along the edges. They now stand 100 feet tall. Mistletoe drapes itself, like

OPPOSITE: This lantern is one of the few garden ornaments. Louise purchased it in Japan, believing its surface, with the mottled colors of aging stone, complement the rusty, red foliage of a Japanese maple. "I like to have a different view, I call it a painting in nature, out every window. Adding subtle contrasts in texture and color gives me pleasure."

SWIMMING POOL

PLAY HOUSE

TO MEADOW

ALLEN GARDEN

IVY BED

WELL HOUSE

ACER PALMATUM

POOL

PERENNIAL GARDEN

ACER GRISEUM

AZALEAS

SPIRIT HOUSE

NANDINAS

TERRACE

ACER PALMATUM

BIRD FEEDERS

HOUSE

FRONT ENTRANCE

GARAGE

SPRING BULBS

MAGNOLIA GRANDIFLORA

DRIVEWAY

CORNUS KOUSA

SPRING BULBS

MAGNOLIA BED

ACER PALMATUM

ROCK GARDEN

AZALEAS

TO ROAD

antique fringed shawls, over their branches.

Early each morning, joined by her miniature schnauzer, Klaus, Louise takes a walk to the meadow's end "after a cup of coffee, but before breakfast." She passes the swimming pool and playhouse that have been there since her parents' day and are now enjoyed by her seven grandchildren. "We lived in the playhouse while our house was being built," Louise recalls. "The far corner of the meadow is about a half a mile away," she says, "and walking to it clears the cobwebs. I think that's why I feel so good." It is a time to enjoy her garden and to plan her day, mentally juggling her domestic and garden tasks with appointments and meetings on civic issues.

PREVIOUS PAGES: The garden beds within Louise Allen's brick enclosure are accented with boxwood hedging and large box balls that follow the lines of the walls. Perennials—peonies, foxgloves, 'Miss Lingard' phlox, Russian sage, yarrow—are chosen in a soft palette of white, lavender, and yellow. ABOVE: The rich copper pealing bark of an *Acer griseum* is set off by creamy double-petaled dogwood blossoms.

Her schedule could daunt someone half her age. "There are so many good causes," she says. Over the years she has been the spearhead of a number. Her husband calls Louise's support during his terms as mayor invaluable. "She's a remarkable woman, a leader in her own right. She is gifted in being able to gather people together to get a project done. She does it in a quiet, nice way."

"My civic work has meant a great deal in my life. It's an anchor," says Louise. Her list of "projects," in which she began to invest her energies at age 19, seems endless: a children's hospital, a family counseling center, a school, the Atlanta Botanical Garden, the Georgia Conservancy, and

LOUISE ALLEN'S RECOMMENDATIONS

FOR NATIVE TREES AND SHRUBS FOR SOUTHERN GARDENS

TREES

BOTANICAL NAME	COMMON NAME
Amelanchier arborea	Shadbush, serviceberry
Chionanthus virginicus	Fringe tree, graybeard
Cladrastis lutea (syn. *C. kentukea*)	Yellowwood
Cornus florida	Flowering dogwood
Cornus florida 'Pluribracteata'	Double-flowering dogwood
Crataegus spp.	Hawthorn
Fagus grandifolia	American beech
Gymnocladus dioica	Kentucky coffee tree
Halesia carolina	Carolina silverbell
Ilex opaca	American holly
Liquidambar styraciflua	Corky sweet gum
Liriodendron tulipifera	Tulip poplar
Oxydendrum arboreum	Sourweed
Magnolia grandiflora	Southern magnolia
Magnolia macrophylla	Big-leaf magnolia
Nyssa sylvatica	Black gum
Pinus echinata	Shortleaf pine
Styrax grandifolium	Snowbell, storax
Tsuga caroliniana	Carolina hemlock

SHRUBS

BOTANICAL NAME	COMMON NAME
Aesculus georgiana (syn. *A. sylvatica*)	Georgia buckeye
Aesculus parviflora	Bottlebrush buckeye
Clethra alnifolia	Summer-sweet
Edgeworthia papyrifera	Paperbush
Hamamelis vernalis	Red witch hazel
Hamamelis virginiana	Yellow witch hazel
Hydrangea arborescens 'Grandiflora'	Snowball hydrangea
Hydrangea quercifolia	Oakleaf hydrangea
Hypericum densiflorum	Dense hypericum, St.-John's-wort
Ilex opaca	American holly
Illicium floridanum	Florida anise bush
Illicium parviflorum	Anise bush
Leucothoe axillaris	Dwarf dog-hobble
Lindera benzoin	Spicebush
Liriodendron tulipifera	Tulip tree
Lonicera sempervirens	Trumpet honeysuckle
Pieris phillyreifolia	Dwarf pieris
Rhododendron alabamense	Alabama azalea
Rhododendron austrinum	Florida azalea
Rhododendron canescens	Honeysuckle azalea
Rhododendron × *hybridum* 'English Roseum'	Hybrid catawba rhododendron
Rhododendron maximum	Rosebay
Rhododendron prunifolium	Plum-leaf azalea
Viburnum acerifolium	Maple-leaf viburnum
Viburnum alnifolium	Hobblebush
Viburnum prunifolium	Black haw viburnum

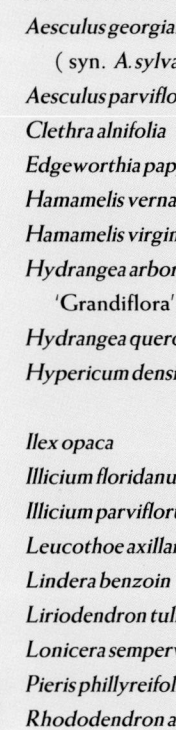

her current primary focus, the Atlanta Historical Society.

Because of her love of gardening, she determined that the gardens at the society should be developed, each with a unique character, for the public's use and pleasure. "You know," she reflects, "gardening, particularly in the 1960s, when the pressures of our political life could have taken a toll, was great therapy for me. Digging in the earth takes my mind off difficult things. I believe gardens can offer refuge for others as well." Thirty-three acres at the society now present the horticultural history of the Atlanta region in a series of gardens that include the Swan House formal garden, the Tullie Smith farmhouse garden, a rhododendron garden, and an Asian-American garden. Louise's own club, the Mimosa Garden Club, took on the challenge of converting an over-grown late-nineteenth-century rock quarry into a planned natural landscape with more than 150 native plants.

While Louise is always modest about the force of her behind-the-scenes efforts, it was she who inspired, organized, and marshaled the efforts of local garden clubs to plan, plant, and maintain the gardens. It was she who went to individuals and foundations to fund the projects. Yet she steadfastly maintains, "It is the people who do the work. When we established the gardens at the society thirty years ago, thirty-two garden clubs joined forces to create them. While I would not diminish the role of the staffs of organizations, the volunteers are the unpaid army who get the jobs done. Without them, all those unsung people, none of it would happen."

"I have always loved the smell of earth.

Especially the fungal smell of the earth in a midwestern spring."

Betty H. Blake

An Alpine Adventure

BETTY H. BLAKE

ONSTED, MICHIGAN

Betty Blake walks slowly through her garden with a vigilant eye, bending to free a tiny anemonella from the stronger pulsatillas that march, like merry brigades in purple helmets, through her spring garden. Digging out a lake iris (*Iris lacustris*) from its crowded colony, she gives it a new home between two rocks. The brown tips of a winter-burned juniper nipped off, she makes little piles of the clippings on the stone paths, to later be gathered and deposited on the compost pile. She still uses the same pair of Felco pruners that she bought in 1961. Betty eschews gloves, even though an occasional poison ivy assailant gives her blisters. "I was born to have dirty fingernails," she says, holding out her hands. Reaching over to ruffle its foliage, Betty congratulates a

mother *Trillium grandiflora* for producing the three little offspring at its feet. Both she and the plants seem to enjoy the intimacy of physical contact.

Betty did not start gardening with alpine plants, the drabas, androsaces, saxifrages, sempervivums, and penstemons she now favors. In fact, she says she did not become a gardener until after her marriage to David Blake, a young businessman, in 1939. When the Blakes moved from Topeka, Kansas, where they had grown up and gone to college, to Michigan, Betty started her first garden on a 40-foot-wide city lot in Detroit. She began with roses, a collection that swelled to 160 different varieties, mostly old and species. Betty visited graveyards and old farms to take cuttings of

questions have been answered, I plant. And I move a plant if it isn't completely happy."

Perhaps, with that attitude, the intense scrutiny of each plant and attention to its particular culture, it was only a matter of time before she joined the community of rock gardeners. She recalls her introduction and instantaneous conversion: "In 1960 a friend told me that there was a British organization—the Alpine Garden Society—with a seed exchange. In those days I thought twice about spending two, three, four dollars on seeds. So, I have to admit, my first impulse was that of a cheapskate—free seeds, how wonderful! I had no idea what I was getting into—my obsession, I guess, could be called a sickness. I joined, and I've never looked back." She pauses in the story and remembers, "And the North American Rock Garden Society wrote to me the following year asking me to join its ranks." She

PREVIOUS PAGE: At least 26 truckloads of limestone and sandstone were imported over a three-year period to form walls and paths around the Blakes' property. The walls follow existing rock formations; there are no square corners. The results are irregular and mysterious, as though the handiwork of ancient Druids. THIS PAGE, ABOVE: To pamper plants, Betty's husband, David, erected a lath house to cover newly germinated seedlings and delicate specimens, providing diffused light and preventing the rain from battering

plants. Six cold frames are part of the nursery complex. In them, plants are plunged, pot and all, into sand. RIGHT: A view from above shows the crazy-quilt-like configuration of beds outlined by paths. OPPOSITE: Betty stands at the base of a 12-foot-high circle of stone, dubbed The Silo. No longer vertical, the walls slant and slouch as though built centuries ago. The ageless quality of the garden suits Betty's aesthetic. "I love the feeling of gardening among old rock formations. We have added to nature. But the outcroppings were here."

roses long out of circulation. "I'm a natural-born collector," she says. And a sleuth and a student.

Though she may not have been a gardener, Betty always had a keen interest in plants, earning a degree in botany from Washburn College. That early dedication to serious plant study is a discipline she has continued throughout her life. When she's discussing plants, several reference books and specialty catalogs lie open on her kitchen table. Handy, too, is a notebook containing a list, including the source, of every plant that enters the garden, often denoting its bloom cycle. "But," Betty says, clear about the distinction, "I'm not a designer. I am interested in plants. I am interested in placing them where they will thrive. I like the way they look in certain combinations, but I consider their needs first. What exposure do they prefer, what conditions? When those

wondered how the group knew of her impending passion. Years later, when she was the treasurer of the Great Lakes chapter, she questioned a board member; he laughed and said, "We have our methods."

Betty soon joined the Scottish Rock Garden Club as well. With seed lists from the three organizations now offering more than 6,000 varieties each per year, the selection is vast and varied. Each group allows members 20 to 35 different seed selections annually. "More are awarded if members contribute seeds," which Betty always does.

Betty remembers receiving the first seed list. Even with her education in botany, the 3,000 possibilities available at that time "staggered" her. She determined to refresh her memory on taxonomy and to investigate the unknowns before she ordered anything, so she took a year to study the

offerings' identities and cultural requirements. Meanwhile, in anticipation of a new passion, she built a raised bed, contained by a stone wall, in front of her roses. "I had to separate my territory from the children's and the dog's."

In 1972 the Blakes hankered for rural living, for more land, for a larger garden. They began a hunt. After consulting aerial maps of the region, they settled on the Irish Hills in southern Michigan, named by the Irish immigrants who arrived in the 1820s and 1830s; the area's rolling hills and strings of clear lakes brought to mind their homeland. The Blakes bought 71 acres, which over the years has grown to 425 with the addition of small parcels. "David collects land like I collect plants," explains Betty.

Single-handedly David reforested the open land. Since moving there he has planted 44,000 trees, mostly whips—butternuts; American chestnuts; Colorado, white, and black spruce; red and white pines—that he

An array of wooden troughs designed by Betty and whiskey half-barrels purchased from Hiram Walker's, across the Detroit River in Canada, provide sheltered lodging for predator-prone alpine plants.

purchased in large quantities from state conservation agencies and nurseries. "It meant that I wouldn't see David all spring," Betty recalls.

The site the Blakes chose for their home and garden was on an outcropping on Michigan's terminal moraine, rock deposited when the glaciers' flow stopped and the ice melted. "Igneous rock, granite, flint—these rocks are hard," Betty says. "They had to be tough to survive the glaciers' movement." A steep north-facing slope with a 20-foot drop-off suited the newly born rock gardener in Betty. The house was built on the southern extremity. David designed a sprawling home faced in limestone to blend with the natural terrain. Without exposing what lies behind it, the 85-foot facade of the house shelters the garden and hides it from view.

Curved stone paths lead around the house. Under the protective cover of junipers and a 19-year-old Japanese maple,

troops of primulas, trilliums, and double bloodroots provide the first hints of what is to come. At the east end of the house the garden is suddenly revealed. Several levels fall off dramatically to a semicircular meadow that wraps around the gray stone-filled garden and complements it with a carpet of green. Mown paths lead farther into a woodland, where the vista is closed in by trees, David's whips grown to mature size.

Stone walls, steps, and paths wind from level to level in mazelike fashion, making the acre and a half that the garden covers seem larger. There is no beginning or end. With uneven settling, the walls seem age-old, like prehistoric relics or abandoned cellar holes. Paths and a terrace are punctuated in an arbitrary fashion by more than 30 whiskey half-barrels and troughs that are home to hundreds of alpine plants, which could not survive in competition with the larger, more aggressive plants that edge the terraces and walls. Receiving elevated treatment, in both place and

stature, alpine plants are protected in their miniature gardens from predators such as rabbits, deer, and slugs.

The insidious slug problem was one of the factors that inspired Betty to build the cedar troughs in the first place. "They don't like to make the long trip up the sides," she says. "However, when adding stone to a trough, I check to make sure I have not unwittingly imported a slug."

The armies of marauding, destructive deer have proved more difficult to control. Few conifers are still in the same architectural form they were a few years ago, and "the yews are down to the nubs." Besides yew, arborvitae is no longer usable, Betty says. So far the hemlocks and spruce have been spared the deer's unwanted pruning. Betty enjoys the Canadian hemlocks, *Tsuga canadensis* 'Jacqueline Verkade', a small slow-growing shrub, and the compact, graceful semiweeping *T. c.* 'Nana Gracilis'. She touts the horizontal *Picea abies* 'Repens' and the dense tight foliage of *P. a.* 'Pygmaea'. When she and David first arrived on their land, Betty recalls, two

low-lying acres near their house were carpeted with thousands of trilliums. "It was a beautiful sight to see," she remembers. But as the deer population has increased, so have their appetites. Not a trillium remains in their woodland.

Betty is particularly interested in native North American plants, but she has also introduced plants from all over the world into her garden. Besides perennials and dwarf conifers, she has collected deciduous shrubs to add texture and contrast in the garden. She points to a *Cornus hessii* with small rounded, pleated foliage. She has several willows, which she reports are extremely hardy and tidy. *Salix reticulata*, her "best one," has leaves the size of her thumbnail. The catkins stand up one and a half inches—which is the full size of the plant. The miniature *S. lindleyana*, which hails from Nepal, has fine foliage and red catkins that turn black with maturity. *S. yezoalpina*, a prostrate variety, has larger reticulated leaves that emerge covered with silver hairs in the spring. "And don't forget the cotoneasters," she reminds, "*Cotoneaster microphyllus* 'Cooperi' is a lovely dwarf I brought here from Detroit twenty-one years ago; it's still healthy."

Betty acknowledges that the Midwest may seem an unlikely place for plants accustomed to the high altitudes, cool air, and sharp drainage of the Rocky Mountains to thrive. In Michigan temperatures can reach 100 degrees in the summer and −20 in the winter. Humidity can likewise stress plants, yet, she says, it is not so severe that an alpine house is mandatory. It is the erratic winters that do the most damage. Snow can be nonexistent, or it can fall in December and last until March. The month of March is the deadliest. As the snow melts and the ground remains frozen, prohibiting proper drainage, water can sit on the plants' roots. Under those conditions, touchy plants succumb.

Betty uses cavities in found stone to create gardens. Here the red foliage of *Sempervivum* 'Packardian' complements the tiny green *Sedum kamtschaticum*.

"Because of the inclement weather in a Michigan spring, we have to squeeze six weeks' worth of work into two weeks. It's a task!" Betty observes. Summer can be a challenge, too. "When we get a two- or three-week stretch where the temperature hits a hundred, we can lose some neat plants." Betty still bemoans a recent summer's casualty, a precious *Campanula zoysii*, "so small you can hardly find it with a magnifying glass."

Betty's deliberate choice of the north-facing slope for the garden offers certain advantages throughout the year. Drainage and air circulation are better there than on a level

surface, the winder freeze/thaw cycle is less extreme, and the soil stays cooler in summer. "The tops of the plants get sun, but their roots do not get heated unduly."

The Blakes' property also provided raw materials—stone, sand, gravel—compatible for rock gardening. David, hardscaper at heart, climbed on his tractor to revise nature's shortcomings. "David likes to build. He's an artist with a front-end loader." Betty adds, "Major soil preparation" was a priority, too. "We had to make our own loam; we had only clay." At one point, David ordered ten manure-spreader loads of animal droppings from the county fairgrounds deposited and mixed with the soil. The Blakes also "dumped in" loads of corncobs and "bees wings," the tissue that holds the corn on the cob. Each year they drove around town and filled a truck with 1,000 bags of leaves that people had left on the curbsides. Composted, it turned into rich leaf mold.

LEFT: Pockets in the walls are home to plants such as the lavender-flowering *Pulsatilla vulgaris,* the small light green rosettes of *Sedum glaucophyllum,* and *Aquilegia canadensis.* Betty has found she prefers vertical pockets to horizontal ones and suggests "the smaller the plant, the better. Seedlings work best. Water in well from the side—not from above —gently. Repeat watering often."

When nature's amendments were not close by, David, always the romantic, traveled to fulfill his wife's desires. To celebrate their 34th wedding anniversary, the couple drove to Castalia, Ohio, where they'd heard a farmer had dug tufa, porous limestone, out of his fields. His price was "three cents a pound. David bought me a ton and a half of tufa," recalls Betty. "Some of my friends didn't understand the gesture; I thought it was wonderful." With the help of a U-Haul trailer, they brought the stone home and placed it strategically around the garden and in the troughs. Tufa is a hospitable environment, Betty notes, as it consists of calcium and magnesium carbonate. Many alpine plants are partial to growing in it. "And others, such as lewisia, which generally likes limestone, will grow in it quite happily, too."

Betty feeds her plants in the spring, generally using a slow-release, 20-20-20 three-month fertilizer. She points out that early applications of phosphorus promote bloom. After July, she may give the plants an additional soluble, high-potassium solution. "As I do with the old roses, I want to give them potassium to help them close down for the winter." Going into the fall, she makes sure she does not give them any nitrogen, however, which would encourage foliage growth and make them more susceptible to winter damage.

Betty sows seeds all year round—about 200 varieties. Her kitchen counter, with views to the bird feeder, is her indoor workshop. Betty's planting medium consists of equal parts coarse sand, peat moss, compost, and chicken grit or "Oil Dry," a substance used to absorb oil on garage floors; lightly moistened, the Oil Dry has the consistency of crushed flowerpots. "It absorbs water and doesn't do any of the bad things, like float or disintegrate." To sterilize the mixture, she closes it in a plastic bag and puts it in the microwave with the probe set at 180 to 185 degrees. "When the probe turns off, I leave the bag in for another half hour."

The planted pots—"one pot to a customer"—often go to the root cellar, a subterranean room lined with shelves, conveniently located at the bottom of the basement stairs. The temperature never quite reaches freezing or exceeds 42 degrees. Plants that are slow to germinate, such as gentians and certain campanulas, can stay there for a year before heading out to the lath house or cold frames. Most plants need to be transplanted, "potted up," at least once before being set out in their permanent homes. Like the theory of the Heir and the Spare, Betty keeps a backup clone of each unusual plant that she sends out into her garden.

A half dozen *Anemonella thalictroides* 'Betty Blake', one of Betty's discoveries, happily nestle at one end of a cold frame. "I found the plant in the woods near Nineveh, Indiana, in about 1975." Each plant produces clusters of tiny double flowers, a half inch in diameter, on long wiry stems. Betty used to call the plant 'Lime Ice'. Peripatetic little plant that it is, it traveled with a friend to Washington, where it was seen and acquired by the owners of Grand Ridge Nursery, near Seattle. Before offering it to the market, the owners, Steve Doonan and Bill Pearson, asked Betty if it could bear her name. "Not being a real dummy, I said yes."

The reward of rock gardening is admiration, respect for these amazing little plants, their size, their resiliency, their beauty, their rarity, and, for some, their challenge to the gardener to propagate or grow them successfully. Betty speaks of how effective the shrubby penstemons can be growing in a wall. "*Penstemon fruticosus* ssp. *scouleri* is an excellent plant, with good survivability; I have a lovely white variety now." And *Helianthemum oelandicum* "makes a tiny mat no bigger than my hand, covered with yellow flowers that last and last." She takes a quick breath and continues, "*Dryas octopetala* is fast growing, with a large creamy white flower like an anemone and silky seed heads. Twenty years ago I bought my *Erythronium albidum* var. *mesochoreum*, the nodding, white trout lily; it had fourteen blooms this year. I was given the tiny yellow-flowering *Draba bryoides inbricata* twenty-five years ago; all my plants, those little cushions, have come from that one plant."

Care of plants is constant, and like a kindly country doctor, Betty Blake makes her rounds, a trip that takes about three hours, in the morning. These days, she takes a short break from her chores in the middle of the day and then heads back out again. "The urge to see things grow was in me all right," she says, "I guess from the beginning. I garden for the pure pleasure of it."

CLOCKWISE FROM TOP RIGHT: Amenonella thalictroides *'Betty Blake'*. Reliable Draba dedeana. .Primula *hybrid, a long-lived and easy plant, Betty received the seed in an exchange with a correspondent in the Czech Republic.* Draba rigida bryoides, *"a great trough subject, reliable, hardy, and long-lived. It increases in diameter and does not die out in the center."* Saxifraga sp., *"prime tough material for tufa and rocky crevices."* Anemonella thalictroides, *a woodland plant that Betty occasionally uses in troughs; she cautions that "it seeds around."* A Primula *hybrid, also from Betty's friend in the Czech Republic.*

BETTY BLAKE'S CEDAR TROUGHS

Toward the end of the settling process, a piece of tufa may be placed, like a miniature mountain range, down the center of the trough. More sequences of watering occur. "Troughs are a tough place to grow plants. They are subject to wind, exposure, and cold." The tufa, with its nooks and crannies, can offer protection for plants. As in the larger landscape, the rock retains the heat of the day, tempering the plants' climate. The trough surface is covered with pea gravel or crushed limestone of about quarter- to half-inch size. Betty reminds, "These gravels are components of the soil mix; they are not merely coatings but are the major part of the upper three to four inches in the troughs."

"I was tired of bending over so far. And I was tired of losing tiny plants in the ground," Betty recalls. "So I had these troughs built. Now working with plants is like working at my kitchen counter." She laughs, "Of course, I do all my sowing of seeds at the kitchen counter, so it's a height I like."

Ten years ago, Betty designed her first "waist-high" trough. Her standard size is six feet long, three feet high, and three feet wide. Made to last, each trough is built of cedar boards, attached to a cedar frame. She uses no preservative on the wood. "Cedar has a long life span; this ten-year-old trough is still in excellent shape." The trough structure slants out slightly at the top. A steel tie-rod, attached to the middle of each long side and near the top, prevents the sides from bowing outward. There is no bottom.

The trough frame is placed on a flat location with a base of crushed gravel, "which makes it easier to level." The open bottom is lined with hardware cloth. A trough's preferred site has some afternoon

shade to protect plants from baking in the western sun. The frame is filled with rock to within one foot of the top. "Good drainage is of the utmost importance."

Betty first pushes soil, "not your best," down between the stones and smooths it over their surface. Then a planting mixture of soil, sand, and gravel—approximately equal parts of each—is added until it is even with the top edge of the trough. Into it Betty incorporates "generous amounts" of compost. "The mixture is thoroughly watered, and watered and watered," advises Betty. As the mixture settles, it further fills the crevices between the stones. More is added if needed. "If I'm a good girl, this process should take at least a month. If it doesn't rain, I water every two or three days. I want the medium completely settled before I begin to plant." She continues, "And if the medium doesn't drain well enough, I take some out and add scoops of gravel. I made myself miserable in the early days before I followed this regime. And I am still suffering from those early shortcuts."

If the tufa does not contain the desired holes for tucking a plant, Betty creates her own. She uses an electric drill with a half-inch masonry bit, "more or less, depending on the size of the plant," to make a hole. She then inserts a tiny seedling and subsequently hovers over it with water until it appears to be independent.

Ongoing watering is determined by the condition of the plant and the moisture content of the surrounding medium, which Betty monitors by probing it with her finger. "In a drought situation, no more water is used than necessary, to minimize the possibility of root rot and to keep the plants in tune with weather conditions."

While Betty places single whiskey half-barrels along the paths of the garden, she likes clusters of large troughs. The placement of a group of three near her lath house and cold frame complex makes for fewer steps back and forth between seedlings' nursery care and their final happy homes. "I spend a lot of time at those troughs, and I want to make the job easy."

With an Artist's Eye

HENRIETTA E. S. LOCKWOOD
BEDFORD, NEW YORK

In refining the property where she has lived and gardened for more than half a century, Netta Lockwood has been governed both by artistic instincts and by the land itself. Visitors see her triumph to be the a classically designed perennial garden located a short walk from the house. Netta laughs when people ask, "Where is your garden? We hear you are a good gardener." "When I tell them it's in the second field out there, they say, 'What? That is no place for a garden'. I say, 'It's the place, it isn't the garden.'" The land offered a flat, protected field, like the stage of an open-air theater. A fitting location, subtle and unexpected, for a garden.

Netta and her husband, John, a lawyer, bought the 1790 farmhouse and 35 acres in Bedford, New York, early in their marriage as a country retreat. The modest house had no electricity and no plumbing. Fireplaces were the only sources of heat. But it was not what the house lacked that made an impression, it was what the land offered. "The reason we bought the place was because the land was so beautiful—it had everything. From the high point it had great views. It had woods. And the hillside drops down by a series of rock ledges to the orchard, and then it drops again."

The Lockwoods began what they view as their tenure of stewardship in 1938. Netta says she and John "wanted to let the land speak for itself. It was our teacher." Gardening, she believes, begins with observing. "I operate like that," she explains. "I am one of those intensely looking people." The young Lockwoods assessed what nature had bequeathed them with their purchase. An apple orchard fanned out behind the house, and the couple gave it their immediate attention. They designated a portion of their household funds for revitalization of trees. "Not adding new ones, just taking care of the old ones—and pruning the orchard." She adds, "As I think back, it was kind of odd that newly marrieds should put tree care in the budget, along with food." Their original orchard of 85 apple trees now numbers 18 carefully edited and elegantly pruned specimens.

A tour of the garden, usually beginning in the orchard, is in part a tour of a tree collection. Trees are a major focus of Netta's work; many she has grown from seed or cuttings in one of her five greenhouses. She has cared for each like a protective mother and has gained opinions about their contemporary garden uses. The styrax, "with its pale pink

"I think my artistic training is one of the

things that has helped in gardening, helped me place trees or move something a few inches.

I have an innate feeling that if it isn't right, it shouldn't be there."

Harriette E. S. Lockwood

bells in spring and oval seeds in fall," Netta touts for modern, small gardens. She favors *Symplocos paniculata;* her first originated from a cutting in her family's garden. In the spring the symplocos bears masses of fragrant creamy flowers, and in the fall it earns its common name—sapphire berry—when the blue fruit, like heavy jewels, weighs down its branches. Usually grown in shrub form, a tall, self-seeded example presides, like a confident matriarch, over the Perennial Garden. Its children, adopted through the many plant sales Netta supports with donations, have made it famous. A honey locust (*Gleditsia triacanthos*) by the house was a gift from Netta's beloved mother-in-law, Elizabeth

Lockwood. Netta credits her mother-in-law, who led a campaign of tree planting in the Long Island Hamptons, with her own initial passion for trees. "She nurtured the wonderful feeling I have for trees." That locust, an old thorny variety, Netta believes to be one of the loveliest of dappled shade trees; only the men who must prune amongst the thorns disagree.

Gardening is part of Netta Lockwood's inheritance. In the early years of the century, Netta's mother, Mable Cabot Sedgwick, laid out a series of gardens at Long Hill, a 114-acre property in Beverly, Massachusetts. Netta remembers that her stylish mother, who "wore those

muslin dresses," always had "grass green" on her clothes.

In 1907 Mrs. Sedgwick published *The Garden Month by Month,* a 500-page compendium of hardy plants and their time of bloom, color, height, and cultivation preferences. A dedicated, hands-on gardener, she wrote in her preface, ". . .he who truly loves his garden will not relinquish altogether the happy task of creating it. For him it is the centre of bright imaginings." That creative seed was sown in Netta when she was very young, though at first it blossomed in the guise of an artist. After making the move from Boston to New York City following her wedding in 1932, Netta immediately began classes at the Art Students League, which she continued to take for many years.

She and John, a native New Yorker, were living in a penthouse apartment on 96th Street. The penthouse, "a most inconvenient place inside," nonetheless boasted a greenhouse and a terrace. It was there that Netta's gardening urge germinated. The small greenhouse offered her the opportunity to start plants from seed. And on the terrace she began "to grow things in tubs. I grew all the dullest flowers, morning glories and petunias. But I was immediately excited by the possibilities." Motivated to learn more, she enrolled in a horticulture class at Columbia University.

PREVIOUS PAGES, LEFT: While Netta's elegant Perennial Garden is designed in quadrants with acknowledged historical references to formal English and French parterres, she insists that her love of the land is the main reason she is a gardener. "The land is the garden," she says. RIGHT: Lush with bloom, standard fuchsias such as the cultivar 'Chinese Hat', which Netta has trained, and 'The Fairy' roses hold court in the terrace flower beds, their feet tickled by petunias, lamb's ears, artemisias, and alyssums. THIS PAGE, RIGHT: "My grandfather wrote to a colleague in Rome, 'Please bring me twelve decent statues.' Of course, by 'decent' he meant 'dressed,'" Netta recalls with a laugh. This is one of them. My mother brought it to her garden at Long Hill, Massachusetts. And now I have it here." OPPOSITE: The apple trees, meticulously pruned each year, were on the property when the Lockwoods bought their land. A path leading from the house to the Perennial Garden in a field up on the hillside runs between the trees.

About the same time, John's civilian wartime assignment took the young couple on numerous trips to Latin America, where Netta made "a beeline for botanical gardens." She became interested in tropical trees and plants, a core of interest that has continued throughout her life.

Unfortunately, Netta's gardening mother passed away, but her stepmother, Marjorie Russell Sedgwick, a great plantswoman, encouraged Netta's gardening inclination whenever Netta visited Long Hill. Marjorie Sedgwick also

introduced Netta to tree peonies with a "gift of Dr. Rock" (*Paeonia suffruticosa* 'Joseph Rock'). Enchanted by tree peonies' blooms, Netta has made them the cornerstones of her Perennial Garden, growing many from seed. Since they do not come true, most are unnamed varieties. She leaves the fuzzy, star-shaped seed heads on the plants all summer and counts and records the yearly number of blossoms each produces.

Despite her gardening heritage, Netta claims that it was really the Bedford farm that made her a gardener. She realized she was not going to "be the world's greatest painter," but her artistic instincts could be transferred to gardening. From the beginning, Netta believed that the indoors and the outdoors, the house and the grounds, should be tied together with transition spaces that make the flow appear seamless. She highlighted the land's natural features and sited new buildings to take advantage of its views and protected corners, of its nooks of seclusion and points of high drama. She says her aim is to create "a picture out every window."

ABOVE: Although they give the impression of being equal geometric quadrants, none of the four units in Netta's Perennial Garden is quite square. The main axial paths of closely mown grass are six feet wide; the paths within the squares, just two and a half feet wide, are laid with pine bark mulch. LEFT: When Netta's father offered to have the swamp across the road made into a pond, she was reluctant to alter any aspect of the topography. To this day, digging it to a depth of 11 feet has been the only change to the land. The pond's banks became the site for an arboretum, for experiments with trees, many of them native.

The property was graced with a network of stone walls that created natural divisions and formed muted backgrounds. It even had its own quarry. Over the years, buildings were renovated and new ones built, the orchard was restored, and the gardens expanded. Terraces, with brick or stone surfaces to accelerate drainage under plants, were added outside the house and guesthouses. Stone steps and paths, placed with Netta's unerring artist's eye, offer pleasant walks and unexpected vistas.

One mown path, its width planned for the comfort of tandem strolling, winds through the orchard to an opening in a stone wall. In a field 200 yards above the house, the Perennial Garden, "a jewel in the crown, full of color and interest," basks in a sheltered southern exposure. Divided by wide axial path, it measures 64 by 61 feet, and is laid out in four sections of approximately 25 feet square each. A series of rocky ledges planted in soft grays and greens—lamium, artemisia, nepeta—rise behind, like the draping of a neutral, but carefully planned, backdrop.

For this garden Netta incorporated design ideas from old gardening books, and the basic parterre plan is an adaptation of one illustrated in Thomas Hyll's *The Gardeners Labyrinth*, first published in 1577. "The old designs had so much character," she says. The two diagonally opposite quadrants are laid out in the same pattern: one pair in circles, the other in diamonds. All are edged in old brick. To keep the garden's pattern clearly visible at all times, Netta does not allow the plants to become too tall. Always vigilent she prunes, pinches, and judiciously removes self-seeders throughout the growing season. "The garden is especially beautiful in the winter, when it is covered with protective Christmas tree branches."

In the center of each square, an iron "umbrella" acts as a support for Netta's prized clematis collection. The umbrellas, designed for climbing roses, were brought from France by Netta's mother as a gift to the young gardener. The entrances, many marked with Netta's collection of tree peonies, are also defined by shrub-size dictamnus (both *Dictamnus albus* and *D. albus* 'Ruber'). But in the "Hot Bed," a generous show

ABOVE: **Netta's first greenhouse is a classic Lord & Burnham model. Having seen others that stood out "like sore thumbs" in the landscape, she excavated and had it built with the floor two and a half feet below grade, making the building appear much smaller. It is stained a soft green to blend with surrounding shrubs and trees.**

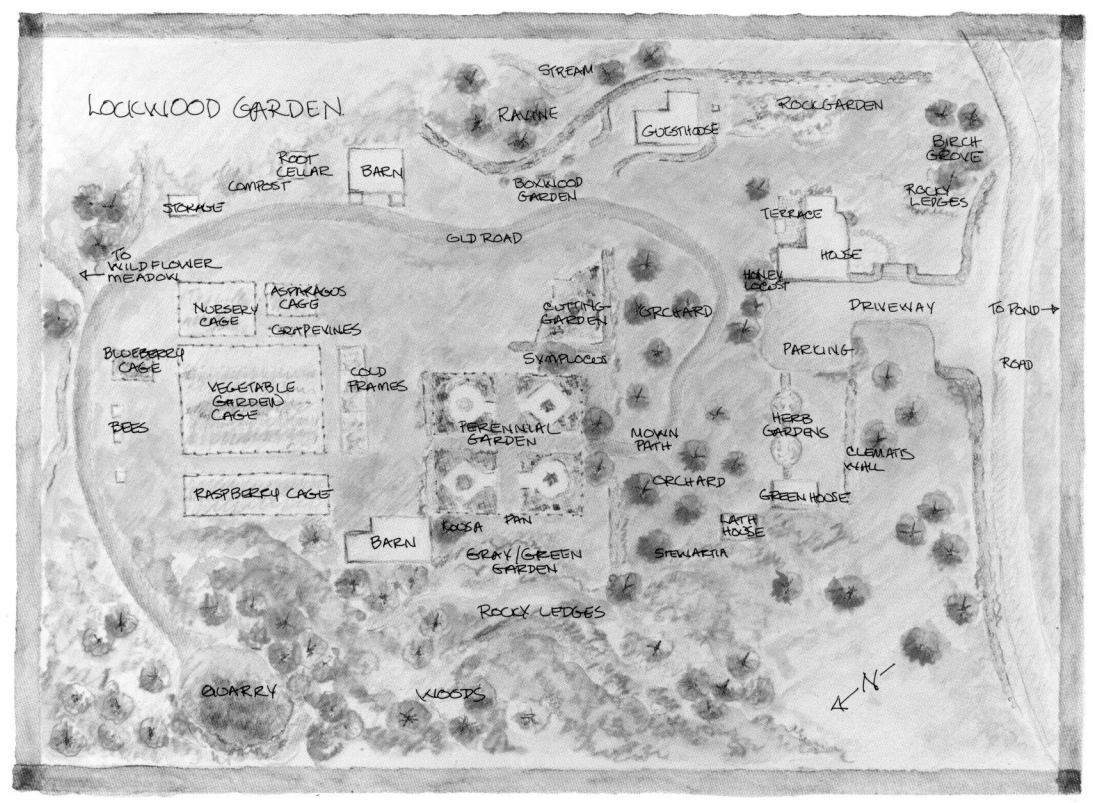

NOTES ON GROWING CLEMATIS

HENRIETTA E. S. LOCKWOOD

ADAPTED FROM "ON CLEMATIS," THE GARDEN JOURNAL,
THE NEW YORK BOTANICAL GARDEN, 1966

I find that clematis thrive best if set in a rich, cool, sweet but above all well-drained soil. Planting in a hole approximately two feet wide by two feet deep is worth the effort, as there are records of clematis living for well over half a century. Add a handful or two of limestone to another couple of handfuls of rock phosphate to furnish food. Provide rubble and sand for drainage. Compost adds quality to the soil. When all is prepared, spread the roots of the plant out carefully.

Set the crown a couple of inches below the level of the soil, and gently tap the soil down. The roots and crown should be protected from the animals; wrap them in a wire mesh cylinder, extending approximately 12 inches above the ground. Cover with a mulch to keep the roots cool. Add further mulch in fall for winter insulation. Each succeeding spring, give the plant a handful of potash to improve its color, and in the fall the same amount of bonemeal or superphosphate (well watered in) for food. I find that plants require about one inch of water a week, or a half gallon per square yard.

Because clematis climb by twining leafstalks, a support must be provided at once. Spring growth is particularly rapid. It is natural for the plant to climb upward. On young plants the fast-growing tips must be pinched out to allow the roots to balance the top growth and form a well-furnished base.

To prune or not to prune? North of New York City the winter does most of the pruning. Therefore in spring the dead wood needs to be removed (starting at the top of the plant). A simple, general rule is to hard-prune the later-flowering varieties and leave the early ones alone.

Clematis are subject to few pests and diseases other than "wilt." This sudden wilting of the plant, or a portion of the plant, is usually due to a fungal disease (*Ascochyta clematidina*). Sometimes, however, it is caused by old woody stems too thick to let the water rise. Spraying the foliage and surrounding soil with a fungicide acts as a deterrent. If wilt is observed, cut below the wilting point (and destroy the diseased piece), even if this is to the ground, and keep the plant well watered. A weak solution of a plant food often aids, and new shoots will usually appear.

Clematis have been one of Netta's passions since the time she was a young girl traveling abroad, where she became fascinated with clematis's wide array of color and form. Many, with the aid of a permit, she imported years later. Netta has grown and shown clematis, winning numerous awards.

Throughout Netta Lockwood's property, pieces of wire mesh are placed over walls for her prized collection of clematis to wind on comfortably. They frolic through trees, holly or hemlock, and shrubs, particularly azaleas, as well. To thwart the unrelenting rodents' appetites, roots are now wrapped in wire protection at planting time.

A FEW OF NETTA LOCKWOOD'S FAVORITE CLEMATIS

- *Clematis alpina* (formerly *Atragene alpina*). The alpine virgin's bower. Soft blue, nodding, four-inch flowers. Will bloom in shade.
- *Clematis cirrhosa.* White, bell-shaped flowers and fernlike foliage. Winter-blooming. Must be pot-grown in areas where temperatures fall below 32 degrees.
- *Clematis florida* 'Bicolor' (syn. 'Sieboldii'). The center is made up of a rosette of purple staminodes that persist after the sepals fall. Prune after blooming. Must be pot-grown in areas where temperatures fall below 32 degrees.
- *Clematis montana* and hybrids. Pink and white flowers. Will grow to great height and bloom in shade.
- 'Betty Corning' (Viticella group). Pale blue flowers.
- 'Étoile Violette' (Viticella group). Profusion of medium-size purple blooms.
- 'Henryi' (Lanuginosa group). Large white flowers with long, pointed sepals and a center of dark stamens.
- 'Huldine' (Viticella group). Cup-shaped, four-inch pearly white flowers. Strong-growing.
- 'Lady Betty Balfour' (Viticella group). Deep purple flowers with yellow stamens.
- 'Lord Nevill' (Patens group). Deep blue flowers. The beautifully formed sepals have a wavy edge.
- 'Minuet' (Viticella group). Two-inch, creamy flowers banded by purple.
- 'Mrs. Cholmondeley' (Jackmanii group). Enormous, flat, light blue flowers. The most continuously floriferous of the large-flowered hybrids.
- 'Perle d'Azur' (Jackmanii group). Light blue and free-flowering.
- 'Prins Hendrick' (Patens group). Extremely large and ruffled flowers. A shy bloomer.

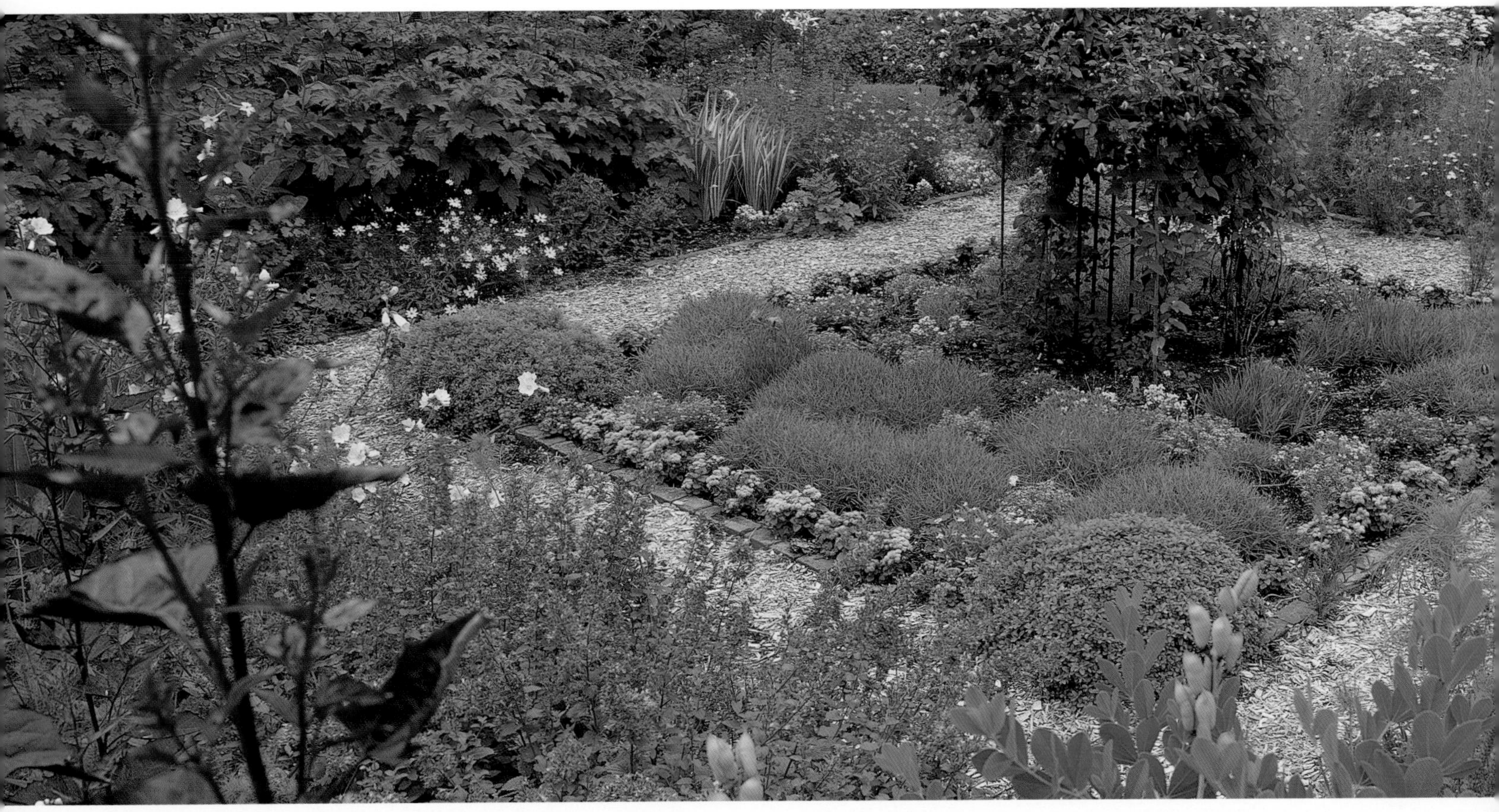

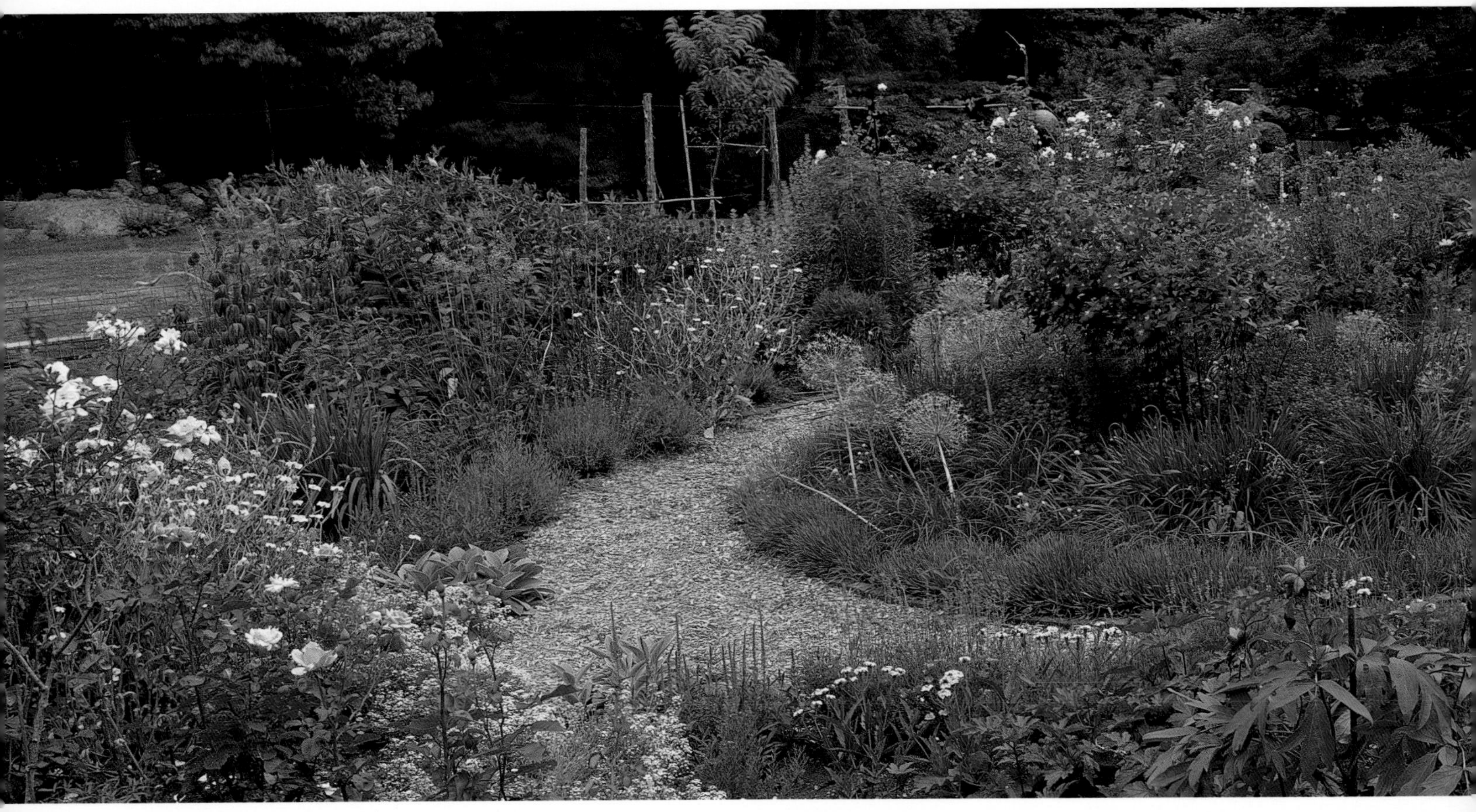

Each bed in the Perennial Garden has a color scheme and a plant theme. Purples, lavenders, and pinks, with notes of chartreuse, dominate, and neat edgings of ageratum, allium, or germander define the patterns. Clipped littleleaf box (*Buxus microphylla* 'Kingsville Dwarf') accents the corners of a diamond-shaped bed (TOP). In another circular bed (BOTTOM), the shapes of flowers are predominantly "spheres," featuring a range of alliums, like the glorious showy *Allium christophii*, and the spicy little heads of globe amaranth.

of variegated-leaved nasturtiums (*Tropaeolum majus* 'Alaska') takes color command. All the nasturtiums are grown from seed annually, approximately 60 plants. Helter-skelter, they toss their heads, in shades of red, yellow, and orange, and sprawl languidly out into the path.

Primroses, euphorbia, nigella, lady's mantle, *Salvia horminum* 'Clarissa', sweet William, and the golden-leaved matricaria have self-seeded throughout the beds with lively spontaneity. The perennials are joined by a range of annuals, such as *Calceolaria mexicana*, *Echium* 'Viper's Blue', angelonia, tweedia, nicotiana, and petunias. Netta observes that almost one third of the plants in the Perennial Garden are annuals, "to make it colorful all through the season." Surrounding beds contain taller plants, such as thalictrums, veronicastrums, globe thistles, and lilies. A display of the elegant, self-seeded *Atriplex hortensis*, a deep bronze-purple accent splashed by a painter's brush, links the beds together.

The garden complex has spread around the Perennial Garden: a 45- by 80-foot vegetable garden, a raspberry cage, a blueberry cage, an asparagus cage, a cutting garden, and the essential nursery, 23 by 27 feet. Like toy soldiers, three beehives are lined up at the back of the garden, the bees' constant humming accompanying birds' song.

Farther down the hill, reached by more grass paths, a deep rock-ledged ravine falls abruptly away to a boggy bottom. Selective clearing has nudged the stand of trees—hemlock, oak, and maple—to branch and leaf high, creating a soaring green canopy overhead. The guesthouse, built to look like a barn, stands above the hollow, its bedrooms feeling like a Peter Pan treehouse.

The windows face down on a carpet of ferns, trilliums, and native cimicifuga, divided by a winding path that leads to a stream. While in many areas the Lockwoods put Mother Nature on a gentle tether, here she is allowed full freedom. And the "wild things" grow, highlighted, one by one, as sunlight passes through the trees with the directional intensity of a theater spotlight.

A new project begins each year, sometimes at nature's

whim. A beloved, 150-year-old white oak fell in Gloria, the hurricane of September 1985. A sad moment; the guardian, which had stood above the house since the Lockwoods' purchase, is gone. But, Netta notes, it fell away from the house. "Trees do not want to hurt people." Something so distinctive had seemed permanent. But it was not, and a new garden, with a little pool, was created in the rocks that had surrounded the roots of the old tree. That, too, changed, as the tree's roots dried up and shrank, and the rocks no longer held water.

Now the area, a sunny Mediterranean garden planted with prostrate junipers, artemisias, sedums, nepetas, and Siberian irises, is an extension of the guesthouse terrace. Netta remarks, "I immediately thought of a Green Taverna," and she installed fig trees in pots and strung grapes across the tables. Ten pots of blue agapanthus wave their blossoms, as though in orchestrated unison, in the summer breeze. The walkways around the guesthouse are lined with exotics such as camellias, crape myrtles, and oleanders enjoying their summer airing.

Changes that are not an act of nature happen slowly. "It seems to take me a bit to think about change." Netta stops and thinks for a minute, her painter's eye gathering today's impressions of the landscape. "In fact, it is *essential* to take time. You don't want to startle. You want new additions to work into the whole. And that takes slow consideration."

LEFT: The vivid 'Alaska' nasturtium fills the "Hot Bed." BELOW: Clematis, which is one of Netta's specialties, were the impetus for a series of eight cold frames, some as deep as two and a half feet. "John gave me one each year." (Marauding animals have become so bold that the cold frames now are lined with hardware cloth and covered with wire.) RIGHT: A welcoming, rustic gate opens to a cutting garden, which provides flowers for the house.

"I've always liked the idea of creating vignettes

in a garden, isolated pictures that one can stop and enjoy."

Jocelyn Horder

At the Water's Edge

JOCELYN HORDER

POULSBO, WASHINGTON

"I'm not as sad about the old pine's death as people think I should be," says Jocelyn Horder, philosophically accepting the immutability of nature. The 130-year-old *Pinus strobus* skeleton towers over her Point Garden. Etched in black against the sky, it stands on the highest spot of a tiny peninsula that juts into Liberty Bay, an arm of Puget Sound, and faces the Olympic Mountains.

Birds—gulls, crows, hawks, osprey, herons, even a rare eagle—target it in their travels. Woodpeckers and flickers, seeking bugs, are removing its bark piece by piece, causing white streaks, like brushstrokes, on the dark surface. "That pine was probably brought here from the East, perhaps as a seedling across the Oregon Trail, as the East is its native

habitat. It will be completely debarked one day. Change and evolution are part of gardening," Jocey says. "When the tree is gone, I'll replace it with something else."

Jocey speaks with fondness of the couple, Sara and Uno Brauer, who purchased the tract of land in 1889. Uno Brauer became a part-time minister in a number of Swedish Baptist churches in the Seattle area. The story goes that he rowed across the bay to preach his sermons. His own church, started in a tent, was built just up the road. The Brauers cleared their land and farmed it. They planted an orchard and raised chickens, and Sara gardened.

Members of the Brauer family lived in the house until five years before the Horders purchased the property in 1980.

live on the water—and to be a part of the history of a place."

The Horders commissioned Garrett's brother Morley P. Horder, an architect, to design their home. Jocey determined she would "experience nature" from all areas of the house and be able to walk outside from each room. The distinction between indoors and out would be blurred with floor-to-ceiling glass, and from her desk, Jocey would look out straight past the pine to the bay. The house, the Horders instructed, should be unobtrusive in the landscape.

The result is a one-story, glass-and-brick house. At 48 by 48 feet square, "with no basement and no attic," it occupies almost the full width of the peninsula. Since the road is located on higher ground with a view directly down on the house, Garrett's brother suggested a sod roof, believing that a grass-covered roof would make the house blend with its surroundings—Jocey's future garden.

The roof, slightly elevated in the center to ensure run-off, was covered with roofing material, like that used on flat-roof industrial buildings. A two-inch layer of pea gravel was added, then two layers of commercial sod were applied back to back, the first layer face down and the second face up. Since it is the sun that ultimately destroys roofing material, presumably with grass as its cover, the roof will last indefinitely.

The roof is like a miniature meadow. Since it is given no supplemental water, little growth occurs. On rare occasions the grass closest to the edge of the roof has to be trimmed with a weed eater, but otherwise it is maintenance-free. "The first year," Jocey recalls, "when it rained, dozens of angleworms crawled out and fell on the pavement; that was a somewhat startling effect, but then they disappeared. The grass does drop its seeds into the garden, and the seedlings have to be pulled, but the roof is a lot less work than the meadow behind the perennial garden."

Jocey reminisces about her garden's evolution as evening falls, with the sun dropping directly across the bay over the mountains. The water is still and streaked in pink. After a day of activity from kayaks to cruisers, all that remain are little boats with their sails furled; they rest at anchor. Jocey sits on

PREVIOUS PAGE: Around the man-made pool, ground covers such as *Bolax glebaria, Saxifraga cuneifolia, Vaccinium vitis-idaea,* and *Paxistima canbyi* fill in the crannies. Dwarf rhododendrons— *Rhododendron* × *cilpinense, R. racemosum, R.* 'Gumpo', *R.* 'Avril', and *R.* 'Kogane'—add accents of color; selected small plants such as the bulb *Rhodohypoxis baurii,* a saturated pink, light up dark corners. A mature multitrunked *Prunus cerasifera* provides shade for ferns. ABOVE: The remains of an old pine tree, now half its original size, form a 40-foot organic sculpture. Stripped of its needles, it offers an ongoing exhibition of bird life. The swing was put up by Jocey and her son soon after they moved onto the property. RIGHT: In the retaining wall that creates a terrace for the vegetable garden, crevices are planted with *Sempervivum soboliferum* and *S.* 'Lavender and Old Lace'. OPPOSITE: Jocey is accompanied on her garden rounds by Sable, a lively German shepherd, who somehow "knows not to walk on a planted bed."

During those unoccupied years, the house was vandalized and, ultimately, rendered unsalvageable. Before having it razed, the Horders went through the contents, but the only remnant of the family was a ship's log kept by a Brauer sailor who traveled the route between Seattle and the Orient.

Jocey remembers the day when her husband, Garrett, called her from work and said, "Would you like to live on Brauer's Point? It was put up for sale today." They had often sailed past the spot and admired it from the water. Yet at first Jocey said no, because the bay was too shallow to accommodate their 48-foot sailboat. But the couple quickly decided to sell the boat, purchase a smaller one, and make the move. They commissioned a 38-foot boat to be built with twin centerboards, so they could pull it out of the bay onto their mud flat. "We were boaters," Jocey says. "Living here afforded a unique opportunity to watch the spectacles of weather, to

a bench in her latest garden, looking down over what she has created: diverse gardens that run seamlessly together. She says she cannot choose a favorite area. "There are several worlds here. That's what I like about it.

"After I married in 1949, my interest in gardening took off, yet my gardens remained pretty simple until I came here. Family events centered around boating. There was not a great deal of time for gardening."

Jocey's first attempt at the new site was planting lupines and daisies from a packaged wildflower mix a friend had given her. Jocey scattered the seeds on the Point between the house and the water's edge—without amending the soil. "Things died, and I learned very quickly that even a meadow in that soil wouldn't work. As a gardener," she says ruefully, "it is surprising that I didn't look at the soil before we bought this property. It was boggy, sour clay, so awful I cannot even describe it. If I had known how bad it was, I'm not sure I would have even moved here." She realized that a

ABOVE: Over the last 15 years, native grasses have invaded and replaced the original sod that covers the roof of Jocey Horder's home; some of it has been taken over by moss. To define the Point Garden, the Horders commissioned a local landscape designer, Dan Robinson, to bring in moss-covered granite from the Cascade Mountains, which was set to look as if the Point had always been a rocky promontory. LEFT: In May, Russell hybrid lupines are a forest of spikes, their colors seemingly chosen to reflect the old brick used in the walls of the house.

major alteration to the soil and accommodation for drainage would be necessary to make a serious garden.

The Point needed to be rethought. "The challenge was to make a garden that did not obstruct the view. I needed to design it with short plants. And since I would be looking at it year-round, I wanted it to be primarily evergreen." Granite boulders trucked in from the Cascade Mountains became the bones of the garden. Between the stones, new soil, mixed with sand, was added. In a nod to the aged feeling of the garden, a number of old stumps and "snags," remnants of cedar trees that had been burned near the coast, were placed as though they had washed up on the shore. Gravel paths lead to seating areas.

As the Point Garden was taking shape, Jocey also developed the area on the opposite side of the house around the front door. It was in-

tended to create a sense of welcome as well as to integrate the house into the landscape. Mounds, accented by decaying stumps, were made with the same mountain stone. A man-made stream terminating in a pool runs under the approach, and

waterfalls provide the restful sounds of water falling on stone. The water is moved round the clock by a recirculating pump. "We had to put pieces of screen over the pipes, so that the clamshells dropped by the gulls won't get caught in the mechanism."

At one point Jocey stocked the pool with goldfish, but when the tides came up and washed saltwater into the pool, it made the fish sick. "Anyway, the herons, kingfishers, and raccoons kept eating them, so I gave up." The otters do not care about the purity of the water, though, and occasionally arrive for a romp—up one side of the Point, through the pool, and down the other back into the bay.

The main garden above the cove is a perennial garden, which Jocey says she really had never done before. "The idea of perennials—campanulas, delphiniums, phlox—was too much like what my mother had. It took me until just a few years ago to become interested in them." When her husband said, "Go ahead and have fun with it," she launched into it "big time." The border, which began to take its final

OPPOSITE: A breezeway links the house with the parking area; at its corner a wisteria drips luxuriant cascades of lavender flowers. ABOVE: An enclosed bonsai garden, with worktables and a brick wall with a shelf, is located outside Jocey's bedroom door, allowing her to keep close watch over her bonsai charges, which now number "a manageable thirty." In the foreground are grouped a 100-year-old three-trunk "grove" of *Acer palmatum*, a *Crataegus* seedling, and a *Chamaecyparis pisifera* 'Squarrosa Pygmea Aurea'. LEFT: The man-made waterfall at Jocey's front door is a well-composed still life. The red foliage of *Acer palmatum* 'Dissectum Atropurpureum' is set off by the soft greens of *Armeria juniperifolia* 'Bevan's Variety', *Heuchera glabra*, *Spiraea betulifolia* var. *lucida*, and *Polystichum munitum*.

shape as recently as 1990, starts at a guesthouse and garage, which was built close to their original boundary, and extends almost to the end of their land—a full 192 feet.

Unlike the constraints she imposed on planning the Point Garden, which required small plants she could see over, the perennial border offered her the opportunity of introducing a completely different repertoire: plants with stature or robust foliage. She chose thalictrums, salvias, *Angelica gigas*, rodgersia, *Filipendula rubra* 'Magnifica', *Sedum* 'Autumn Joy', *Helianthemum* 'Eloise'—all in a palette of pinks, lavenders, purples, and russets, accented with yellow foliage, such as that of golden sage or elder.

To control the bank and to give the Perennial Garden a raised effect, Jocey placed pieces of railroad ties as an edging. "The design was a mistake," she says. "It was done while I was away. I had wanted a castellated effect, with gradual ups and downs. Instead it was installed with each *piece* a different height, and I have never liked it. But you learn to live with some things. Some you can change and some you can't." Of the daily annoyances, she says, "The biggest problems in my garden are slugs and horsetail [*Equisetum hyemale*], which seem to like every environment on the place." She flicks a slug to the ground and gives it the heel of her sneaker.

A well at the top of the hill supplies water via pipes to the Perennial Garden. Having learned about the necessity of soil amendments the hard way with the first garden, Jocey added "manure, humus, mulch" to the Perennial Garden from the beginning. "This lean sandy soil had absolutely no food in it."

Rising behind the Perennial Garden is a meadow, which Jocey cuts with a weed eater twice a year. She has planted so many trees on the hillside,

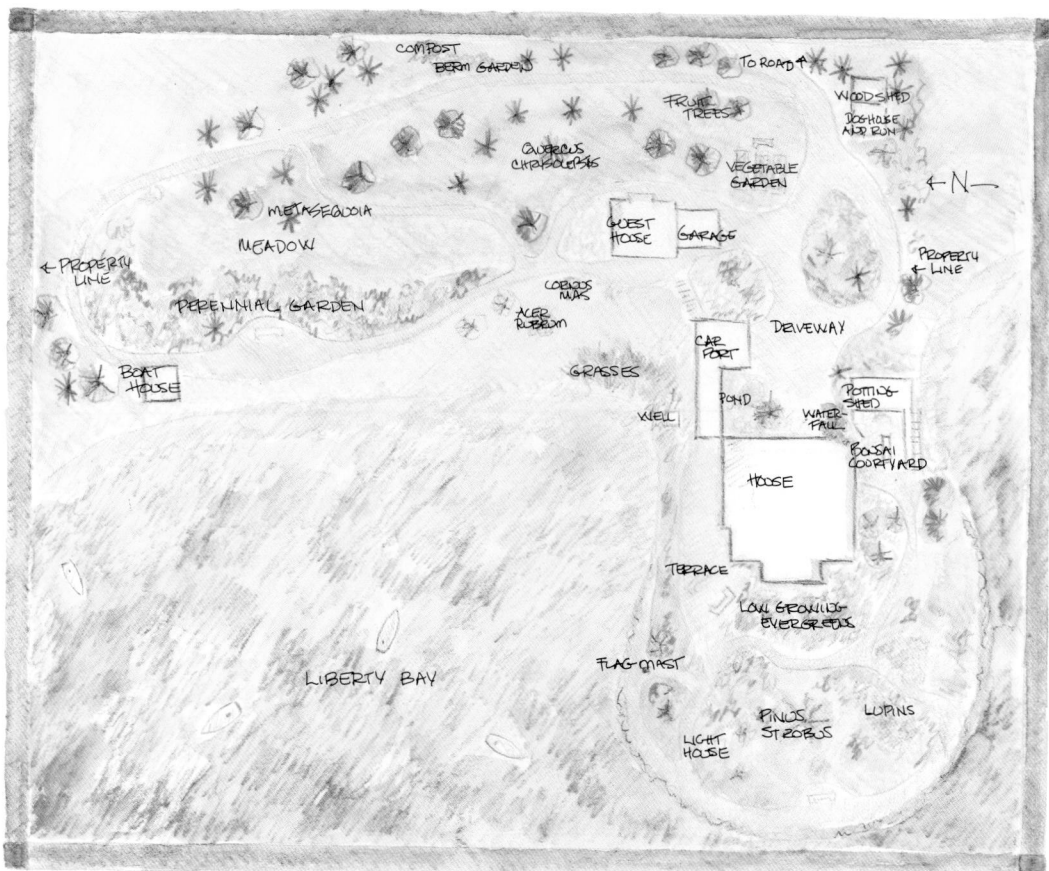

some still small, that caution must be taken with the cutting, and besides, the meadow is too steep for a mower. "For the first cut, I wait until the clover is through blooming, because it is so beautiful. And then for the second cut, until after the Queen Anne's lace in the fall."

Jocey's gardening interests have always focused on trees and shrubs. As a child she was never interested in small plants. "I only wanted to learn about trees," she remembers. "People generally plant big trees; I'd rather start one from seed and be able to watch all its stages." A *Quercus chrysolepis* reminds Jocey of the day 15 years ago when she and her grandson collected "fistfuls of acorns" on Mount Whitney.

The tree is a memorial to that outing. A *Quercus phillyreoides* was grown from acorns picked up on a beach in Japan. A katsura (*Cercidiphyllum japonicum*), a *Koelreuteria paniculata*, a *Picea breweriana*, and a *Sorbus forrestii* were also grown from seed. The sorbus is about to bloom for the first time. "It will be fun to see it." An eastern balsam fir (*Abies balsamea*) was placed at the edge of the mown path, "so I can caress the needles as I walk by." She looks down the hillside. "When all these trees have reached maturity, it will be a forest here."

She pauses to look at a rhododendron volunteer seedling at the base of a tree trunk. "This came from somewhere in the garden; I'm watching it in place." Jocey often moves volunteer seedlings to her "intensive care unit," a 4- by 24-foot raised bed that is located near a potting shed and workroom, just outside her bedroom door. There, in the protected environment backed with a pergola, she isolates plants until

A *Viburnum plicatum* var. *tomentosum* 'Mariesii', the focus of the island bed, stretches its white-flowered branches over the driveway. It glows on a foggy morning. Jocey admits, "I'm not particularly a white-flower fan, but given their own areas, white flowers can be lovely."

they are ready to be placed in the garden. "I've always wanted big trees and woods, and I don't have those here, so I have to be satisfied with certain specimens. I love growing plants

JOCELYN HORDER'S FAVORITE FERNS

Jocey Horder became interested in ferns in 1975, when she was invited to attend a Fern Study Group at the Northwest Horticultural Society. Growing 50 species in her garden, she touts ferns as unappreciated plants suitable for mixture into many styles of gardens. She reminds that ferns are found in a wide range of habitats. "There are woodland and dryland ferns."

Wherever possible, Jocey creates environments hospitable to ferns: slightly acidic, humus-laden soil with good drainage and rocky crevices. Most woodland ferns prefer dappled shade, not heavy shade, she says. However, she also grows some ferns in the sun, since, she says, "it is a shame to relegate such a range of textures to the shade." She notes that in the sun, ferns will probably grow to only about one third their expected size.

In 1986 Jocey joined the American Fern Society, and in 1989 she became a charter member of the Hardy Fern Foundation, of which she now serves as a board member. "Our chief purpose," she says, "is to promote knowledge about hardy ferns that grow in the different areas of the country. We are establishing a comprehensive collection of the world's hardy ferns for display, evaluation, public education, and introduction to the gardening and horticultural community. We now have nine satellite gardens that test ferns for hardiness in their areas." Reports of the assembled results—what grows where—are sent to members via a newsletter.

For six years Jocey was in charge of the spore exchange for the American Fern Society. She has begun many ferns herself from spores. She either collects the spores from the fertile fronds of her own fern or acquires them from fern spore exchanges. She chooses a sterile plastic container, often as small as two by two by four inches, with a transparent plastic top. The clear lid allows light in but retains the moisture content. "You are creating a terrarium environment with constant humidity—just like the Victorians did."

She grows the spores in peat pellets.

She instructs, "First, thoroughly moisten peat pellets with hot water, then drain off the excess water. When cool, sprinkle the dustlike fern spores over the peat and close the lid tightly. Keep in good light but away from direct sun. In one to six months the spores will germinate and take on a greenish cast, looking like fine moss. Then a prothallus, which looks like a tiny heart-shaped leaf, will develop, under which, if sufficient moisture is provided, the sperm fertilizes the egg, which produces a root and a tiny leaf. This can take two to twelve months. When the leaf looks like a small fern, it can be carefully pricked out and potted up in a light, lean potting mix. It must be kept protected and moist until hardened off.

"There are excellent reference books that detail the nature of the fern reproductive system, collection of spores, and methods of growing them. It is a fascinat-

Blechnum spicant *and* Polystichum setiferum rotundatum cristatum *nestle in the fertile area around an old tree trunk.*

ing area of horticulture," Jocey says. She particularly recommends *Ferns: Wild Things Make a Comeback in the Garden* by C. Colston Burrell, the Brooklyn Botanic Garden; and *Ferns for American Gardens* by John Mickel, the New York Botanical Garden. "But beware," she adds, "ferns can quickly become an addiction."

LARGE FERNS

BOTANICAL NAME	COMMON NAME	HEIGHT
Dryopteris affinis	Golden-scaled male fern	2–3'
Dryopteris championii	Champion's wood fern	1–3'
Dryopteris × complexa		2–3'
Dryopteris wallichiana	Wallich's wood fern	2–4'
Matteuccia struthiopteris	Ostrich fern	To 5'
Onoclea sensibilis	Sensitive fern	1–3'
Polystichum munitum	Western sword fern	3–5'
Polystichum neolobatum	Long-eared holly fern	1–2'
Polystichum polyblepharum	Tassel fern	2–4'

SMALL FERNS

Adiantum aleuticum subpumilum	Dwarf western maidenhair	6–8"
Asplenium adiantum-nigrum	Black spleenwort	6–12"
Asplenium trichomanes	Maidenhair spleenwort	4–6"
Woodsia polystichoides	Holly fern woodsia	6–8"

FERNS THAT WILL TOLERATE SUN

Adiantum pedatum var. *aleuticum**	Dwarf western maidenhair	6–8"
*Asplenium trichomanes**	Maidenhair spleenwort	4–6"
Blechnum penna-marina	Little hard fern	6" (in sun)
*Blechnum spicant**	Deer fern	12" (in sun)
Cheilanthes, all species	Lip fern	6–12"
Matteuccia, all species	Ostrich fern	To 5' (in sun)
Polystichum munitum	Western sword fern	15" (in sun)

*If roots are protected by rocks or a log.

from seed." She has received many seeds through subscribing to explorer seed programs and through the seed exchanges of organizations such as the North American Rock Garden Society. "It is easy to get carried away, and I usually have about five dozen going at a time. It's exciting to watch them germinate, to start up, to gain a good root system." Often they remain in the nursery for three or four years. "Of course, I then have to find a good home for them after I grow them."

A large stump, placed near the entrance of the house "to add height, arrived with moss, dicentra, and huckleberries growing on it." These natives, she notes, were already in their habitat. Their home was moved to her home. Jocey left them in place. A pileated woodpecker works on the stump constantly, seeking the carpenter ants for his midday meal.

Jocey considers herself "a frustrated botanist; I'd always like to know more than I do." Though she never studied horticulture, she agrees that her degree in art from the University of Washington may help her in the refinements of

gardening. "But I never sketch things when I plant; I just bring home a plant and find a place for it. Until the perennial garden, I was always cautious about color. Now I'm excited about playing with different combinations."

The cultivation of bonsai is also a lifelong interest, kindled by a chance lecture at the Seattle Garden Club by the revered teacher Yuji Yoshimura. Jocey's original study group, about 12 equally dedicated people, have stayed and worked together for 40 years. At its peak, her collection of bonsai numbered about 150.

In keeping with her thorough, disciplined approach to gardening, Jocey logs all her plants with both botanical and common names, source, location, flower color, bloom date, "and other pertinent information" into a computer for quick and constant reference. At last count the entries numbered 1,706 plants and growing. "For all plants that have departed the garden, a total of 389, whether by death, sale, or gift, I have a category: the category is labeled 'croaked.'"

Ten years ago, the Horders were able to purchase three empty house lots next to their original property, giving them ownership of most of the cove. "I now have about two and a half acres, depending on the tide." The land rises abruptly to the road above. "If we had owned that additional land when we came here, we would have built at the top. Our present house site would have been our boatyard." Garrett Horder, a marine insurance broker, passed away in 1986. "His life was the sea, and it was mine for a long time, too." Since Garrett has been gone, gardening has taken over Jocey's time. "I keep saying I will not add one more bed. Then last year I added one at the top of the hill. But this is the last. Absolutely."

These days, with back trouble—"I can't look a shovel in the eye anymore. I've turned into a pointer: 'prune this, plant this there'"—her "right hand," Denise Kelly, must do much of the work at ground level. "I could not make it look like this without Denise—we're a team.

"Gardening, for me," Jocey muses, "is the excitement of watching things grow. I stand and look around and think, 'All these plants have come from a seed.' I'm greedy about the seasons, always looking forward to the next one."

BELOW: Reflecting her love of woody plants, Jocey's 192-foot Perennial Garden is anchored with trees and shrubs. A tall, columnlike *Sequoiadendron giganteum* 'Pendulum' was the first tree she planted in the bed. Golden foliage is offered by *Sambucus racemosa* 'Plumosa Aurea' and *Philadelphus coronarius* 'Aureus'. *Acer palmatum* 'Kashima', *A. p.* 'Seiryu', *Picea mariana* 'Nana', *P. omorika* 'Nana', *Sequoia sempervirens* 'Aptos Blue', *Sambucus canadensis* 'Variegata', *S. c.* 'Purpurea', and *Cotinus coggygria* also add a variety of color with their foliage. *Rosa* 'Dapple Dawn', with its peachy pink flowers, blooms all summer. LEFT: A detail of one of Jocey's compositions features the pinkish-lavender flowers of *Polygonatum bistorta supurba*.

A Secure Harbor

MARION PRINCE HOSMER

YORK, MAINE

Marion Hosmer has the soil and the sea in her blood. "I come from a country family who always worked the earth. My grandfather was determined from the time he was four years old to be a farmer. And the rest of my ancestors all went to sea." As she glances across the garden she has worked for almost 50 years, a break in a line of shagbark hickories affords a view directly out to the Atlantic Ocean, only 500 feet away.

Her husband, Calvin, she says, "came from the same New England stock." In fact, she and Calvin both grew up in Sharon, Massachusetts, a convenient halfway point between Boston and Providence. "We belonged to the same group of children who played together, went to school together, rode horses together, went to dancing school together." Marion jokingly adds, "So we have no excuse if we don't get along. We knew from the beginning what each of us was like."

Marion and Calvin were married in 1928. Their first home was on a quiet road in their native Sharon "where we were the only people." But as the town of Sharon grew, it began to "feel like suburbia." The quiet isolation Marion and Calvin had grown to value was disappearing. With their two sons, Calvin and Tom, in tow, they looked to the North. For

12 years they canvassed the coast of Maine, searching for land. Marion remembers, "Cal got a geodetic map, and we explored every single point and estuary." In 1948 they purchased a farm, 150 acres of field, woods, and marsh winding along the ocean and a harbor inlet.

A one-story, rustic cottage that had been built in 1939 came with the land, and after making it habitable, the family moved in for their first summer. They even spent portions of the winter in the cottage, "to see if we really liked year-round living here," and found that they did. A serendipitous offer on their Sharon house cemented their decision to relocate permanently.

Officially full-time residents of Maine, the Hosmers walked their coastal land and formed plans for adding a house, barns, and a garden; for keeping their horses; for raising beef cattle, pigs, and chickens. The place would once again be a farm. Calvin designed an imposing, four-square stone house. "Cal was a flour merchant, with his business in Boston. But architecture is his passion. He is just a natural." Built at the highest point, a crown about 25 feet above sea level, it holds a clear view to the sea. "At night the lights

"If I could grow only one thing, I'd grow fruit trees; they are so beautiful all

the time. Beautiful in the winter with the buds, beautiful in bloom, beautiful bearing fruit."

Marion Prince Hosmer

from four lighthouses are so brilliant that they flash and glow on our bedroom ceiling." The house was situated due south to hold the sun's warmth on its facade and in the garden that soon took shape. Dry stone walls were erected in front of the building to protect the plants from the salt spray.

The rocky soil was replaced with rich topsoil amended with manure and other nutrients such as greensand and rock phosphates. Eager to put her hands in the earth, Marion filled the Front Garden, as she named it, with roses, lilies, and delphiniums. The color scheme of the Front Garden has always been yellow, white, blue, and "shades of those colors—with a little pink to pep it up."

When the Hosmers purchased the property, it was over-

grown and untended. They gradually cleared it, their husbandry spreading like ripples across a pond. As they worked, they uncovered many stone walls. "We built up the old stone walls along the roads that had tumbled down. And we planted flowering crabs—'Golden Hornet', 'Young America', 'Van Eseltine'—along the walls. And the lovely *Malus toringoides,* which I raised from seed."

The Hosmers learned that higher walls, tightened by mortar, were needed in harsh weather as a barrier from the wind and salt spray. And Marion, with the plant collector's impulse operating at full throttle, wanted more space for her garden. They expanded the Front Garden's layout to its current 75-foot length and hired a man, "just out of jail" for

PREVIOUS PAGES, LEFT: The Front Garden is surrounded by a mortared stone wall. "For," as Marion Hosmer observes, "when a nor'easter blows, the spray reaches all the way to the house." RIGHT: The burying ground, surrounded by stone walls, is home to perennial borders edged with grape hyacinths and drifts of naturalized daffodils. In the spring thousands bloom, a yellow carpet under the old hickories, lilacs, and apples that dot the property. THIS PAGE, ABOVE: Eight Italian pineapple finials mark the corners and height changes on the wall. The pineapple ornaments, traditional New England symbols of hospitality, reflect the Hosmers' open-door policy. RIGHT: While Marion has often trained her own espaliered and standard fruit trees, those on the south face of the house were purchased from Long Island master Henry Leuthardt, already in espaliered form.

dense windbreaks and natural divisions between gardens. "Friends often ask, 'Why on earth do you keep those old lilacs in your view?' But knowing we were going to be here year-round, we didn't want to have the waves dashing in our faces. And we felt it was more interesting to get different views, rather than have the whole thing spread out in front of you at once."

some minor infraction, to do the extensive stonework. The resulting wall, eight feet high on the sides, steps down gradually to four feet at its lowest point. In the center a solid, double gate opens to the lawn beyond.

Early on, the Hosmers assessed what they had inherited with the land, and they built on that foundation. A legacy of lilacs was left untouched. "They are so fragrant. The fishermen tell us that when the winds are offshore, you can smell them eight miles out at the Isles of Shoals." The bushes form

On another high point on the land between their house and the sea, the Hosmers discovered an old burying ground, suffocating amidst the brambles, sumac, and wild cherries. Marion recalls, "The Raynes family settled the place in 1638, and this was their family plot. Someday," she adds, "of course, we will join them. But gardeners live a long time. We have to get up in the morning to see what grew in the night."

129

To gain access to the burying ground, an opening was cut through the lilacs, an enticing entrance with the feel of *The Secret Garden*, which Marion says she's "reread and reread." It became the Hosta Path. Marion favors large gray-leaved hosta varieties and those with golden edges. They are given plenty of room to spread.

Over the years the Hosmers added more acreage, some of which they have deeded to the Rachel Carson Wildlife Conservancy. At one point a nearby farm, where Marion enjoyed walking and bird watching, became the focus of her desires. "Cal used to ask me what I wanted for my birthday and Christmas, and I responded, 'The Reilly place.' It took awhile, but he got it for me.

"The plan for this place is all our own. It grew as we opened new areas and made them available." Marion cites many influences—historical sources; visits to gardens at places such as Williamsburg, Mount Vernon, and Monticello; and extensive travel in Europe, particularly during the years their son Calvin, a career army officer, served in Germany. Marion recalls repeated readings of Sarah Orne Jewett's memories of summer on the coast of Maine in *The Country of the Painted Firs*. The couple studied English gardening magazines, such as *Country Life*, to which they have subscribed for over 40 years. "We're Anglophiles," she admits.

One of the first major projects, borrowed directly from one of the English periodicals, was the selection and planting of espaliered fruit trees against the walls of the house. On the south side, eight trees—apples, pears, and a plum—thrive against the warmth of the stone facade: 'Cornish Gillyflower', 'Stayman's Winesap', 'Early Sweet', 'Strawberry Chenango', and 'Spitzenberg' apples; 'Clapp's Favorite' and 'Sheldon' pears; and 'Stanley' plum. Each is meticulously pruned three or four times during the growing season, the side shoots always taken off to about eight inches and the forward shoots to about four inches. "You must always prune enough for the tree form to show."

At first thinking only of the ornamental value of fruit trees, Marion determined to add an orchard for its sheer beauty. She learned that a nearby orchard of 25-year-old 'Cortland' apple trees that had been owned by the Goodrich Tire family was to be cut down to make way for a hay field. "So we hired a tree man with a digger and a bucket, and he moved twenty-seven trees; we lost only two." She lined the exterior of the horse pasture, where, in September, the prolific-bearing trees, now 70 years old, look like an emerald chain studded with rubies.

ABOVE: Marion planted a white border along the outside of her garden wall. The blooms of a kousa dogwood in a woodland bed across from the white garden echo the white of the foxgloves. LEFT: An enticing path leads directly from the Front Garden gate through an opening in the aged lilacs, along mown paths edged with wildflowers, to the rocky shore.

To ensure an abundant harvest, Marion initiated a spraying program, researching the five necessary stages: "dormant," in early spring; "pink," when the buds are separated in clusters and show pink; "petal fall," when 70 percent of the petals have fallen; "weekly," after the petal fall until August 1; and "the final spray," around August 15. She religiously continues that program to this day. "We get excellent apples," she proudly reports.

Once bitten by the fruit bug, Marion found that apples were not enough. She installed an orchard to the north of the house, adding stone fruits—peaches, apricots, cherries. She experimented with more apples, modern dwarf varieties that are easier to maintain and to harvest. Always marrying the graceful with the pragmatic, she designed the orchard to funnel the trees back to a single point. There a stone bench faces the marsh—a quiet nook for rest and contemplation.

Not to be limited by Maine's climate, Marion also grows more tender fruit trees—'Bing' cherries, 'Garden Gold' nectarines, and 'Bonanza' peaches—in tubs. Stored in the barn for the winter months, where they share accommodations with more than 100 potted lilies bound for spring

OPPOSITE: The exterior facade of the Hosmers' magnificent house was built from the old farmers' walls of native stone that networked the property.

perennial beds, they bask like pampered children in the summer sun in front of the barn. Unlike the 25-year-old apple trees she purchased in the beginning, Marion now buys 2-year-old whips. She nurtures them in a shrub frame, tucked discreetly behind a hedgerow, and plants them out when she deems them strong enough to stand on their own. She stops and smiles, "I really love those baby trees."

The south side of the barn provides a natural, warm growing surface. Over each door Marion has trained a patriotic array of grapes—red 'Delaware', white 'Niagara', and blue 'Concord' and 'Worden', the latter "an earlier, larger, and sweeter variety of 'Concord'."

Besides fruit, Marion has always enjoyed growing vegetables, and a 20- by 35-foot "catchall" garden was added outside the kitchen door. Woven through the hills of squash, rows of broccoli, and lettuce are colorful ribbons of cutting flowers. One corner is dominated by a compost-filled tomato ring, while additional long, narrow beds, one on either side of the vegetable/cutting garden, contain currants, raspberries, jostaberries (a cross between a black

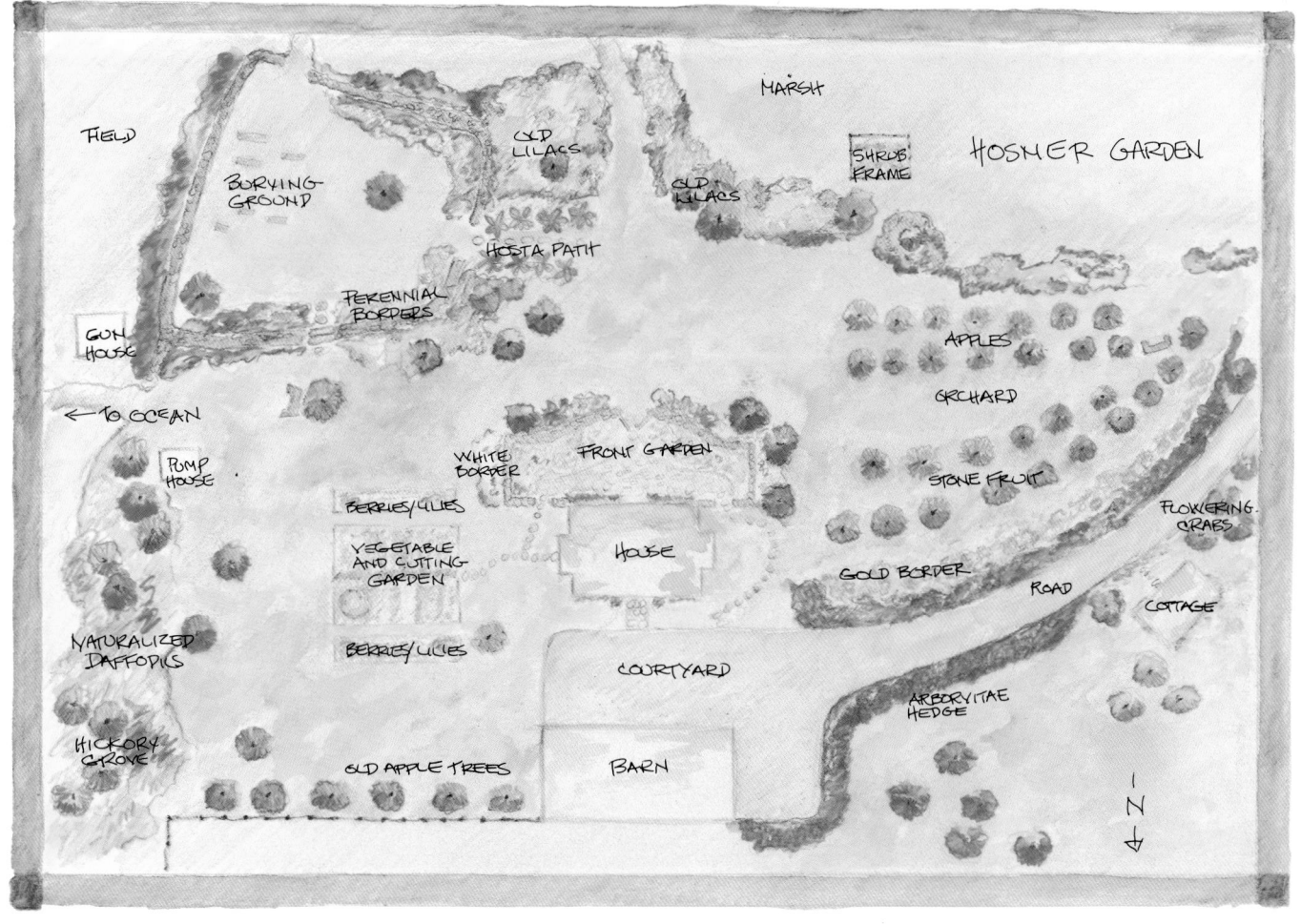

currant and a gooseberry), and gooseberries trained as standards. The beds are finished with seasonal color, such as the bold red of rows of tulips in spring and bright purples provided by asters in fall.

There is no color scheme in the catchall garden, unless "joyful" or "exuberant" could be the name of a palette. "I just put everything in and let it grow." Favorite exotics—the orange-red sprekelia (*Sprekelia formosissima*), the Jacobean lily, and the gleaming white Peruvian daffodil (*Hymenocallis narcissiflora*)—are planted annually purely for use in vases. Their bulbs must be taken in each winter. Marion cautions that, unlike the treatment given gladiolus bulbs, which are shorn of foliage and wintered in a cold place, the leaves and roots must be left on the hymenocallis. They must be coddled and cozy while they sleep. Marion stores the bulbs, bagged and labeled, next to the hot water heater in the cellar.

Keeping track of all these plants is part of

BELOW: In the "catchall" garden, rows of vegetable beds alternate with flowers for cutting. Additional long, narrow beds contain currants, raspberries, jostaberries, and gooseberries.

Marion's discipline. She has maintained a remarkable series of garden journals, dating back to the garden in Sharon, more than 65 years ago. "Not," she says, "like Washington or Jefferson. My journals aren't chatty. Just the facts." Marion records all planting plans. She registers the name and date of each plant that enters the garden, as well as its planted site, bloom time, even behavior. Some plants, she reports, such as daffodils or lilies, have mysteriously disappeared for years and then returned unexpectedly one season. By going to her journal and checking the location of the plants' reappearance, she can quickly retrieve their names. Entries list when vegetables are sown and harvested. Fruit records are as precise as a child's medical records, including dates of the spraying regime, the ripe fruit, and the harvest.

The journals, in ten-year increments, are stored in loose-leaf binders, so that pages can be moved for easy ordering. The current journal, "at the ready," sits on her library desk. To

MARION HOSMER'S "JAPANESE TOMATO RING"

Many years ago Marion Hosmer read an article about growing tomatoes around a vertical ring filled with compost. She tucked the idea in her Garden Journal, and, as with other tips she draws on

when "the spirit moves," one spring she decided to build a ring herself. She placed it, like a decorative column, in the corner of her vegetable/cutting garden.

Using chicken wire and metal fence posts purchased at a hardware store, Marion constructed a circle of wire four feet in diameter and about four feet in height. In it she deposits all the spring-cleanup debris from the garden, material that would usually be placed on the compost pile. She adds some thin layers of soil and fertilizer as the pile builds. Twelve tomato plants, still in their pots, are planted tightly around the ring. As the plants grow, they are tied to the wire and pruned to single stems.

By late summer, the wire is completely covered with thickly growing tomato

plants. In the compost at the top, Marion also plants cucumber seeds, and the cucumber plants hang down over the wire like Victorian festooning. Moisture and nutrients from the decaying compost constantly feed the tomatoes and cucumbers, providing a lush display and a continuous supply of food. In a normal summer, the rain keeps the pile moist. And, Marion reminds, if the summer is dry, wetting the compost with a hose is a water-conserving measure: the compost maintains the moisture longer than ordinary garden soil would. It feeds the plants slowly and regularly. "They take what they need, when they need it." She laughs and adds, "And if you get tired of the ring, you just remove the wire and spread the good, rich compost over the garden."

have ten years of information always at hand, Marion believes, is a crucial tool in making gardening decisions. "I can look here and see 'March 10—Put the tubs of fruit trees outside.' Or when I set the geraniums outside and whether I repotted them last year. Now, that's good to know."

Moving, adding, changing—and dealing with wild creatures' appetites—are all part of the process of gardening. Birds and animals constantly challenge her patience and ingenuity. When the birds "took to plucking the apricot buds off and throwing them on the ground," Marion festooned the trees with Scare Eye balloons, making the trees look like they were on parade to a Halloween party. To deter deer, the garden is dotted with soft-drink cans with wicks hanging out of them. Filled with what? "Well, if you must know, urine. I learned that trick from a man who visited from a big orchard up north. And it works, too." Cans of the same solution and bars of cheap, smelly soap are hung at deer-nose level on the tasty yews as well. At night a blinking light by the kitchen door and rap music barking from a plastic-wrapped radio spread an eerie glow and an unlikely noise over the cutting garden. Pretty strong ammunition. It is successful—for the moment.

Marion muses about the development of her interests over her more than 80 years of gardening, since she was a little girl gathering wildflowers in the fields of Massachusetts. She admits to being a collector, calling her garden "a horticultural zoo—one of everything." She never tires of observing and adding knowledge. "Plants make you sentimental. I have kept many way too long. But they are like old friends. I talk to them and encourage them." She tells a plant when she is going to prune it or divide it, when she is removing its seedpods. Like a good disciplinarian, she admonishes it when it displeases her. While each plant receives her devoted attention, particularly in her later years, it is trees that have captured her passion.

"They say that when you begin to garden, you start out with annuals, and then you add perennials. Then you go on to shrubs, and finally you end up growing trees. That's my story."

Her story, too, is one of generosity, of opening her garden gate to many groups as well as to individuals. And in her life she has taken an active role, as officer, committee member, and president, in various organizations. "I enjoy having people come to the garden, because when you love something so much yourself, when you've put so much work into it, you enjoy sharing it with others."

BELOW: Rebuilt stone walls, remnants from the early farmer's boundary lines, run along the road that leads to the Hosmers' home. Marion planted the edges with a double line of crab apples. Openings lead into fields and marsh land. Paths are kept mown throughout the season, allowing the Hosmers to walk the far reaches of their property.
OPPOSITE: Marion prizes the elegant Japanese relative to the native jack-in-the-pulpit, *Arisaema sikokianum.* It has silver-streaked foliage and a flower, or spadix and spathe, of pure white.

"Knowing the Latin names of plants has its value,

but the ultimate value of gardening for me is to feel a part of the earth."

Harriet McMahon Turtell

Gentle on the Land

HARRIET McMAHON PURTELL

MILWAUKEE, WISCONSIN

Harriet Purtell gardens on five acres by the Milwaukee River. The land is pie shaped, with 700 feet of river frontage forming the "crimped crust." The property, mostly woodland, triangulates up a gentle slope to the house site and a spectacular, enclosed vegetable garden, which is "the point of the piece of pie."

Acquiring this wooded piece of land at the water's edge had been Hattie's longtime dream. She and her husband, Edward A. Purtell, Jr. (known as Ted), and their two children lived on higher ground, less than half a mile away, for more than 20 years. Their first house, a "formal redbrick Georgian," was in the middle of an open treeless farmer's field. "I didn't like it at all," Hattie says. "There are two kinds

of people in this world: those who want to live under open sky and those who want to live in a cave. I'm the cave type. I like the trees around me and over my head."

One day in 1974 Ted, a real estate broker and contractor, came home for lunch and said, "The piece of land you love is for sale, and I'd like to buy it for you." She recalls, "I should have jumped for joy, but instead I picked up my shovel and headed for the property. I am probably the only person I know who determined whether she would own a piece of land with a shovel. But I had tried to garden on miserable clay soil, and I could not face that again.

"I turned one shovel over and was thrilled. The entire property was rich, dark river soil. *This*, I said to myself,

139

ate degree in botany and "got so cranked up I just kept on going." She earned a master's degree in botany in 1985.

When Hattie picked up the shovel again, with more education under her belt, she studied the ecosystems on the land and took inventory of what was there. She determined that she would conduct intense cultivation close to the house, but the remainder of the land she would manage, not change. Hattie began both tasks simultaneously, planning an ambitious vegetable garden to provide organically grown food and initiating a program to preserve and reinstate native plants in the woodland.

"Some of these trees," she says, "are over a hundred years old. To have trees this old is unusual, a privilege, since much of the land in this area was turned into farmland in the nineteenth century. But the farmers never bothered to develop this land, as the river floods, sometimes twice a year.

is *really* a place to garden." Hattie and Ted bought the land and built a house with a wood-shingle roof and clear pine siding that has weathered to blend with the forest. The great trees—maple (*Acer saccharum*), northern red oak (*Quercus rubra*), bur oak (*Quercus macrocarpa*), beech (*Fagus grandifolia*)—some three feet in diameter, create a dense umbrella overhead. "We took only one tree down, and that was to put in our driveway," Hattie reports. "You get these gifts from the Big Gardener, Mother Earth, and you have to take care of them."

Other than planting a modest vegetable garden, Hattie did not begin to garden right away. Instead, she put the shovel away and determined to go back to school. She had begun teaching at the River Edge Nature Center, where she had previously taken courses in native plant conservation, and realized she would be a more effective teacher—and gardener—with further education. She enrolled at the University of Wisconsin–Milwaukee to finish her undergradu-

PREVIOUS PAGE: Hattie Purtell built a rustic enclosure out of cedar for her vegetable garden, feeling that the informal style suited the site. Electric wires have been added over the top of the fence to a height of five feet, with additional wires strung to seven feet to deter the voracious deer that persistently threaten her gardens. THIS PAGE, ABOVE: The wooded property is crisscrossed with paths swathed in wood chips; at the places where Hattie paused repeatedly when initially walking the land, she set benches, made mostly of stone or occasionally from logs from fallen trees, for private moments of reflection and appreciation. OPPOSITE: Hattie cultivates her organic vegetable garden manually, believing a rototiller burns up organic matter too quickly. She uses no chemical sprays or fertilizers.

To give the natives a chance to thrive, the Purtells are clearing the forest floor of invasive alien species such as *Lonicera tatarica*; buckthorn (*Rhamnus catharticus*); reed canary grass (*Phalaris arundinacea*), which was introduced from Europe to feed cattle; and garlic mustard (*Alliaria petiolata*). The first year alone, they removed eight truckloads of debris.

Clearing interlopers encourages the "forest-floor community," particularly the wildflowers, which offer one of the richest arrays in the area. The first flush after the snow and ice melt brings the spring ephemerals, including the marsh marigold (*Caltha palustris*) and trout lily (*Erythronium americanum*), which appear and live for six to eight weeks, disappearing back into the earth to feed it nutrients. The skunk

cabbage (*Symplocarpus foetidus*), trillium (*Trillium grandiflorum*), spring beauty (*Claytonia virginica*), and false rue anemone (*Isopyrum biternatum*) follow, with *Allium tricoccum* and wild geranium (*Geranium maculatum*) making successive appearances throughout the season.

Native understory trees and shrubs—alder (*Alnus rugosa*), pagoda dogwood (*Cornus alternifolia*), nannyberry (*Viburnum lentago*), hazelnut (*Corylus americana*)—are also afforded room to spread, and additional specimens are being reintroduced by a planting program—with varying degrees of success. The deer are the main dilemma throughout Hattie's restoration. "To this day," she moans, "the deer undo almost everything I try to do." Small plants must be fenced against them.

Despite the deer's appetites, the forest seems lush with vegetation, and its crosshatch of pathways make it inviting. "I figured

The long narrow beds and grass paths of George Washington's garden at Mount Vernon were a model for Hattie's vegetable garden, although she has only studied them in photographs. Where plants need to climb, Hattie constructed *tuteurs* (supports) and decorative tomato cages. A pair of trellises hold gourds and tiny pumpkins, 'Baby Boo' and 'Jack Be Little', "for the kids."

out the directions of the paths just by walking until they felt good under my feet," she says. She covered the foot-worn paths' surfaces with wood chips, which were deposited by the town, happy to unload this refuse at no charge.

With the forest floor's revitalization under way, Hattie realized that the family needed some open areas near the house. She resolved that those would be small prairie gardens, sites where she is taking liberties in her purist approach. "This land was all woodland when we arrived, and so, while prairie is natural in other parts of Wisconsin, those sun-loving plants were not strictly native on our property. They are native, but not indigenous."

She added a pair of clearings on each side of the driveway. One, planted with bright monardas, yellow coneflowers, starry campion, and black-eyed Susans, is a haven for butterflies; in the other, an eight-acre field

in front of the house, she mingles flowering plants and grasses. Nonnative oxeye daisies (*Chrysanthemum leucanthemum*) moved in immediately. "As pretty as they are, they will have to be removed. Prairies *are* grasslands," Hattie reminds, "not flower gardens." However, to make the area colorful, she is trying to introduce a higher than normal percentage of forbs, or flowering plants, such as purple coneflower, Culver's root, prairie smoke, and rattlesnake master among the grasses. Since the spot is one of the few open areas on the property, a log bench has been sited at the opposite edge for stargazing, a favorite pastime for Hattie and Ted.

Closer to the house the paths, often made of stepping-stones, are more defined. Little lawn exists.

A graceful group of aspens (*Populus tremuloides*) near the back door shades plants used by Native Americans: wild ginger (*Asarum canadense*), chocolate root (*Geum rivale*), green dragon (*Arisaema dracontium*), false Solomon's seal (*Smilacina racemosa*). A bench is tucked into the foliage. "We aim to keep the place as natural as we can." Hattie says with a laugh, "People

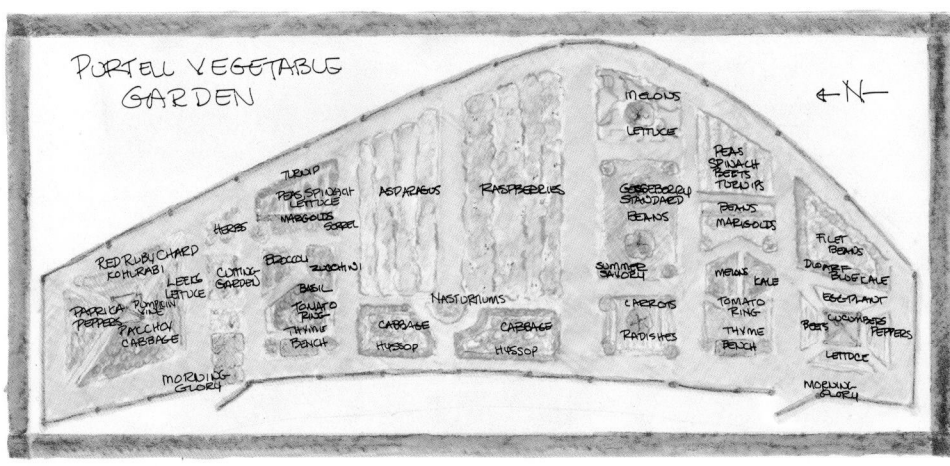

ask, "Why don't you cut a real view of the river?' and I answer, 'No way.' They say, 'How can you live with all that wild stuff?' and I say, 'Quite happily.'"

Hattie cites the influence of Jens Jensen, the early-twentieth-century landscape architect who was a proponent of prairie preservation, naturalistic design, and the use of simple natural materials. She has also studied Japanese design principles, such as that of "hide and reveal" or the use of "borrowed scenery," and has applied them in her garden. The river, for example, does not belong to her, but, as her borrowed view, she chooses where and how it will be seen. "The Japanese may frame the view of a mountain; I look for the right spot to watch the current splash around a boulder."

Only in her vegetable garden has Hattie attempted to bend the landscape to her bidding. Yet though the plantings are more structured, the overall design reflects her respect for the land. The garden occupies a crescent-shaped niche, tucked off the drive and surrounded by trees. For the necessary fencing against the deer, Hattie chose to keep the structure rustic, believing that the rough cedar posts and crossmembers integrate into the landscape more unobtrusively than would more formal materials. As she unlatches the gate, she recites a mantra, "This is my garden, and I welcome you, so come in."

The garden, Hattie decided, would be ornamental as well as utilitarian. She sketched her plan, which has remained basically the same, with a few decorative additions. For those she commissioned a local landscape architect, Judith Stark, for assistance. The garden is laid out in rows and squares, with some beds divided into even smaller triangles and squares. Focal points such as a tomato cage or oversize cast-concrete planters draw the eye to the lush red fruit or to cascades of 'Alaska' and 'Empress of India' nasturtiums.

To retain moisture and to inhibit weeds, the beds are mulched about two inches deep with a mixture of cocoa beans and rice hulls, in a three-to-one proportion. The rice hulls lighten and help aerate the mixture, as well as preventing the "skin" from matting. Paths are made of cedar chips; those that dissect beds must be replaced each spring, for when the beds are turned and compost is added at the beginning of each season, narrow paths lose their definition. Compost, cooked in bins near the garden, is mixed with manure or mushroom compost and also fed to the perennials, herbs, raspberries, strawberries, and asaragus.

The vegetable-growing process begins in early winter at the dining room table, which is always stacked with catalogs. Ninety percent of Hattie's vegetable garden is grown from seed, a task she begins in February. "In 1996 I grew 93 different varieties. I guess that's a little insane. But the most fun and the biggest challenge of the whole vegetable garden is starting plants from seed." She says as she heads down the basement stairs, "What else are you going to do in the winter? It makes me feel so good to have 'children' in the basement."

OPPOSITE: **A rustic arbor leads from Hattie's greenhouse, garage, and cold-frame complex through a green corridor to the vegetable garden. The placement of a** *tuteur,* **sited to catch the evening light at the far end of the walkway, is an example of Hattie's fine-tuned design sense.** ABOVE: **In front of the Purtells'** house, purple coneflower (*Echinacea purpurea*), Culver's root (*Veronicastrum virginicum*), prairie smoke (*Geum triflorum*), rattlesnake master (*Eryngium yuccifolium*), *Physostegia virginiana,* and wild quinine (*Parthenium integrifolium*) mingle with grasses. Tiny flags note the locations of new plants.

She shows her seeds' birthing station, as clean as the nursery of a pediatrics ward. Two frames have been constructed to care for all her charges. Each structure is five feet tall and five feet long. Shelves hold the trays of seedlings, planted in a sterilized germination mix, under six double banks of fluorescent tubes. Each bank is four feet long. The lights can be raised or lowered on chains as the little plants grow. Heating pads with thermostats rest under those plants that need a boost of warmth to germinate.

Seeds, at least 100 packages, are stored in zipper-sealed plastic bags in seed-saver boxes, organized by family; a chart, generated on her computer, keeps track of the botanical name of each variety, its common name, its family, the date planted, germination time, and its required temperature for germination. Some plants, such as chervil, like to pop into action at 55 degrees, whereas others, including cosmos and morning glories, need 80-degree temperatures.

Hattie has a 10- by 22-foot greenhouse, which she fills with her potted plants for winter protection. She does not use it for vegetables. The vegetable seedlings head directly from the basement into the garden on a staggered schedule. Those that can survive the danger of late frost—peas, spinach, onions, lettuce—emerge first, followed by the warmth-loving babies, members of the cucumber or tomato families, who make their entrance around Memorial Day.

The two basement frame stands generate an eighth-acre garden and fill it to the brim. "I like to see a garden billowing," Hattie says, back in the garden. The asparagus, a "big billower," has been given a central position right down the middle of the garden. It waves in the breeze, glistening with dew in the early morning light. Raspberries arch to their sides, like red-tipped fountains of green. And four gooseberry standards, which Hattie trained from whips, nod their heads in unison. All sparkle as they are backlit by the rising sun. "My favorite hour is six in the morning. I love to come out here in my nightgown and listen to the birds and insects at work. It is more beautiful than any cathedral. The garden's beauty is as important to me as its productivity."

Hattie underscores the importance of knowing a plant's family. It makes vegetable gardening much more efficient.

HATTIE PURTELL'S
POINTERS FOR VEGETABLE GARDENS

Hattie says the efficiency of her garden is helped by two principles: intercropping and companion planting. She reminds, "A garden is an ecosystem, with plants working together to form the whole. For example, one plant can provide filtered light for another. A deep-rooted plant can break up the soil for a shallow-rooted plant, and certain plants can emit odors that repel harmful insects." Intercropping allows the maximum productivity of the bed. By planting successive crops next to each other, when one is mature and harvested, the other takes over its space. Long-term crops are interspersed with early or late crops. Onions are planted between cabbages; lettuces with zucchinis. When the onions are harvested, the girth of the cabbages is ready to cover their empty home. Early 'Presto' turnips make way for spinach, and when the lettuces have gone into the salad bowl, the zucchini takes over.

Companion planting, she observes, is less scientific. Tradition holds that certain plants grow better when shoulder-rubbing with well-chosen neighbors, and by the same token, some plants "detest" each other. Basil and tomatoes are pals, in the garden as well as on the plate. Basil is meant to deter whiteflies from tomatoes and to improve their growth and flavor. However, basil and rue do not get along, perhaps because the first is sweet and the latter bitter. Hattie planted a border of globe basil around baby bok choy, and the basil did not grow. "No question in my mind that those two plants did not like each other."

Some pairings are purely for the magic of a marriage. While summer savory seems to add vitality to beans, and eggplant is happily partnered with red-leaf lettuce, both complement each other as well. And the blue-green foliage of the 'Pronto' beet and the red-edged kohlrabi are a knockout couple. Some well-behaved plants, which queue without resistance, such as hyssop, chives, *Allium senescens* var. *glaucum*, or dwarf blue curly kale, define the edges of the beds, like tiny hedges.

Nasturtiums and the much maligned but perky little marigolds, with their strong scent, are meant to keep all sorts of pests at bay. Petunias, which have also borne their share of disdain, work hard for the cause—they trap insects on their sticky stems. Self-seeders are welcome in Hattie's garden, too. Dill and cosmos travel around the garden to her applause. If they choose the wrong spots, they are tweaked out quickly.

Opposite are Hattie's favorite vegetables, chosen for flavor and beauty.

BRASSICACEAE

VEGETABLE	VARIETY
Baby Pak Choi	'Mei Qing Choi'
Broccoli	
Cabbage, Dutch Savoy	'Baby Promasa'
Cabbage, Flowering	'White Pigeon'
Cabbage, Red	'Scarlet O'Hara'
Kale	'Dwarf Blue Curled Scotch'
Kale	'Red Russian'
Kale, Flowering	'Miniature'
Kale, Flowering	'Peacock'
Kohlrabi	
Oriental Greens	'Tatsoi'
Radish	'Early French Breakfast'
Turnip	'Presto'

CHENOPODIACEAE

Beet	'Pronto'
Beet	'Sangria'
Spinach	'Nordic IV'
Spinach	'Wolter'
Swiss Chard	'Charlotte'
Swiss Chard	'Red Ruby'

COMPOSITAE

Lettuce	'Fall Mix'
Lettuce	'Lollo Rossa'
Lettuce	'Spring Mix' (from The Cook's Garden)
Lettuce	'Summer Mix'
Lettuce	'Valeria'

CUCURBITACEAE

Cucumber, Armenian	
Cucumber, Lemon	
Gourd	'Small Mix'
Melon	'Carmel'
Melon	'Charentias'
Melon	'Galia'
Melon	'Moon and Stars'
Pumpkin	'Baby Boo'
Pumpkin	'Jack Be Little'
Squash	'Zucchetta Rampicante'
Zucchini	'Milano Hybrid'

LEGUMINOSAE

Beans	'Jacob's Cattle'
Beans	'King of the Early'
Beans	'Lowe's Champion'
Beans	'Speckled Yellow Eye'
Beans	'Vermont Cranberry'

VEGETABLE	VARIETY
Beans	'Andrew Kent'
Beans, Bush	'Filet', 'Finaud'
Beans, Pole	'Trionfo Violetto'
Peas	'Knight'
Peas	'Sugar Mell'

LILIACEAE

Chives	
Garlic Chives	
Leek	'Bleu de Solaise'
Onion	'Snow Baby F-1'

SOLANACEAE

Eggplant	'Violetta di Firenze'
Pepper, Sweet	'Early Italian Pimienta'
Pepper, Sweet	'Kolasca Spice Paprika'
Tomato	'Big Rainbow'
Tomato	'Brandywine'
Tomato	'Camp Joy Cherry'
Tomato	'Carmello'
Tomato	'Costolluto Genovense'
Tomato	'Red Current'
Tomato	'St. Pierre'

UMBELLIFERAE

Carrot	'Caroline'
Carrot	'Chantene'

Pristine, abundant, and healthy cabbage, lettuce, and broccoli attest to the merits of Hattie's organic approach to gardening.

First, crops must be rotated on at least a three-year cycle, to prevent disease or insect infestation. That means that even a plant from the same family should not be placed in the same bed the following year. For example, if a tomato plant, which is a member of the Solanaceae family, has been in a bed one year, neither eggplants nor peppers, also family members, should be planted in that spot the following year. "While I do have to redesign the garden each year, it sounds more complicated than it is. Many of my beds are in quadrants, and I can move the plant around the quadrant. Therefore it is four years before the cycle is repeated." Second, knowing the cultural requirements of one member of a particular family means that in general those same considerations follow throughout the family. "All Solanaceae like heat," she says, "and members of the Brassicaceae family, like cabbages or turnips, hate it; they are cool crops."

Hattie is committed to growing more open-pollinated plants, those pollinated by wind or hardworking insects, as they become available. She hopes to eventually eliminate all hybrids in the vegetable garden. (A hybrid is created by breeding two different strains of a plant, such as a tomato, in an effort to obtain the best qualities of both on one plant.) While a first-generation hybrid will come true to its variety, by the second generation a hybrid will not. Collecting seeds of hybrids is useless, because the plant will revert to its original parentage or result in a genetic mutant. "Open-pollinated seeds," Hattie underscores, "*will* come true."

She observes that according to charts released by the United States Department of Agriculture, America has lost more than 5,000 different varieties of vegetables since 1903 in favor of more uniform but less flavorful hybrid varieties. "Fortunately," she notes, "there is a new wave of consciousness," and numerous seed companies and seed-saver societies all across the country are collecting and offering heirloom seeds. "These plants are our history, our heritage," she says.

"If I can leave two things to my grandchildren, it is to respect the soil and to treasure the seeds—to preserve the earth to keep it chemical-free, and to remain in awe at the miracle of the seed. I am very lucky to live on the edge of a river, on land with wonderful soil. My goal is to live gently on this land and to leave it as healthy and in as good a shape as I can." Wandering through the network of curving paths in the woodland, Hattie says quietly, "We are only caretakers on our land. We are not really its owners."

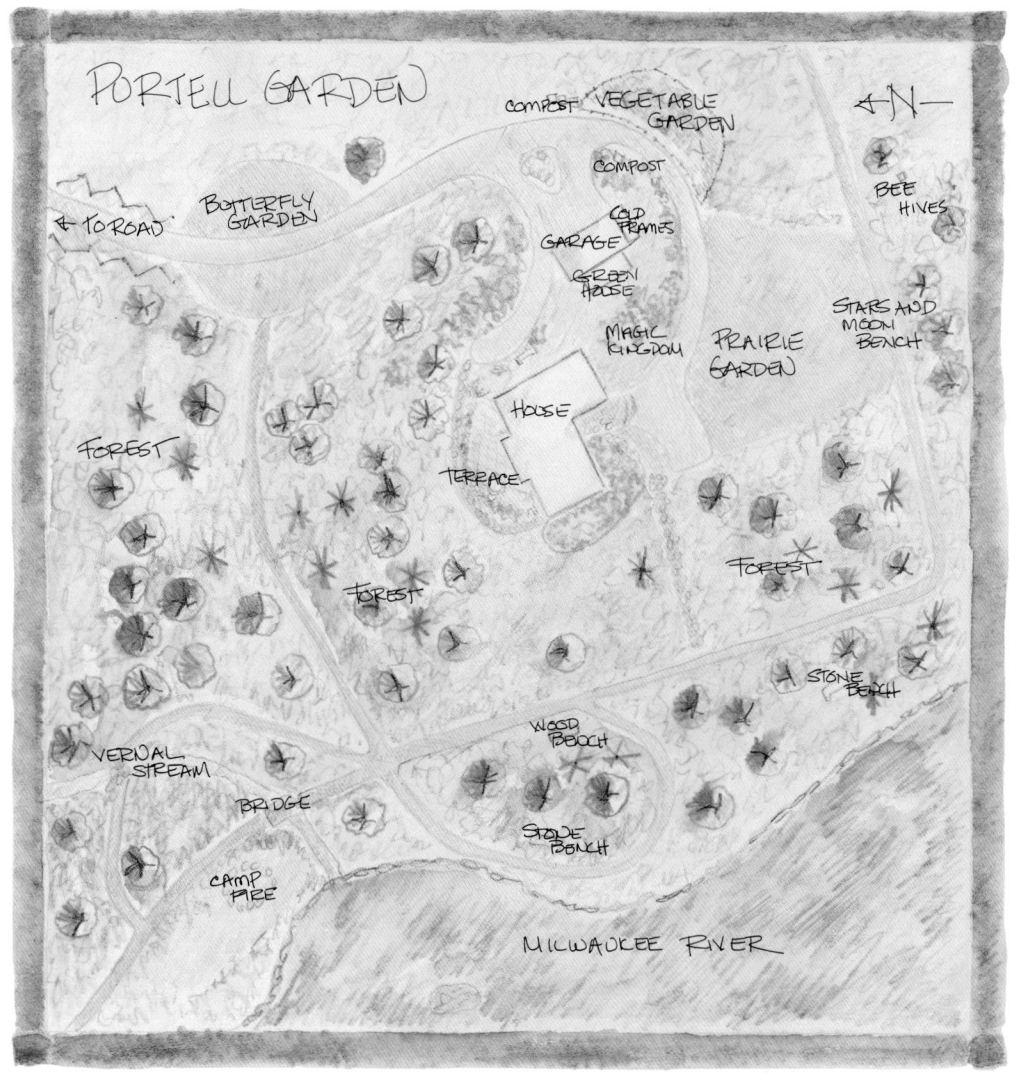

RIGHT: Native crab apples (*Malus ioensis*) and hawthorns (*Crataegus* spp.) hide a favorite family domain: the Magic Kingdom. A brilliantly colored facade and tower, painted in primary hues, looms behind a curtain of trees. Hattie cautions visitors that they are welcome only if invited by small people. The territory belongs to her four grandchildren and various other relatives of wee stature.

The Art of Simplicity

IONE CHASE
ORTING, WASHINGTON

Over the past 35 years, Ione and Emmott Chase have carved out a garden on a high plateau that faces the Cascade Mountains with Mount Rainier as its centerpiece. Sprawling from a house with features adapted from Japanese architecture are a stroll garden, a rolling meadow, and a naturalistic woodland. Each, in a different way, is the result of the couple's celebration of nature's gifts—in geography and in plants. The garden, in Ione's words "is really very simple. It evolved over time, and we did it with our own hands."

In recognition of the Chases' extraordinary accomplishment, the Board of Directors of The Garden Conservancy voted in 1994 to accept the Chase garden into its ongoing program to preserve unique American gardens. Incorporating recommendations from the Chases themselves, the conservancy is designing a plan that will both restrict changes to the Chase property and maintain the property as a public garden with the help of a local organization. It is the goal of the project to develop a plan for the organization to assume ownership, operations, and support of the garden for the pleasure of future generations. Reflecting on the process of creating her garden, Ione says, "I believe that if you have

a dream, you should go for it. That's what we did here.

"I grew up in this logging country," she continues, "and it's the only place I've ever wanted to live." She spent her childhood years in a village in the foothills of the mountains, just a few miles away. Her parents took their four children on picnic outings in their Model T along the dusty wagon road that skirted the present garden. They made rest stops and ate picnic lunches on a sandy spit—"with our buckets and shovels, playing as children do"—that today marks the lower corner of the Chases' property.

Ione and her husband, Emmott, grew up together, attending the same grade school and high school. They fell in love in their teens. Ione went away to college: first to study art history at the University of Puget Sound and then, since she was skilled at designing and sewing, to learn patternmaking in Long Beach, California. When she had completed the six-month course in California, Emmott asked to borrow his father's car to bring her home. "Not without marrying her," Emmott's father said. That was all the encouragement the young couple needed. Ione recalls, "I knew I couldn't live without him." It was 1933.

"If you love plants, if you collect plants, simplicity can be the hardest thing

to achieve. If you get too many different plants, the simplicity slips through your fingers."

Ione Chase

PREVIOUS PAGES, LEFT: **While** Ione Chase's meadow is planted in a naturalistic style, she plans each area with a finely tuned sense of design by layering complementary colors and contrasting textures and shapes. RIGHT: An intricate network of paths traverse the Chase garden. Steppingstones and bridges were cast in concrete poured near their permanent sites in simple forms made of 2x4 or 2x6 lumber. The forms were moved into place by using four-inch alder logs as rollers.

THIS PAGE, ABOVE AND RIGHT: A stone bench is set at the edge of the woodland, where once a year, in December or January, Emmott mows the herbaceous woodland carpet to the ground. Plants sleep in their own compost and return in the spring with renewed vigor. OPPOSITE: Looking across her garden to snow-covered Mount Rainier, rising like a gigantic mirage out of a sea of clouds, Ione says, "I like to feel open space around me. Like the old song says, 'Don't fence me in.'"

his worst piece of land; it wasn't suited for farming. They valued only farmland in those days." The Chases made a proposal to the owner, and in 1943 they purchased 14 acres, half of which they later sold to a friend for $425. "Things have surely changed," Emmott observes wryly.

Before developing the property, Ione studied books from the local library and became interested in Japanese houses and gardens. "We hired an architect. We told him we wanted something simple, uncluttered, and that from every room we wanted to be able to walk outdoors." In 1959, 16 years after their land purchase, they began to build a house, doing much of the work themselves.

With so much construction to accomplish in the immediate environs, it was five years before Ione really started to garden. She was 55 years old, but from that point on, gardening quickly became her full-time occupation. "I cannot imagine life without it," she says. "I learned by plunging in. I just got down on my knees and started. I'm self-educated. I learned the botanical names of plants, because it helps me communicate at

nurseries or with other gardeners. And," she smiles, "don't think I don't talk to the plants, because I do." She pauses, "Experience is always the best teacher. Speeches are fine and books are fine, and I do a lot of reading and looking, but mostly I learn by doing. And I've always been strong."

Slowly and deliberately, the Chases began to transform the property, with a commitment to preserving the native plants. "I love the natives," Ione says as she runs her hands along the arch of a Solomon's seal and rustles a patch of vanilla leaf. The Chases cleared the dense brush but left the great trees: Douglas firs, western red cedars, and "our state tree," the hemlock. "They are all second growth, but they

Emmott went to work for the Electron division of Puget Sound Power and Light Company, over the years climbing the ladder from "common laborer" to supervisor. He brought his bride to a house in the company-owned complex at Electron, where they lived for the next 25 years. There Ione began to garden, "looking only at the wall of the house next door. It was on a very modest scale. But gardening was in my blood, I guess."

The Chases nurtured their dream of owning land. Remembering the site of her childhood picnics, Ione took Emmott to see the property, situated on a bluff, dropping 200 feet down to the Puyallup River. Ione says, "The owner thought it was

are now close to eighty years old. The area around here has been logged for the second and third times. These trees are probably the only ones left that are this old. Some are a hundred and fifty feet tall," Ione notes. Garbed in lineman's gear and secured by a belt around his waist that circles a 3-foot tree circumference, Emmott routinely climbed 60 to 80 feet up into the treetops to clean out dead wood.

For the layout close to the house, the Chases hired landscape architect Rex Zumwalt to draw a plan, which Ione still unrolls on the table for reference from time to time. The couple executed the landscaping themselves; they built decks, laid out the ponds, hammered together forms, and mixed concrete. Initially, they followed the architect's plan, and they planted trees where trees were noted. But over the years, Ione says, "We took things out. I am always striving for simplicity."

The Chases made additions as well. Both respect stone, a resource in scarce supply in

Ione's open meadow is a thoughtful composition of discreet beds formed by a labyrinth of paths. On one side is a man-made reflecting pool; on the other, the woodland forms a dense, dark background.

this terrain of sandy loam. Emmott recalls, "Not a rock is here that we didn't haul in. We brought stone from the Puyallup River Bar and the logging roads on Mount Rainier. Some were two or three tons in weight." "And then we carefully arranged them," Ione adds. Indeed, many of the garden's accents and ornaments are just well-placed stones.

Around their house, the Chases built reflecting pools, walkways, a free-form patio/dance floor, stepping-stones, and bridges—all using concrete as a base. In some cases the pieces are made entirely of concrete; others are exposed aggregate—concrete mixed with stones or gravel of varying dimensions. The couple did virtually all the concrete work and stonework themselves, using homemade lumber and improvised metal forms and $\frac{3}{4}$-inch gravel, which Emmott says is referred to locally as "three-quarter minus." The mistake the Chases say they made on some of the larger areas was not using reinforcing steel, an

economy measure they both regret. The terrace cracked in the 1964 earthquake. As a compensation for their error, plants have made their homes in the cracks, which Ione feels softens the effect of a large span of concrete.

The Chases also planted trees. They rescued six-inch alpine firs and mountain hemlocks that were in the path of the bulldozers on roads being built "in the high country. We brought them home and put them in our nursery until they were ready to be planted out." Electron encouraged employees to take small trees from under the power lines, so the Chases retrieved several three-foot-high hemlocks.

Ione propagated juniper from cuttings, finally planting 25 that have grown into an impenetrable hedge along the rim that drops off to the valley floor. Nine quaking aspens were spaced in a cluster to frame the view of the mountain. One survives; the others succumbed to disease. Next to the terrace in a square bed filled with round riverbed stones stands a lodgepole pine (*Pinus contorta*), one of a group that the Weyerhauser Company was giving to the public many years ago. "Usually these pines grow tall and straight, but in the lot were a couple of oddballs. I thought, 'Hmm, maybe this is a dwarf.' I've encouraged it to grow in an S-shaped sweep, sometimes hanging a rock, like a weight, from its branch. It's been a conversation piece.

"Mostly," Ione reflects, "we have cared for the natives. They are often the most beautiful. We don't *need* to bring in a lot of exotics. It's nice to read about them, and see them, but I don't really need them." Yet she is not a purist, and she continues to investigate new plants and their habits. Visiting nurseries, she claims, has taught her volumes over the years. "When exotics fit, or when they are a gift, then I welcome them." A five-foot katsura (*Cercidiphyllum japonicum*), cloaked in chicken wire against the deer, is being pampered at a path's corner. "I'm curious to see if it's a female," she says, "for, I'm told, the branches will spread out more horizontally than in the more vertical male."

The woodland, which covers about an acre and a half, is divided by a network of paths that lead around clusters of trees, old stumps, or fallen trees. Ione points out the "nurse stumps," where younger trees have made their homes, as though nestling into the comforting folds of the flesh of an old nanny. A young vine maple's roots twist through the rich composted remains of a decomposing fir. Beds of moss expand through glades edged by *Anemone nemorosa*, columbine, *Cornus nuttallii*, disporum, *Synthyris reniformis*, and false Solomon's seal (*Smilacina racemosa*). Ione shakes her head, "I don't approve of calling any plant by the name 'false.' The false lily of the valley, *Maianthemum dilatatum*, has to endure that indignity, too." She emphasizes, "*No* plant is false."

Plants, gathered in colonies, thrive in the mulch created by needles shed by the conifers overhead. Once established, plants mostly multiply on their own; occasionally Ione steps in. About five years ago, she collected trillium (*Trillium ovatum*) pods as they were about to open and rubbed them on the ground. "They were so sticky, I couldn't get them off my hands. I swear every seed grew." Unfortunately, the deer, which "find them very tasty," are depleting the community.

The woodland feels primeval, as though untouched by humans. These plants have occupied the Northwest forests for centuries. Sun flickers down through the old trees, its fall a shower of delicate light. Ione strolls slowly, checking the conditions of inhabitants. "I often take a walk through here first thing in the morning. This is perhaps my favorite place. I don't like anything too tampered with by man."

The Chases used strips of tin purchased from a local metalwork shop to create forms for the curved shapes of the free-form pool in front of the house. Ione set the strips in place, bending the tin to her desired configurations and stabilizing the strips with wooden pegs at one-foot intervals.

Closer to the house, the garden is spare in keeping with its Japanese influence. Looking at it, Ione observes, has a calming effect. A bridge constructed of strips of wood crosses a shallow, curved reflecting pool and leads to the house's entrance. A raised mound, spread with gravel, is accented by a few rocks. "I like to place a stone as though it would have been there naturally—by nature's grace." *Penstemon davidsonii* makes its home neck-deep in the gravel, warmed by the sun. A porch covers part of the terrace, which falls away to another pool.

Gravel paths lead farther out into the "meadow." Thick with weeds when the Chases began, the three-quarter-acre area was developed portion by portion. They mowed each

selected section and covered it with several layers of newspapers. Then they blanketed the paper with six inches of raw sawdust, bringing in truckloads "twenty yards at a clip." After a couple of years, they hired a man with a rototiller to incorporate the remaining decomposing sawdust and paper into the soil. Ione was ready to plant.

In the meadow Ione planted perennials in vast, undulating waves of color. They shimmer like moving reflections on water. Masses of heather mingle with extended families of geraniums, hypericums, and iberis. Dianthus nudge phlox. Thyme and Ione's favorite, dragon's blood sedum (*Sedum spathulifolium*), creep under veronica and helianthemum. Ione notes that many of the colonies came from just one plant, the "workhorses." In 1962 she had just one clump of heath, *Erica carnea* 'Springwood White', which she broke into little pieces, "each with a hairlike root." In each case, as insurance, she planted three together, with the expectation that at least one would live. The heath now covers beds that total 10 by 180 feet. Just one coral-flowered plant of *Lewisia cotyledon* planted ten years ago has seeded itself, sometimes with Ione's help, all along the north side of the house and out into the garden. Its progeny is salmon, pink, and white. Providing its cultural requirements—dry feet and protection from rain with the overhang of the house—has made the lewisia flourish. "You don't need a lot of money to make a garden like this," she advises, "just persistence—and an idea."

While the meadow is a carpet of brilliant hue, Ione often interrupts color with the white flowers of phlox, iberis, arabis, and even larger-scale plants such as rhododendrons or *Magnolia stellata.* She believes white gives the eye a rest and prevents disparate colors from clashing, allowing the gardener to use a broader range of color. White also adds "sparkle and life to a dark area." She points out that many woodland plants— including bloodroot, Solomon's seal, trientalis, aruncus, tiarella—flower in white, lighting up the forest floor.

Individual trees and shrubs accent the meadow's beds. "When you walk around the bend in a path, something should strike you—a rhododendron, an azalea, a tree can do it." Although Ione has a clipped hedge of *Ilex crenata* next to the house, she says she would never plant such a structured form away from a building. Rather, large groups of each plant flow in natural-looking formations; when they are trimmed, they are never forced into "false shapes." Ione does

OPPOSITE: **The Chases' magic mountain, Mount Rainier, provides a spectacular show throughout the year. Often cloud covered, it appears and disappears at nature's whim. "It's all in the light, isn't it?" Ione says, "I guess we have the ultimate 'borrowed view.'"**

not like topiary. But this does not mean she eschews pruning. "When a tree is pruned, you see its structure, its lines. Seeing the tree as a series of lines, or a single line, rather than as a mass, adds to the simplicity of the whole."

The paths through the meadow basically track the routes of "getting from one place to another." She adds, "Yet I try always to remember the Hogarth Curve, or a 'lazy S,' in finalizing placement. You see it all the time in the mountains. People make paths by going around an object on their right and then going around an object on their left. A curved line is a line of beauty."

Ione says she never really made a planting plan; pencil never went to paper. Early on,

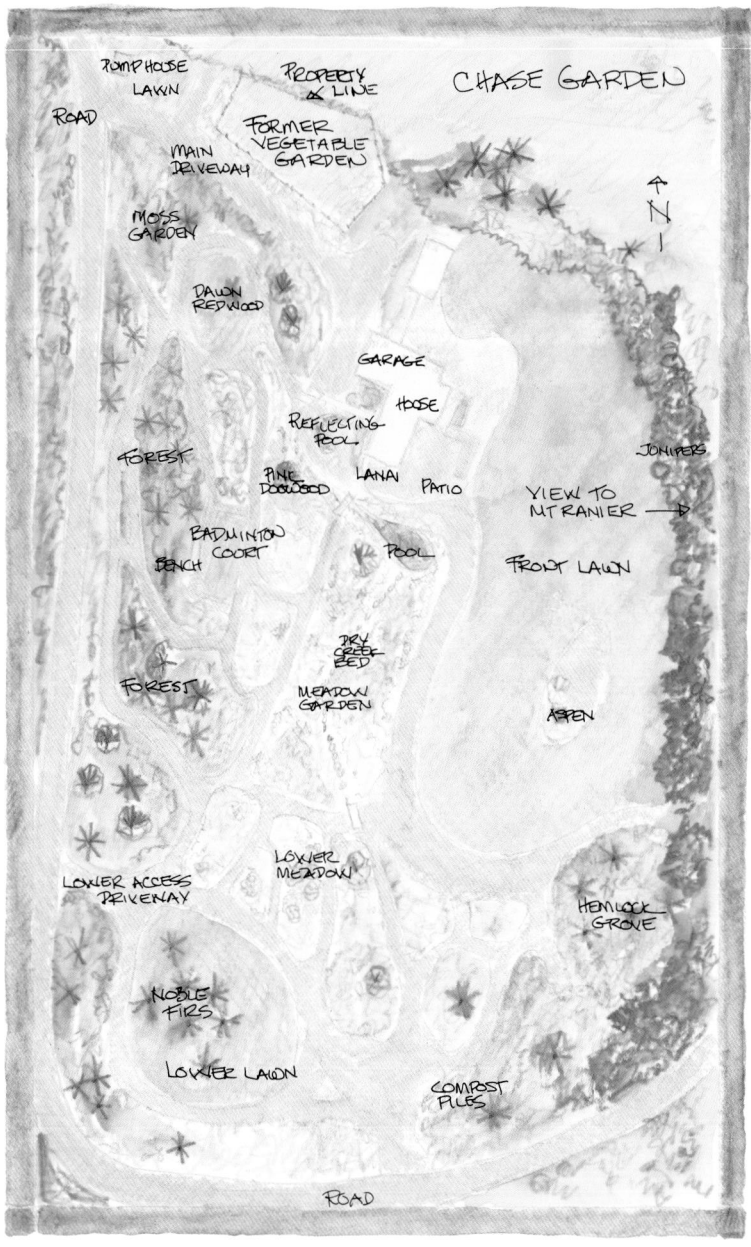

masses of plants came from divisions or from seed. These days she often buys plants in multiples, as many as six to ten of a kind. She thinks about contrast of textures between different plants as she determines their locations. "I take a new plant in my hand and walk around, putting it on the ground in several places. I try to imagine it full grown. Then I spot the rest of the group around it in the same manner, until I am satisfied." Ione claims she follows few studied design principles; rather, she works by instinct. "I just follow my nose, making brushstrokes with plants. I feel like I'm painting a picture with plants. A painting that I will enjoy."

In the early days Ione did not religiously amend the soil, but now each transplant or new plant is given a mixture of 50 percent sand, 30 percent peat soil (a rich substance made of decayed wood and vegetation that is found in bogs), and 20 percent barnyard manure. She also often "scratches" the mixture around established plants.

The "yard," as the Chases still call their garden, receives meticulous care. "It's all a matter of housekeeping," observes Ione, "whether indoors or out." She quickly adds, "The key to control is not letting things go to seed." Since Emmott's retirement 11 years ago at age 75, the couple have averaged at least five hours a day each working in the garden. "We inched our way along, until we reached the property's edge. We could go no farther."

Great drifts of plants, many divided from just one original parent, appear woven together with a master's hand. "If you love plants, if you collect plants, simplicity can be the hardest thing to achieve. If you get too many different plants, the simplicity slips through your fingers."

The Chases' travel has been primarily in the Northwest. They have hiked, "particularly in our own Olympic Mountains," to see plants in their natural habitats. "I just wanted to see the dodecatheon and the *Lewisia tweedyi* in the wild. And the dear little *Fritillaria pudica* growing in the worst soil, but still happy." They have journeyed little abroad. "We've been too busy here. I would have liked to have gone to Japan, especially Kyoto," Ione muses. "I have no regrets. Anyway, it is not artificial environments that interest me. It is only private gardens, other people's handiwork that I want to see."

She turns toward Mount Rainier, which has dropped the clouds, like a silk shawl cast aside on a warm, summer night. As the low, evening sun becomes golden, the mountain turns to bullion. "The beauty of living here has always been the big sky, so much sky," Ione observes. "I stand on the brow of the hill and feel like I could fly."

CHASE GARDEN NATIVE PERENNIALS

FOREST-FLOOR WILDFLOWERS

BOTANICAL NAME	COMMON NAME	FLOWER COLOR	HEIGHT
Achlys triphylla	Vanilla leaf	White	Leaves 12″, spike to 15″
Actea rubra	Baneberry	White, red berries	2 to 3′
Asarum caudatum	Wild ginger	Brown	Evergreen trailer, 3 to 4″
Cornus canadensis	Bunchberry, creeping dogwood	White, red berries	4 to 6″
Dicentra formosa	Pacific bleeding heart	Pink, clusters	15 to 18″
Disporum hookeri	Hooker's fairybells	White, orange fruit	2 to 3′
Maianthemum dilatatum	False lily of the valley	White, red berries	10 to 12 ″
Oxalis oregana	Red sorrel	White, pink	4 to 6″
Smilacina racemosa	False Solomon's seal	White plumes, red berries	2 to 3′
Smilacina stellata	Star-flowered false Solomon's seal	White	12 to 15″
Tiaralla trifoliata	Western foamflower	White	15″
Tolmiea menziesii	Piggy-back plant	Brown	15 to 18″
Trientalis latifolia	Western starflower, Indian potato	Pink	4 to 6″
Trillium ovatum	Western trillium	White, aged red to violet	14 to 18″
Vancouveria hexandra	Inside-out flower	White	15 to 18″
Viola glabella	Yellow wood violet	Yellow	10 to 12″
Viola sempervirens	Evergreen violet	Yellow	3 to 4″

EDGE-OF-FOREST OR OPEN-FIELD WILDFLOWERS

BOTANICAL NAME	COMMON NAME	FLOWER COLOR	HEIGHT
Aquilegia formosa	Red columbine	Red and yellow	2 to 3′
Aruncus dioicus	Goat's beard	White	3 to 5′
Brodiaea hyacinthina	Fool's onion	White	2 to 3′
Camassia quamash	Common camas	Blue	2′
Erythronium oregonum	White fawn lily	White	12 to 15″
Erythronium revolutum	Pink fawn lily	Pink	12 to 15″
Fragaria chiloensis	Coastal strawberry	White	4 to 6″
*Iris**	Pacific Coast hybrids	Lavender, white	15 to 20″
Penstemon davidsonii var. *menziesii*	Davidson's penstemon	Lavender	2 to 3″
Sedum spathulifolium	Stonecrop	Yellow	Leaves 1″, flower stalk 4″
Sisyrinchium californicum	Golden-eyed grass	Yellow	8 to 10″
Synthyris reniformis	Spring queen	Lavender	4 to 6″
Xerophyllum tenax	Bear grass	White, clusters	Leaves 2″, flower stalk 3 to 4′

FERNS

BOTANICAL NAME	COMMON NAME	HEIGHT
Adiantum pedatum	Maidenhair	2 to 3′
Asplenium trichomanes	Maidenhair spleenwort	6 to 8″
Blechnum spicant	Deerfern	2 to 2½′
Polypodium glycyrrhiza	Licorice fern	12 to 18″
Polystichum munitum	Sword fern	3′

* Iris douglasiana, Iris innominata, Iris purdyi, Iris tenuissima (natural and man-made crosses with variation in color and height)

List prepared by Rosina McIvor.

"I love the fact that I am tending someone else's treasure.

It gives me a wonderful sense of belonging, of attachment, of comfort."

Dorothy Hannon Gardner

A Gardener's Legacy

DOROTHY HANNON GARDNER

WINNETKA, ILLINOIS

"The bones of this garden are really fine," Dorothy Gardner observes, surveying the series of formal gardens originally laid out in 1927 by her mother-in-law. "She had no landscape architect; she designed this garden completely on her own. To complement her Normandy-style house, she created a garden that is French in influence, with allées, parterres, and separate 'rooms.'" Dorothy opens a black iron gate leading into the White Garden. "French, of course," she says of the delicately tooled filigree. "My mother-in-law was a Francophile." She smiles and adds, "And I am one, too."

"There are so many similarities between my mother-in-law and me, it is almost spooky," Dorothy continues. "She was educated in Switzerland and spoke French." Dorothy acknowledges that she, too, speaks French, having attended a French grammar and high school in Kansas City, Missouri, where she grew up, and received a master's degree in French literature from Middlebury College in Vermont. Dorothy has taught French and lived in France. She pauses to add the pièce de résistance of the story on the two women's affinities: "And her name was Dorothy, too."

For a total of 70 years, with no break in sequence, two women, a generation apart, have tended the same garden. Though the women spent only one summer afternoon together in this garden, where they drank tea, the second Dorothy Gardner speaks with great fondness of the woman she knew for only a brief time. "I certainly did not know my mother-in-law well, yet I feel deeply connected to her, and very lucky to have inherited such a meaningful legacy. My husband, John, was an only child, and his parents really hoped that he would want to live here."

For several years after the senior Dorothy Gardner passed away in 1976, the young Gardners, Dorothy and John, brought their children north from their Chicago apartment to spend weekends at John's family home. They joined John's

father in caring for the garden. Young Dorothy had always wanted to garden, had created small ones in her apartments, had even grown corn and tomatoes on her fire escape, but this garden was her first "serious gardening experience." She recalls, "John's father was a great tutor. And I learned by doing." She smiles, looking skyward, "My mother-in-law is probably shaking her head at what I still don't know, but I do feel like I am communicating with her."

Following the death of John's father in 1980, the Gardners decided to move into John's parents' house. Changes to the structure were necessary to accommodate their four children and contemporary lifestyle. The Gardners kept some of the French antiques and paintings but blended them with art deco and twentieth-century works that were more to their taste. The most dramatic addition is a garden/music room and greenhouse that sweeps across the back of the house. "We wanted to make our living space

PREVIOUS PAGE: The 10 by 50 foot lap pool's shaped ends reiterate the curved line of the arched wall. The pool, made of black gunite, is bordered with bluestone; the coping is Vermont slate. Mechanicals, even the ladder, are hidden beneath removable pieces of the stone. At each corner of the surround, an oversized lead container spills white pelargoniums (*Pelargonium* 'Snowmass'). THIS PAGE, ABOVE: Punctuated at each of the four corners with five-foot standard *Malus* 'Tina', the borders in Dorothy's White Garden are planted with *Nepeta* × *faassenii* 'Snowflake', *Gaura lindheimeri* 'Whirling Butterflies', *Linaria purpurea* 'Alba', and *Lamium maculatum* 'White Nancy'. OPPOSITE: Carrying on the family tradition for the love of gardening, Dorothy Gardner says, "While other people play golf, we garden. We work at it all weekend long."

more integrated into the garden, diffusing the separation of indoors and out. Ours are long hard winters," Dorothy says, "and we felt these rooms should allow us to feel that we were living in the garden throughout the year."

Wishing to know more of the history of the house and garden, Dorothy was pleased to discover a cache of clippings and notes that her mother-in-law had used for reference in the conception of both the house and the garden. "You can almost see the workings of her mind as this place came to be.

"My mother-in-law's story is a romantic one," observes Dorothy. "The land, house—and even the Crown Derby china—were wedding presents from her aunt." The acre of land on which the house sits is part of a series of residential properties that skirt the Indian Hill Country Club, established in 1913. The house was designed by the prominent Chicago architect Philip Maher. "My mother-in-law had some definite ideas, and she knew exactly what she wanted." The file of reference material indicates particular features to be incorporated—enclosures, often defined by hedges; walls and gates; parterres in geometric patterns; topiary and espaliered trees; fruits, vegetables, and herbs integrated with ornamental plants; arbors covered with roses; allées connecting separate spaces; and axis lines. Indeed, the house is sited across the middle of the property, almost like a dividing line. A 12-foot arborvitae (*Thuja occidentalis* 'Nigra') hedge hides the only portion of the garden that would be visible from the road.

Dorothy says that as soon as the house was built, her mother-in-law laid out her gardens, and she did them all at once with the confidence of an experienced designer. "She created a sense of space by dividing the garden into rooms, each with a long vista or focal point. The hedges and walls

replaced in 20 years. "They must be mightily pruned twice a year to maintain the necessary columnar effect."

The allée terminates with a nine-foot block-and-stucco wall painted in a creamy color to blend with the exterior of the house. In the center, where the wall rises to a ten-foot arch, a niche holds a statue of Apollo. The graceful figure, another piece of family heritage, originally stood in the nearby Kenilworth garden of John's grandmother Edna Boal Flood, a highly regarded gardener of her era. "While my mother-in-law read and studied gardening extensively, she learned a great deal of it at her own mother's knee," Dorothy muses on the gardening history that infuses the family.

A small pool with a "bubbler" was located under Apollo when the Gardners took ownership. "Things have a way of telling you when to change," observes Dorothy. "The pool sprang a leak. And we wanted a lap pool, since we love to swim. This open allée was the only space for it. The challenge was to design a pool that would appear to be a reflecting pool and also serve for swimming. A great deal of thought went into every detail of it. We didn't want a Roman excess that appeared like a turquoise bathtub—it would destroy the integrity of the garden." She called on Janet

Meakin Poor, a friend, horticulturist, and respected Chicago landscape designer, for assistance. The result, a pool 10 by 50 feet, was installed on the central axis from the living room doors. At four and a half to five and a half feet deep, "it is fine for swim-

ming, which we do twice a day. But there is no diving here.

"I added the trellis over the wall, too," Dorothy recalls. "The wall that terminates the pool axis had numerous cracks and the trellis was meant as camouflage. However, the wall finally crumbled, and we had to have it rebuilt anyway. I liked the softening effect of the ivy-covered trellis, so we kept it intact after the repairs."

In the first Mrs. Gardner's day, the allée was bordered by perennial beds dominated by white flowers, which were planted in tiers. "They bloomed constantly, and were gorgeous at night. Old newspaper clippings make reference to the electrifying beauty of the white garden at evening dinner parties." However, they were also extremely labor intensive, with a total of over 150 feet of bed. Dorothy, who

ABOVE: About every three weeks throughout the summer months, Dorothy's husband, John, prunes the 25-foot crab apple tree meticulously espaliered to the chimney, a two-day task. RIGHT: Dorothy's greenhouse is attached to the family room and kitchen complex. OPPOSITE: In the Herb Garden, perennial herbs— savory, chives, lovage, oregano, thyme, lemon balm, marjoram, and chamomile—are planted in the ground, along with annual parsley and basil. Annuals or tender perennials, such as heliotrope, soft gray santolina standards, and a rosemary tree, are placed in pots and moved into the greenhouse for the winter.

provide privacy—and mystery. It really is an ingenious design. Our contributions have been toward making the garden an active part of our lifestyle." For large parties, which the Gardners often give, the entire garden holds dining possibilities. Tables can be set up around the reflecting pool or a buffet table might be arranged near the teahouse, as well as in the Picnic Area. "We use every inch of this garden," Dorothy says. "It is not for show, it is for living."

The garden's main axis leads from the French doors in the living room down an allée of columnar maples (*Acer saccharum* 'Skybound') that punctuate long hedge-lined beds. Initially, the allée was planted with Bartlett pears, but severe Chicago winters took their toll, and the pears were replaced with the more cold-hardy maples. Only one of the maples has been

is president of the Michael Reese Health Trust (John is a partner in a Chicago investment banking firm), has simplified the planting by converting the beds to carpets of purple-leaved winter creeper (*Euonymus fortunei* 'Coloratus'). She has, however, underplanted the winter creeper with masses of white 'Mount Hood' and 'Carlton' daffodils for a grand spring show. The daffodil foliage, tied with raffia in tepeelike clumps to ripen, is removed in the beginning of July. Dorothy says, "Some years, when I have the time, I even braid the foliage, double the braid, and tie it together. It looks fabulous but takes days." The borders, enclosed on three sides with 18-inch yew (*Taxus* × *media* 'Hicksii') hedges, are backed with a hedge of burning bush (*Euonymus alatus*) 3½ feet high.

Here, as elsewhere in this garden, a variation of surface material, as well as slight level changes, indicates a change from garden room to garden room. An opening in the hedge, like the cross mark in a small *t*, leads down another

ABOVE: A path of chipped
bluestone that ushers under a
half dozen arbors planted
with the climbing *Rosa* 'New
Dawn' separates the Picnic Area
and the Herb, Rose, and
Vegetable Gardens. The rose
beds are mulched with cocoa
bean shells, which gives the rose
garden a delicious chocolate
scent. With the fragrance
of herbs and chocolate, the
site is favored for dining. LEFT:
In the vegetable beds, bamboo
tepees support tomatoes to
form a decorative wall.

allée where grass changes to bluestone chips for the path. This path ends at a gate on the northern boundary of the property, where Dorothy's newly installed potting area is tucked behind a fence covered in the climbing hydrangea (*Hydrangea anomala* ssp. *petiolaris*).

To one side of the allée, the Picnic Area, backed by a perennial cutting garden in soft blues, yellows, and mauves,

The copper-roofed teahouse sited at the end of the Far Allée was originally screened, but the Gardners removed the screens to give the teahouse an open, architectural feeling. A copper sculpture of a Thinker Frog, created by Charleston artist Charles Smith, is fondly dubbed Guillaume ("French for 'William,' our son's name") la Grenouille.

is planted with three crab apples. One is *Malus* 'Beverly', a replacement for a tree John's mother planted, for he carries on a family tradition of making crab apple jelly each fall. The Picnic Area's floor, a rectangle with gracefully rounded ends, is gravel.

Opposite the Picnic Area, a formal layout of rectangular beds contains herbs, roses, and vegetables. The pathways are made of brick, now moss covered, and edged in strips of steel. The Herb Garden, composed of three 6-foot-square beds, used to have hedges of santolina and germander, which rarely survived the winter. Keeping the original design, Dorothy has converted the hedges to boxwood.

Next to the Herb Garden, roses—a mixture of hybrid teas, such as 'Tropicana', 'Peace', 'Mister Lincoln', 'Chrysler', and 'Tiffany', and the grandiflora 'Queen Elizabeth'—fill four 8- by 12-foot beds. The final bed, 18 by 18 feet, divided into quadrants by brick paths, is used for the family's daily fare of vegetables, rotated each summer.

Three enclosed rectangles line the northern boundary. The first, called Bar None Ranch, contains a hip-roofed playhouse, a remnant of John's childhood. Dodge's Palace, the domain of the family's black Labrador, fondly named for a gardener who helped the family for many years, is second; the third space, subtly camouflaged, is an enclosed storage and utility area.

Turning in the opposite direction toward the southern boundary, the cross axial path leads to an area called the Far Allée, which parallels the reflecting pool. It is bordered by a continuation of the arborvitae hedge, behind which is an even taller line of Washington hawthorns (*Crataegus phaenopyrum*). A copper-roofed, six-sided teahouse is the focal point. "It was designed by John's father and built by a Belgian craftsman. My mother-in-law must have spent a good deal of time there, as the teahouse was equipped with a telephone jack."

The garden is as enchanting in winter as it is lovely in the summer. Because of its distinct structure, the bare bones, especially under a cover of snow, retain their elegance. Besides an espaliered crab apple on the chimney in the front of the house, five others, calligraphic without their foliage, grace the house walls. Evergreen hedges contribute bold geometric shape. Discreet lighting has been installed

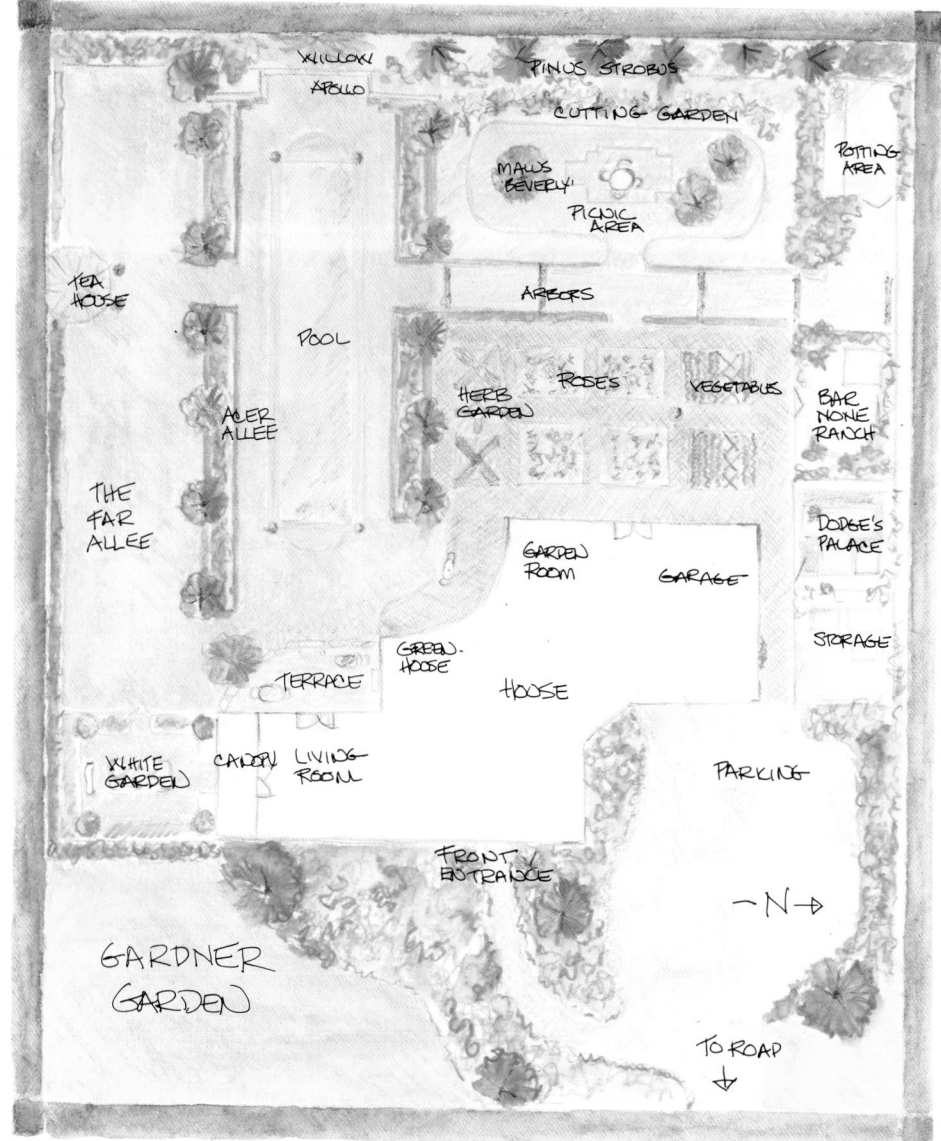

throughout the garden. Each of the columnar maples is lit from beneath. The pool is outlined, and the statue of Apollo highlighted. Dorothy says, "The exterior lighting also ensures that we never see our own reflections in the glass; we need no curtains. I put the exterior lights on every night we are here. It's easy, all on a master switch. The landscape is so beautiful with a light snow cover."

A tour of Dorothy's garden generally begins and ends in the White Garden. Formerly, it was called the Ivy Garden, but three consecutive winters with no protective snow cover devastated the English ivy. Dorothy tired of replacing it. Since the white perennial gardens maintained by her mother-in-law had been eliminated, Dorothy decided to bring the white-flower theme to this small rectangle located directly off the living room.

Keeping the layout her mother-in-law had designed, Dorothy created a cool garden of whites and grays. It is separated, like an elegant parlor, from the larger garden with a boxwood hedge. "I would hope that the atmosphere is ethereal." Artemisias (*Artemisia schmidtiana* 'Silver Mound' and *A.* × 'Powis Castle') billow in delicate gray clouds in the center rectangle. Tiny pea sticks set in the English fashion await to control further growth and keep formal order. Ivy topiaries give height and dimension. A quiet garden, shaded much of the day, it has a dramatic moment at the end of July when the tall 'Casablanca' lilies bloom.

Ornaments create focal points throughout the garden. On the terrace a cherub surrounded by an arch of ivy drips water into a basin. "I've grown accustomed to the tinkle of water. It contributes to the feeling of privacy."

Dorothy remembers the local concern for the future of the garden after her mother-in-law's death. She reminds that in those days organizations such as the Garden Conservancy, of which Dorothy is a board member, did not exist. "The purpose of the conservancy," she says, "is to preserve exceptional American gardens by facilitating their transition from private to independent nonprofit ownership and operation."

Fortunately, in the case of her mother-in-law's garden, Dorothy was able to take over the trowel, and the garden is preserved. For her, it has many layers of meaning. She is able to participate on a personal level in the preservation of a distinctive old garden. "And," she says, "I am passionate about family. Neither John nor I have our parents anymore, but living here makes me feel connected to all of them. We are carrying on family history through this house and the garden. And we are making history for our own children, too."

DOROTHY GARDNER'S PLANTERS

Throughout her garden, Dorothy Gardner uses planters as focal points or accents of color. Containers—ranging from terra-cotta, lead, and ceramics to French wire—provide textures that contrast with the plants. They punctuate corners of beds or are placed directly in the center. Bold specimens are set singly or in pairs, but when Dorothy creates a grouping, she usually varies the heights and kinds of plants. Topiaries—fat balls of ivy, myrtle, rosemary, scented geraniums, curry, and santolina—abound.

"There is great flexibility in incorporating planters into the garden," says Dorothy. "They can be moved on a whim or rotated, like the furnishings in a house."

Dorothy has attached pairs of wire baskets, cascading with ivy (*Hedera helix* 'Glacier'), trailing geraniums (*Pelargonium peltatum* 'L'Elégante'), and impatiens, to the sides of the rose arbors at eye level. Bay trees are placed on either side of the living room's French doors. A pair of antique French sewing tables holding ivy and *Coleus amboinicus* decorate either side of another set of doors. Two 4-foot oleanders define the ends of an outdoor dining area in front of the Cutting Garden. Five oval clay planters reiterate the exterior curve of the garden room. French iron roosters hold ivy on the steps to the White Garden. Wire planters are attached to both sides of the entrance gate. Most of the windows of the house have iron window boxes, holding rows of white pelargoniums, attached under them. "Almost anything can be used as a planter; and that's what makes it interesting," Dorothy says of the 50-plus she has placed around the garden.

In the summer, Dorothy works in an enclosed potting area—"I call it the potting shed, but it doesn't have a roof." She has just installed a 7½-foot-long redwood counter, with a lower shelf to accommodate clay pots in varying sizes. A boxlike structure, 52 by 29 inches, holds a planting medium, mixed and ready for use, composed of roughly four parts potting soil, one part vermiculite, and three parts peat moss. "More or less, as it is all done by feel—I just grab the ingredients the way I cook." She places broken pieces of clay pots in the bottom of planters to ensure good drainage. Repotting is an ongoing effort. As plants outgrow their containers, they've moved on to bigger pots, because, as she says, "the proportion looks better." To prevent air pockets, she waters the plants well to settle the soil before top-dressing the pots.

Dorothy lines wire baskets and covers the surfaces of the rest of her planters with damp sphagnum moss, which helps retain moisture. Watering all these planters, and simultaneously incorporating a liquid fertilizer, is a task, she admits. Some of the smaller ones, those in direct sun, may need a drink twice a day. She often places pots in planters, and she may leave the plants in their plastic nursery containers if the pots are not going to be visible. "While I would never allow the plastic to show," she says, "it does hold moisture longer than clay."

Even clay pots, especially when new, can be improved—or "aged." Dorothy mixes a watered-down solution of latex house paint—approximately three parts water to one part paint—and she applies it to the surface of a dry, unglazed terra-cotta pot with an old rag, rather than the traditional sponge. Muted colors with apropos names, such as "Driftwood" or "Thyme," are her choices.

Most of the potted plants are either annuals or tender perennials. Some planters contain a rich mixture, but others feature only one plant. "I strive for simplicity," she says. "Sometimes the most effective planting is of a single plant or a series of single plants." She favors plants with bold, colored, or variegated foliage—caladiums, coleus, ivy, dracaena, begonias, oxalis—as they keep their fresh looks throughout the summer. Many planters are designed totally with foliage plants, especially those that thrive in the shade. Dorothy says, "Tucking a flowering plant into a planter that is primarily green is like fluffing up a pillow in a room. It says that someone has given the spot special attention." For entertaining, she often puts white flowers into the planters. "White is so pretty at night," she observes.

It would be difficult to incorporate so many tender plants without consideration of their winter needs. "The two things I wanted most when I moved here were a dog and a greenhouse. And I got them both. The winter is so long. With a greenhouse, I knew we could enjoy part of our garden all year long." In the fall the parade of bay topiaries, rosemary, myrtle, curry, lemon verbena, and stephanotis marches from the garden into the greenhouse.

Dorothy chose to have the greenhouse incorporated into the garden-room addition, rather than purchasing a commercially manufactured greenhouse. It is 8½ feet square; it has a ceiling height of 9½ feet, windows that open along the lower edge, and ventilation in the roof. The skylights are fixed. "Of course," she says, "it is too small, but any greenhouse would be too small. It is amazing how many plants I can cram into it, and it still looks wonderful all winter."

Perfection in Miniature

JANE C. SCOTT

LOCUST, NEW JERSEY

In the late 1930s Jane Scott read an article in *Life* magazine about bonsai. In the length of time it takes to read a thousand words, Jane found her calling. "One tree was five hundred years old. I was smitten. It was an immediate love affair that has gone on all my life." For the past 50 years Jane has been dedicated to the ancient and elegant art of growing miniature potted trees. "I'm in it for the years, not for the minutes," she says. It is a commitment that has meant decades of quiet consideration. "I have spent my whole life thinking."

During the war years Jane's desire to learn bonsai had to remain "latent, but very much alive." After the war in 1946 Jane and her husband, George, were among the first to build a new house in Monmouth County, New Jersey, on the tidal Navesink River. "It was so pretty and good for sailing," Jane recalls. They bought an acre of land thatched with poison ivy and coreopsis. High on a bluff facing south, it overlooks a changing spectacle of water activity and weather.

Jane launched into planting the property. "Every tree, every stone, I have put here." The house, set back from the road, is hidden by a screen of dense foliage. Its privacy belies its close neighbors. With many additions and refinements,

the house now spreads around a gravel courtyard. The grounds are groomed and the vegetation pruned to perfection. Even the trees—silvery spruce, hollies, dogwoods, hickories, oaks—and shrubs—rhododendrons, pieris, ilex, leatherleaf viburnums—are shaped, yet they appear uncontrived, as if nature itself had held the shears. "I know the viburnum has lovely flowers, but it never has a chance to bloom, I prune it so often," says Jane, a master of manicure.

Jane admits that her initial forays into the world of bonsai were uncertain. She recalls proudly showing one of her early efforts to Tom Davis, an American colleague of George's who had spent most of his life in Japan. He sat still and silent for "a long while" before announcing softly, "In about five years, you'll have a nice beginning." His response was pivotal in her understanding of the process of bonsai.

At the time, very little literature on the subject was published in English. But Jane found kindred spirits at the Brooklyn Botanic Garden, where she took courses for many years. She met Yuji Yoshimura, a teacher with whom she became friends, and his influence on her work was profound. His book, *The Japanese Art of Miniature Trees and Land-*

"I have always studied form.

With miniature gardens, you are looking at precise formality."

Jane C. Scott

scape: *Their Creation, Care, and Enjoyment,* first published in 1957, has become a constant, well-worn reference.

Jane supplemented her studies with books her friend Tom Davis sent from Tokyo; she knew no one to translate the text into English, but she learned from studying the photographs. Interest in bonsai has grown, more quickly than the trees themselves, all over the world. These days Jane receives as many as six magazines a month on the subject, all published in the United States.

Jane's garden is a study of greens, in infinite variation. Yet there is no grass on the property. Few flowering plants enter the restful environment. And where they do, they hold minor roles. A cutting garden is tucked behind the potting shed. A few blue lobelia spill in unison over the edges of a pot at the garage doors. Trees, in myriad configurations, are the attraction. Jane's is a subtle garden.

Intriguing paths of gravel and steps of stone lead in every direction from the house's main courtyard. The land has been terraced to take advantage of all available space, and its layered character provides enclosed sites for a series of gardens, large and small. Tables and comfortable chairs are placed in shaded corners. On them miniature trees, singly and in planted "forests," await a viewer's attention.

Surprises, a view of the river or an individual bonsai, are revealed around corners. A prize, a cypress forest on a round table, commands the center of one garden. Jane looks at it and

muses, "It seems like an island in an inland sea."

Many of Jane's life-size gardens are circled by trees, creating lush, dark backgrounds for "exhibitions of the smaller bonsai." Shade cast by the trees furnishes tranquil work areas, particularly in July or August's intense heat. Jane often carries a piece to a cool spot to work with it for hours. Stone steps layered with ground covers—ivy, pachysandra, sedum, or *Alyssum montanum*—lead to the largest garden. Multilayered, it, like the smaller gardens, is cupped in enclosure, with more stone steps leading to the higher levels. On one side a weathered potting shed adds architectural interest. Its windows reflect the light on foliage and the sky in moving patterns of greens and grays.

Irregularly shaped horse-stall dividers, bought 40 years ago from a junk man, are laid horizontally; they form display surfaces of various heights. Like shelves, they hold an array of bonsai in a loose, unstructured fashion, presenting them at "eye level" when a viewer is seated. Jane paints the dividers

yearly in the spring with crankcase oil, which prevents them from rusting and maintains their flat, unassuming black color. Their cement-block underpinnings are faced with abundant ivy. On their surfaces, like a jeweler arranging a necklace of emeralds in a boutique window, Jane moves a plant, studies, and looks. Cocking her head, she pinches a tiny conifer's needle, views, and thinks again.

Of the choices of plants to form into bonsai, Jane has tried "them all." She fondly recalls that her first bonsai attempt was probably a pine, "a seedling that had come up in the yard; I turned anything that came up into bonsai." Obviously, large-leaved or big-needled plants do not lend themselves to bonsai scale, and "you don't want anything that grows too tall too fast." Yet while dwarf varieties are often good choices, using them exclusively would be too limiting; any tree can be trained to dwarf proportions. A bonsai artist is a little like an animal trainer who with the flick of a whip commands an elephant to stand on his hind legs with his trunk poised in the air. The performance appears artless, a suspended moment, but count-less hours over years have been logged in the education.

Jane uses a range of conifers: juniper, spruce, pine, cypress. Evergreens she favors are littleleaf boxwood and rhododendron. The deciduous mimosa (silk tree), *Hydrangea anomala* ssp. *petiolaris*, wisteria, and ginkgo have worked well. The seasonal characteristics of deciduous specimens are perhaps more varied, as the loss of foliage exposes the structure of the trunks and branches during the plant's dormancy. And many come into flower, a glorious show concentrated in miniature. She enjoys the excitement of experiment, of try-ing something new. "Something to titillate you." And she is always looking for "babies," instructing friends to watch for seedlings.

Infants live in a protected cold frame at the back of the potting shed. Bowls and pots hold scores of diminutive plants and cut-tings. "Root all good cuttings right away," Jane advises as she dips a juniper pruning into

BELOW: Jane's main garden is cup-shaped, with bonsai set at varying heights to mingle with permanent plantings. RIGHT: Outside the greenhouse, a cold frame 18 inches wide and deep was built for winter shelter. When the temperature rises above freezing, Jane allows each plant a breath of the fresh air.

tepid water and then Rootone. With a chopstick she makes a hole in a sandy bed and tucks the tiny twig in to cuddle between a preemie pine and slightly fatter arborvitae. "All babies, we hope, will be immortalized into great trees."

The baby's next home is the nursery. Surrounded with chicken wire, this area is situated in another corner out of view. There Jane keeps a plant until it has established a good root system, until she feels it is ready to undergo the regimen of training.

As new growth appears, it is trimmed to control shape. While she has many Japanese pruning tools—all kept very sharp by George in his workshop—Jane often removes growth with a dexterous twist of the index finger and thumbnail. Pinching, she points out, is frequently more effective in prun-ing than snipping, as snipping with scissors—especially slightly dull ones—can sometimes cause the surrounding growth to turn brown.

Training the tree is one of the most creative

parts of the process. It is an exercise in previsualization. What would nature do if this tree were to grow on a grand scale, and how does the artist translate that form into miniature? Flexible copper, aluminum, or covered aluminum wire, in different gauges from threadlike to pencil width, is used to encourage the branches to grow in precisely planned directions, especially when curves are desired. The wire stays in place for about a year, with constant monitoring. If it is removed too soon, the tree reverts—or regresses. If left on too long, the wire can leave cuts or imprints in the living tissue. Other materials, such as bamboo splints or forks, can be used to set branches in a particular configuration. Shaping by systematically pruning shoots throughout the growing season makes the subtle refinements.

Tiny ground covers, with foliage in scale with the trees, are worked into the bases of the pieces. Like intricate needlework carpets, they, too, encourage close inspection. Jane favors partridgeberry, with its white flowers in spring and red fruit in the fall; miniature ferns; hens and chickens; mosses; and sedums. Sedums, she says, come in seemingly infinite varieties, some with leaves as small as the head of a pin. She is always looking for new ideas. Of a recently discovered sedum, she says, "If it's little and adorable, why not use it?"

In an indoor workshop, outfitted with a long table and several lazy Susans, Jane works on individual pieces throughout the year. "I use lazy Susans for everything—for work and for display. I need to see bonsai from every angle as I work and

think." She points to a fir. "I've been fooling with that for
forty years—hoping to do something spectacular."

Bonsai must be repotted regularly—on a yearly or bi-
yearly schedule, although some established in large pots
remain for as long as three or four years. Roots must be
trimmed, as well as top growth of foliage or needles. Pot-
bound plants will die; they need the space to make new
roots each year. The size of the roots and the scale of top
growth must be kept in balance, a key to keeping bonsai
healthy. Jane observes, "Nothing would dare die around
here; not with all the attention each one gets."

Watering, like the vigilant pruning, is a constant commitment for those who cultivate bonsai. Often roots are planted
in very shallow soil, "sometimes less than an inch"; some are
even exposed to feature their structural beauty. Many are
snaked around and through rock formations. Every plant
must be watered at least once a day; in the dry heat of summer, some need it twice. Wind dries plants out quickly

ABOVE: Large pieces of slate, some round and some uneven, are propped on different levels to create pedestals for Jane's bonsai. White marble purchased from a defunct meat market offers a lighter background for more contrast. LEFT: The view from the deck cantilevered from the house could illustrate a lesson in an art appreciation manual, with a carefully planned near-ground, middle-ground, and far-ground: from the arrangement of bonsai on a U-shaped display wall through the protective branches of the well-pruned trees to a panorama of the river.

as well. Jane has water faucets in five locations throughout the garden. The task, which she views as fulfillment rather than chore, can be completed in an hour if she is in a hurry, or it can take all day, her preferred pace.

The best way to quench a plant's thirst is "deep watering," submerging the plant once a month in water that also contains fertilizer. She uses a cement-mixing tray or an old washtub. The plant, she says, should stay under water until no more bubbles rise to the surface. With hardy bonsai, she fertilizes, with a balanced 20-20-20, bonemeal or fish emulsion, once a month during the spring, summer, and fall. Her "doses" are usually half the strength recommended by the manufacturer. Tender versions, which warm their toes inside during the winter, receive fertilizer all year round. But Jane laughs, "I never do anything quite as regularly as 'once a month'; I just don't live like that."

Winter care is a challenge, considering the number of bonsai that Jane has nurtured over the years. For plants that remain outdoors year-round, their containers' potential to freeze and crack must be considered. Jane plants hardy bonsai in fine, dense pots that she knows can withstand winter temperatures. Then she wraps each to the top of the pot in salt hay.

A retaining wall behind the potting shed makes a sheltered area about 4 feet wide, 20 feet long, and 3 feet high. In it she "stuffs" the hardy plants, surrounding each with a salt-hay bunting for the winter. The two openings, one at each end, are barricaded with wire, to keep cats, dogs, and raccoons out.

CLOCKWISE FROM TOP RIGHT: *Buxus microphylla* 'Kingsville Dwarf', *Chamaecyparis obtusa, Pinus parviflora, Juniperus, Hydrangea anomala* ssp. *petiolaris, Rhododendron* spp. *Juniperus, Acer palmatum.* CENTER: *Pinus strobus.*

Tender bonsai take up residence in Jane's greenhouse, crowding the usual spare arrangements.

Containers or bases, made mostly of pottery, are important to Jane's work. Substantial, timeless, understated, and spare, the containers bestow a certain beauty by their simplicity. She seeks out pieces in earth tones: grays, rusts, greens, browns; some solid in color, some variegated or shaded. Most are Japanese. Some are glazed on the exterior, but all are unglazed on the inside. Coral and stone, many of the pieces collected on winter vacations to the Bahamas, are another hallmark of her arrangements. Stones that appear to twist, have holes, are graced with unusual shapes, or can be viewed from several angles are particularly prized. The porous pieces or those with natural holes are ideal for planting and water drainage. Containers need drainage holes, one to three depending on the size of the vessel. The exception is for trees whose roots are planted in Jane's recipe of "muck," a concoction of six parts Michigan Peat, four parts Milled Spagnum, and a handful of bonemeal. Beginning at the consistency of mayonnaise, the mixture quickly solidifies, helping the plants' roots to adhere to rock formations.

Many of Jane's containers were gleaned in the course of the couple's frequent travels. George's business, as vice chairman for Citibank, made the travel-loving pair mobile. "We had no children and no pets, and could leave on twenty-four hours' notice." And they did. For a period of 20 years, they spent at least one third of their time traveling—to Europe, to the Far

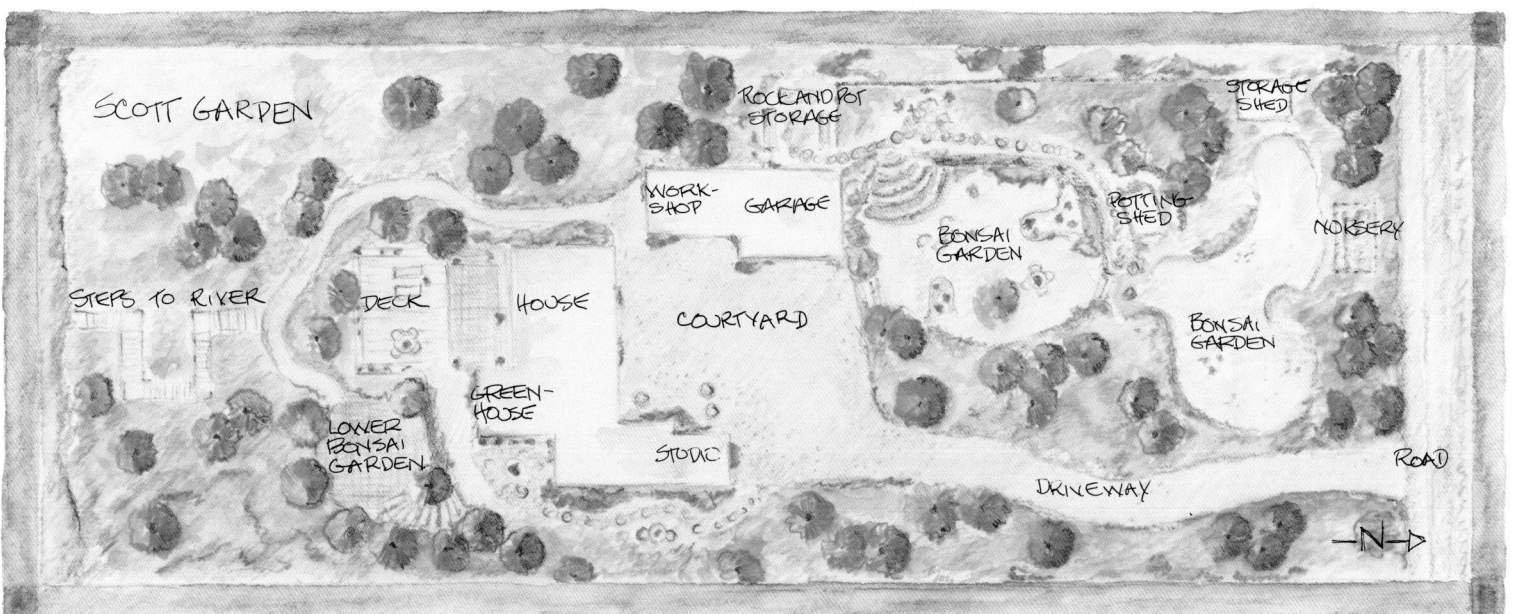

East, to Africa, to South America, to Australia and New Zealand—in two- to three-week trips.

While the men did business, the women entertained Jane and in turn were entertained by her. Jane discovered that she loved to talk about bonsai; she was a convincing advocate. Spreading her message with infectious enthusiasm, she found ready audiences all over the world.

Her travels also provided her with materials and inspiration for her work, which she still modestly refers to as a hobby that "took her by storm." As well as taking aesthetic and technical cues from the Japanese, Jane accumulated many of the tools and containers she uses during her many visits to that country, and a large piece of volcanic rock accompanied her on a plane trip from Iceland. For 30 years, she held a permit to bring plants into the country, but as the United States tightened restrictions on plant import, she found she was no longer free to bring home the plants she wanted, so she gave up the permit. Since then all her plants have come from

Large bonsai are wrapped with a circle of wire, which is filled with fallen leaves or salt hay for protection in the winter.

within the United States. Friends bring unexpected gifts in miniature. George, too, makes his offerings. He carries plastic bags in his golf bag and often brings a bit of moss from one of his ball's woodland adventures. He claims, "Jane's work makes you interested in every little thing."

Jane does not keep records of her plants. She never photographs them. Studying each for long hours, as she nurtures them, she finds they have imbedded themselves in her visual memory. She knows them by heart. Stories, too, are part of their mystique. A 40-year-old plant, she maintains, has done a lot of living. Plants' origins mark both high points and quiet times in Jane's life; many are reminders of her friends. For instance, a sacred ficus, *Ficus religiosa*, with its lacy foliage, is meant to be the tree under which Buddha sat and meditated. Jane savors those histories like fine, aged wine.

Arranging, reworking, and replanting form the mixture of the art that Jane has perfected over the course of 50 years. Add the most important ingredient, she says: "Sit and study."

JANE SCOTT'S RECOMMENDATIONS

FOR TURNING PLANTS INTO BONSAI

Jane Scott advises that almost anything can be turned into bonsai. That, to her, is part of the adventure of bonsai culture. She delights in discovering the tiniest seedling, nurturing it, and turning it into bonsai. In all her years of creating bonsai, she has bought only one mature plant. The rest she has begun from seedlings. She laughs, "Sometimes I don't even know what the plant is, but I want to give it a try."

While Jane admits to being a passionate rock collector, particularly of shapely specimens to use as bases, she adds "I try to underplant everything." The following list of shrubs, trees, vines, and other plants, she suggests, is just a beginning.

BROAD-LEAVED EVERGREEN SHRUBS

BOTANICAL NAME	COMMON NAME
Buxus microphylla 'Compacta'	Dwarf boxwood
Buxus microphylla 'Kingsville Dwarf'	Dwarf boxwood
Ilex crenata 'Helleri'	Japanese holly
Ilex crenata 'Microphylla'	Little-leaf holly
Nandina domestica	Heavenly bamboo
Pieris japonica 'Bisbee Dwarf'	Japanese pieris
Rhododendron kiusianum	Rhododendrom
Rhodendron racemosum 'Compactum'	Rhododendrom

DECIDUOUS CONIFERS

Larix kaempferi	Japanese larch
Pseudolarix amabilis	Golden larch
Taxodium distichum	Bald cypress

DECIDUOUS TREES AND SHRUBS

Acer palmatum	Japanese maple
Carpinus japonica	Japanese hornbeam
Ilex serrata	Finetooth holly
Liquidambar orientalis	Oriental sweet gum
Zelkova serrata	Japanese zelkova

EVERGREEN CONIFERS

Cedrus atlantica	Atlas cedar
Chamaecyparis obtusa 'Nana Gracilis'	Hinoki false cypress
Chamaecyparis pisifera	Japanese false cypress
Cryptomeria japonica	Japanese cryptomeria
Juniperus chinensis	Chinese juniper
Juniperus horizontalis	Creeping juniper
Juniperus squamata 'Prostrata'	Prostrate juniper

BOTANICAL NAME	COMMON NAME
Picea jezoensis	Ezo spruce
Pinus parviflora	Japanese white pine
Pinus strobus	White pine
Pinus thunbergii	Japanese black pine

FLOWERING TREES AND SHRUBS

Amelanchier canadensis	Shadbush
Rhododendron spp. (Azalea)	Azalea
Chaenomeles japonica	Flowering quince
Cotoneaster horizontalis	Cotoneaster
Crataegus laevigata	English hawthorn
Daphne × *burkwoodii* 'Carol Mackie'	'Carol Mackie' daphne
Malus sargentii	Sargent crab apple
Prunus subhirtella 'Pendula'	Weeping Higan cherry
Pyracantha coccinea	Scarlet firethorn

VINES

Hedera helix 'Conglomerata'	Bunchleaf English ivy
Hedera helix 'Glacier'	English ivy
Hydrangea anomala spp. *petiolaris*	Climbing hydrangea
Parthenocissus tricuspidata 'Veitchii'	Boston ivy
Wisteria floribunda	Japanese wisteria

PLANTS FOR INDOOR CULTURE IN AREAS SUBJECT TO FROST

Carissa grandiflora 'Nana Compacta'	Natal plum
Ficus religiosa	Sacred ficus
Gardenia jasminoides	Cape jasmine
Pyracantha koidzumii 'Low Dense'	Formosa firethorn
Rhododendron spp.	Azalea (tender varieties)
Serissa foetida	Snow rose

"In a city like Los Angeles, peace and quiet in the garden is its greatest gift."

Georgianna Bray Erskine

Structure with Style

GEORGIANNA BRAY ERSKINE

PASADENA, CALIFORNIA

Georgiana Bray Erskine has a habit of sitting up in bed in the middle of the night and making a pronouncement for her garden: "A wall, I need a wall," or "The answer is an axis," she has proclaimed. These types of nocturnal revelations come often to Georgie. Her dreams are never small; they rarely take budgets into consideration. Of course, this design technique takes a toll on her husband's sleep— Georgie does not whisper. But the wall gets built, and the axis carved into place.

When Georgie and Paul Erskine, an engineer, purchased their colonial-style house in a residential district of Pasadena in 1961, four years after their marriage, it came with a garden. "Quite a nice California garden, including the inevit-

able swimming pool. The previous owner had been a landscape architect with an interest in trees," Georgie recalls. The property covers a generous acre, but the entire garden was visible at once, giving it "no sense of mystery." However, with three children to raise, the couple deferred an overhaul of the property, choosing instead to educate themselves on garden design before lifting a spade.

Georgie and Paul love to travel, and Georgie believed that visiting gardens, particularly historical gardens, in other countries would be inspiration for making the garden her own. Having studied art history in college, she is a firm believer in "going back to the source. Our culture in southern California is rooted in Spain, so it seemed that looking to the motherland would make the most sense," Georgie remembers.

"Perhaps the most influential garden for me was that of the Generalife of the Alhambra in Granada. It is a series of walled gardens, with long colonnades or galleries. Further divisions are made by hedges, often of myrtle and roses."

Different levels are reached by sets of stairs. "Within the enclosures is the restful presence of water. Not loud splashing water, but quiet fountains, reflecting pools, and runnels." Georgie says, "The fragrance of flowers is intensified because of the walls. The most significant feature is a profound sense of silence.

"The word 'Generalife,'" Georgie continues, "means 'garden of paradise,' or, depending on who is writing about it, 'orchard,' 'garden of feasts,' or 'house of delights.' The strictest translation defines the word as the 'garden of the architect.' I suppose, in a sense, I'd have tried to bring all those meanings together here."

However, when nature forced her hand with a major storm in 1982 that flooded the grounds and washed away some of the garden, it was not Spain that was the catalyst for design change. Rather, a trip to see gardens in Italy resulted in the "axis dream," and the genesis of Georgie's garden plan. "But Italy just confirmed what I had learned in Spain. I also saw an exhibition of Chinese scrolls and was moved by the artists' mythical respect for nature. Those Chinese gardens, like the Alhambra, seemed so quiet. I also determined to divide the garden into rooms," she says, citing the layouts of a number of gardens that she visited in England, particularly Sissinghurst. "I thought those divisions would help supply a sense of privacy or intimacy." Thus the "wall dream."

The Erskines launched into a major garden renovation, dividing the property loosely into thirds, with the curved driveway and house occupying the first third. A six-foot wall built of cement block and covered with stucco made the second horizontal division. "A tall hedge would just

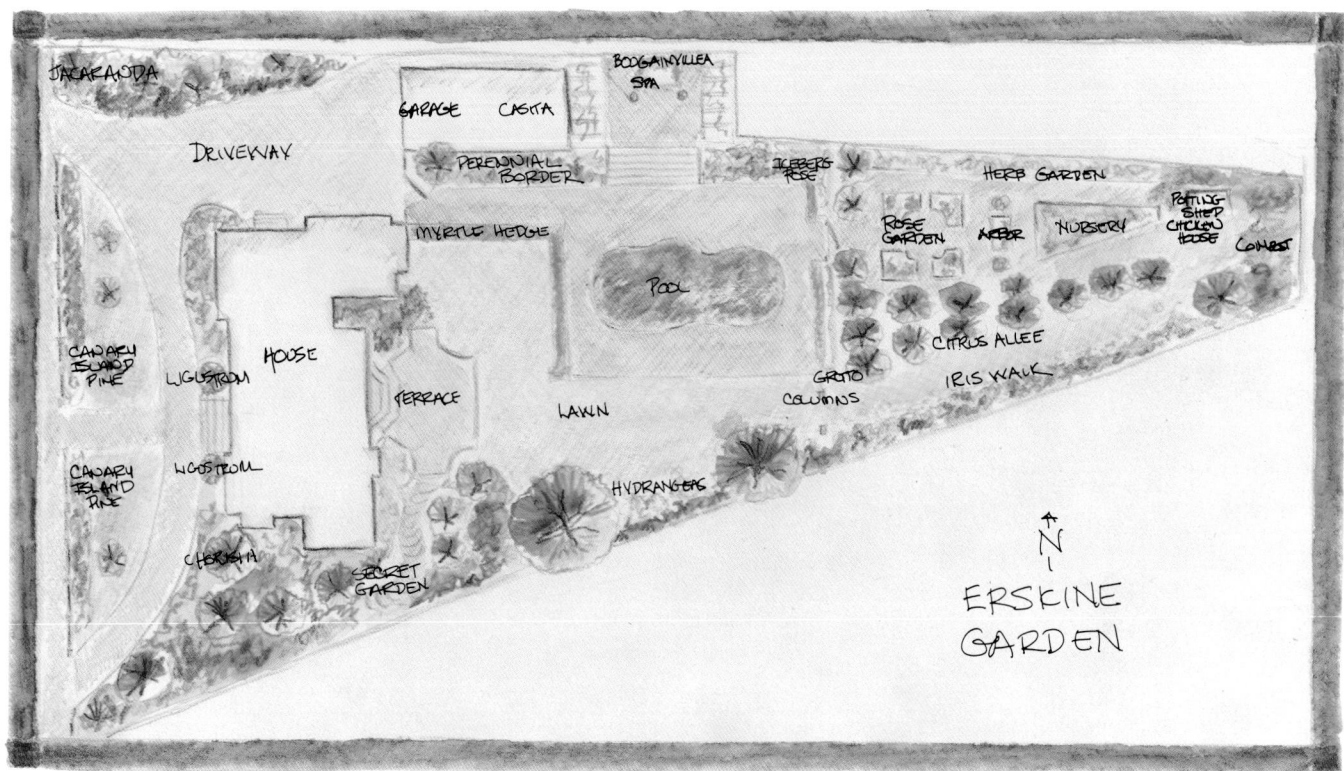

take too long to grow. I wanted instant height," Georgie explains. When she discussed her plan with friends, they said, "What a bad idea. A wall will only make your garden seem smaller." "Exactly," she responded, confident that she knew better.

"And what is a rose garden without a fountain? I found a wonderful nineteenth-century figure, and later the basin." Many adjustments were made to the recirculating pump to ensure that "the fountain's music is quiet."

The axis line, laid out with stakes and string, led directly from the French doors in the dining room to an opening in the south end of the new wall. Capping the columns that flank the opening are two nineteenth-century carved limestone baskets of flowers, purchased in San Juan Capistrano. "The property is a peculiar triangle, and some adjustments had to be made to the axis to accommodate that shape. But the impression now is that the garden is a rectangle." For example, the axis line had to take a sharp turn to the left past the opening, where the path becomes a "citrus allée" and an "iris walk." Georgie laughs conspiratorially, "I wanted both, and didn't have the room, so I combined the two ideas into one allée." The allée boasts a variety of citrus trees, including Eureka and Meyer lemons, Valencia and Washington naval oranges, tangerines, a Minneola tangelo, grapefruit, and a Mexican lime "essential for margaritas."

A free-form swimming pool dominates the center third of the garden. To the north the Erskines built a raised terrace— with a wide stairway as an architectural feature. An elevated

terrace with a brick floor in a herringbone pattern reiterates the brick around the pool, integrating the entire area. Each level is accented with pots of blooming plants and succulent agave, echeveria, and euphorbia.

On either side of the terrace a pergola is host to grapes and wisteria, a green ceiling of cool shade. To the east a built-in barbecue is also constructed of brick. To the west is a charming guesthouse, "our Casita," outfitted with everything from a lace-covered canopy bed and music system to a fully stocked kitchen. "I've always believed you should stay in your own guesthouse before you offer it to guests. How else will you answer all their needs?"

The area around the curved drive leading past the front door is treated in a subtle fashion. When the Erskines bought the house, the front yard was separated from the street by a picket fence "too New England for California. Anyway, it succumbed to dry rot, so that took care of that." The Erskines replaced the fence with brick columns, painted white, and a wrought iron fence.

A pair of tall Canary Island pines (*Pinus canariensis*) with textured bark stand guard on either side of the entrance walkway. A *Magnolia grandiflora* is espaliered the full two stories against the front of the house. (A Japanese maple has received the same treatment on the north end of the house.) Two specimens of *Ligustrum japonicum* 'Texanum', which have been in pots since 1965, flank the front door. Pruned regularly to keep their ball heads neat, they are never allowed to blossom. The plant is also used as a hedge along the fence. *Podocarpus elongatus,* which is usually grown as a tree, is trained in hedge form on either side of the front door.

Next to the driveway, a new border is taking shape. Georgie took its color cue from the purple jacaranda tree (*Jacaranda mimosifolia*) already in place. Purple-leaved plants, such as *Prunus* × *cistena,* and purple-flowering buddleias extend the theme. Then Georgie drops in vivid color, such as *Camellia reticulata* 'Howard Asper,' which was a gift from the botanist and curator who developed the plant at the Huntington Botanical Gardens, where Georgie worked

BELOW: The bricked terrace features a raised "spa," centered on the axis that runs from the pool up the stairs to the property boundary. A massive bougainvillea (*Bougainvillea brasiliensis* 'San Diego') creates a drapery of red velvet. A pair of five-foot structural frangipani (*Plumeria rubra*), grown in pots, produce clusters of fragrant white flowers "blushing pink in the center." OPPOSITE: While ebullient planting is Georgie's signature behind the house, the entrance garden is tailored and restrained.

before she was married. "From December to March it gives red blossoms—six to eight inches across—that are as heavy as baseballs. The flowers are so full, fat, and heavy that all I have to do for a dinner party is put four or five down the middle of the table with some ivy, and I've got it made."

Georgie grows many plants for flower or foliage to use in her arrangements, for which she has been awarded ribbons in competition. Favorites are marguerites (*Chrysanthemum frutescens*), Shasta daisies (*C.* × *superbum*), delphiniums, scabiosas, *Convolvulus cneorum*, Iceland poppy (*Papaver nudicaule*), *Salvia farinacea,* *Pittosporum tobira* 'Variegatum', *Hydrangea macrophylla,* and *Leptospermum scoparium.* "I never buy flowers, I use only what I grow." A student of ikebana, the Japanese art of flower arranging, she currently attends classes in the Sogetsu school of thought, which allows for the freest

interpretation of the tradition and the widest use of materials and plants. "Still," Georgie points out, "it is all based on the mathematical principles of the three basic elements: the *shin*, *soe*, and *hikae*, which stand for 'heaven,' 'earth,' and 'man.'" As in the larger context of her whole garden and its historical influences, she welcomes working within a centuries-old structure. "What I have learned is that rather than a whole bouquet of irises, I get the most power-ful response from a single, perfect iris." As she walks through her garden, Georgie looks for the individual flower that could be brought indoors for heightened appreciation, a search that often leads her to her favorite spot in the garden: her rose garden.

Approached by yet another axis line, one that leads from the driveway along the pool, the rose garden is entered through a weathered-looking gate in the wall. The gate remains closed, suggesting a surprise behind. "I don't want to show my hand all at once, now, do I?"

Georgie's first rose, the floribunda 'Iceberg', was given to her by her mother in 1965. It stands, in graceful maturity, at the entrance to the rose garden and sets the tone for the L-shaped hedges that Georgie planted beside the swimming pool. Thirty bushes of 'Iceberg', planted bare-root, now form a white-flowered screen in April, with generous intermittent repeat bloom for nine months of the year. On the east side an 18-inch hedge of myrtle (*Myrtus communis*) disguises their bare lower canes.

On the north side the roses form the backdrop for a 100-foot-long perennial and annual border, with the old-fashioned flowers—foxgloves, *Felicia amelloides*, lantana, penstemon, yarrow, lobelia—mostly in subdued blues, pinks, grays, and lavenders and with

yellow accents provided by daylilies, yarrow, and marguerites here and there. "I learned about how effective yellow is from flower arranging—put a spot of yellow where you want the eye to focus. It's the same in a border." By the same token, labor-intensive delphiniums, which often require restaking daily, add a touch of grandeur. "And drama is essential—even in a quiet garden."

Seeing plants in the wild has been one of the "bonuses" of the Erskines' frequent travel. "You begin to understand what a plant really looks like and how it grows." In Sicily, Georgie spotted a caper plant (*Capparis spinosa*), with its white flowers with purple stamens, growing through some cracks in rocks; she sought it out when she returned, and placed it in a pot on the hot, dry terrace. "But the vivid yellow alstroemeria we saw in Chile in masses along roadsides, in meadows, in rock crevices bloom in a color that just does not grow here," she says sadly, remarking that her own are pallid in comparison.

Georgie has always brought lessons back from her travels abroad, many of which have come to roost in the garden years later. Musing on her individual style, she says, "Well, I am a bit eclectic." As a student she studied French at the Sorbonne, living with a French family and learning to cook in the French manner (a talent she put to use in the cooking school she operated with a partner in her own kitchen in Pasadena for three years).

"In their meals," observes Georgie, "the French adhere to what they call *tradition de table*, which is a strict formula of order, beginning with an entrée of *saucisson*, soup, or fish, then the *plat*, or main course, and a salad, cheese, fruit, and dessert, if they're being formal. The custom means that there is a time-honored structure that forms the architecture of a meal. Within those constraints, of course, each chef puts his or her own creative stamp on the ingredients, coming up with unique tastes. The French have unabashed daring to try absolutely anything within the tradition. Like dining, I believe that there are principles, established over centuries in gardens, that make the finest gardens.

"Perhaps all this makes me a traditionalist," she says, then pauses with an impish laugh. "Well, a traditionalist with a spirit of adventure."

OPPOSITE: To soften the stucco wall that imposes structure on her garden, without having to wait for a hedge to inch its way to maturity, Georgie planted Boston ivy (*Parthenocissus tricuspidata*)—originally only eight or ten plants—which has covered the surface in green. The wall opening leads to the "citrus allée" and "iris walk." ABOVE: Georgie comes from a gardening family. Her mother, Evelyn Lewis Bray, pictured here, and her sister Lourinda still live in the family house, where an old 'Iceberg' rose like those that bloom in profusion throughout Georgie's garden stands guard by the front door. LEFT: Some of Evelyn's cymbidium orchids and the blossom of a shell ginger (*Alpina zerubet*). OVERLEAF: Following the lead of the Generalife in Granada, but on a smaller scale, Georgie chose myrtle for most of the hedges that form separations throughout the garden. She punctuates the corners where the border is divided by the flight of stairs to the terrace and Casita with jasmine (*Jasminum humile*).

GEORIGIANA ERSKINE'S ROMANTIC ROSE GARDEN

LEFT, TOP TO BOTTOM: *'Brandy', hybrid tea; 'Buccaneer', hybrid tea; 'Bridal White', floribunda; 'Medallion', hybrid tea.*

"I think you have to have roses in your garden. All the romance of life is in a rose."

As part of her garden's redesign in 1983, Georgie imposed a traditional quadrant pattern on her rose garden, with each 7½- by 8½-foot quadrant holding a half dozen rose plants. Under the roses in the side borders, Georgie has planted kitchen herbs and fragrant flowers for cutting. A mass of lavatera grown from seeds given to her by the head gardener at Dunbeath Castle in Scotland ends one path in a splash of pink.

"I had gone to Villandry in France, and I wanted an arbor at the end of my rose garden, like the ones in the vegetable garden there. Of course, we couldn't buy one; we had to build it. I had a wonderful Swiss gardener, Rudy Hofer, then. He could do anything. He took strips of redwood and floated them in the swimming pool for days to make them supple. With them he molded the arch shape of the arbor's top." Georgie points out that the curved edges defining the central circle of the garden were fashioned in the same way. A standard *Rosa* 'Contempo' stands on either side of the arbor.

Georgie feeds the roses a mixture of fish emulsion, cotton seed meal, bone meal, hoof and horn (a waste product of the racing industry), blood meal, and her own compost. Measurements are done by handsful: small plants get one of each; big plants, two. Sometimes, also in the spring, she gives them an organic commercial rose food. "I want them to bloom their hearts out. And they will do that if they feel full and happy."

Pruning is just common sense, Georgie says. "You look at a plant, and it tells you what to do." Dead, straggly canes must come out in early spring. Shaping is a "stand back and look at the plant" decision. "Always prune to an outside bud, which makes the canes grow outward." Her tip to ensure good health: Give the roses a dormant spray in winter. It coats the eggs of insects with oil and helps keep mildew and black spot at bay. In a garden with a certain formality, continued tidying up, including dead-heading, is part of the process, but petals on the pathways adds to its charm.

As for the roses: "'Cecile Brunner' envelops the arbor in pink flowers. It only blooms once a year but makes such a show that it is forgiven for its single performance." She thinks a moment. "The beauty of this garden is that almost every rose has some sentiment attached to it—each was a gift from a friend." She laughs, "Beginning, of course, with the 'Iceberg' from my mother all those years ago. She gave me 'Bridal White' when my daughter Eugenia was married and the reception was here in the garden. I look around and see 'Sonia', which was presented to me by the mother of my goddaughter. 'Allspice' was a fragrant message from another friend. And, of course, 'Olympiad' commemorated the 1984 Los Angeles Olympics. My roses are my memory album."

GEORGIE'S FAVORITE ROSES

ROSE VARIETY	TYPE	FLOWER COLOR/DESCRIPTION
'Allspice'	Hybrid Tea	Yellow, ruffled, honey and tea fragrance
'Brandy'	Hybrid Tea	Apricot, repeat flowering, fruity fragrance
'Bridal White'	Floribunda	White, frequent flowering, fragrant
'Buccaneer'	Shrub	Buttercup yellow
'Cecil Brunner'	Climber	Pink
'Iceberg'	Floribunda	Soft white, repeat flowering, fragrant
'Just Joey'	Hybrid Tea	Coppery apricot, frilled, richly fragrant
'Medallion'	Hybrid Tea	Pale pink to apricot, fragrant
'Ole'	Grandiflora	Warm crimson
'Olympiad'	Hybrid Tea	Brilliant red
'Peace'	Hybrid Tea	Pink, tinged with yellow
'Princess de Monaco'	Hybrid Tea	Delicate pink fading to ivory, fragrant
'Pristine'	Hybrid Tea	White, tinged with pink
'Queen Elizabeth'	Grandiflora	Bright pink
'Rose Gaujard'	Hybrid Tea	Deep pink edges fading to pink
'Sonia'	Grandiflora	Pink
'Sweet Surrender'	Hybrid Tea	Rose pink with a silver tinge, fragrant
'Tropicana'	Hybrid Tea	Apricot
'White Swan'	Floribunda	Delicate, clear white

A Caregiver's Touch

JANE P. OVERESCH
KANSAS CITY, MISSOURI

Surveying her walled English-style garden of richly tex-tured plants, Jane Overesch has good reason to be content. "I have everything I wanted in life: training as a nurse, a won-derful marriage, a good number of children, and a garden."

Jane, a native of Kansas City, studied nursing at the local Research Medical Center. She served as an army nurse in the Philippines and Japan in 1945 and 1946 and returned to Kansas City as a head nurse for her alma mater. Through her work she met her future husband, Harry Overesch, an orthopedic surgeon. It was only after Jane and Bud, as Harry has always been called, were married in 1951, both at the age of 30, that they discovered a mutual bent for gardening. Roses immediately captured their imaginations, and that infatuation lasted for nearly 20 years. But years change per-spective, Jane says, and her focus now is on a broader range of plants, each of which is required to meet a demanding list of criteria. No deadbeats make the grade. "For a plant, par-ticularly a tree or a shrub, to hold its own in my garden, it must have interesting foliage: rich in color or strong on tex-ture; it must have unusual leaf form or a fine overall shape or bearing. Just plain old green doesn't cut it."

The garden has evolved over the 30 years that Jane and Bud have owned their 1900s house, built as a summer residence, on the southern outskirts of Kansas City. The Overesches fell in love with the commodious house, its outbuildings, including a fanciful playhouse, and its broad expanses of lawn the minute they turned into the winding drive.

"We were looking for a house where each child could have his or her own room—our youngest was three and our oldest fourteen when we moved in. We wanted to keep ani-mals. And we wanted to have the space to really garden." The Overesches took possession of the house, located on nine open acres, in 1966. "Thirty diseased Dutch elms were here when we arrived. We had them removed, and we've been planting trees—American hornbeam, bald cypress, cork tree, goldenrain tree, magnolia, pawpaw, redbud, river birch, sophora, tupelo, yellowwood—which are the bones of our garden, ever since."

"With six young children in five different schools, it was a busy time," Jane remembers. "I had to be pretty determined to be a gardener, but I'm an early riser. I can do a lot of work between five a.m. and breakfast." She continues, "Bud and I

"Learning to be tough was one of my most difficult lessons. It isn't easy to harden your heart. As a nurse it is hard for me to eliminate anything, even an ailing plant. But sometimes it just has to be done—quietly—for the sake of the garden."

Jane P. Overesch

PREVIOUS PAGES, LEFT: A fountain is the centerpiece of Jane's Swimming Pool Garden, the former location of the family pool, since filled in to make room for more plants. RIGHT: A diamond of clipped Korean boxwood dominates the English Garden. On the northern edge of the sunken garden, a small building that once housed a cistern for the house's water supply has been transformed into a summer house. THIS PAGE, ABOVE: Sited under mature trees in front of the house's long porch, a circular reflecting pool made of poured concrete mirrors the flickering light as it changes throughout the day. RIGHT: The 'Pink Petticoat' phlox mixed with purple peppers and *Artemisia schmidtiana* 'Silver Mound' makes a signature color combination in Jane's garden. OPPOSITE: "I start out early in the morning with my bucket of tools and tell my dogs 'we're going for a walk'. Sometimes I don't get very far before I see something that needs doing. Other days, I define a project and just work on that."

the dogs (a couple of well-fed, lovable, face-licking golden retrievers), a pondful of goldfish, and four peacocks remain.

In the Overesch rose garden, a formally laid out parterre, more than 500 plants of 100 varieties blossomed. Jane and Bud became showmen, entering and winning competitions with their finest rose specimens. They were active in the American Rose Society, and Bud held offices, including that of district director, in the early 1970s. "When the politics of the rose societies became tedious, Bud lost interest—not only in the organization but also in the roses," Jane says. "He has an old maxim: 'Never buy more roses than your wife can take care of.' That did it for the roses. One day I invited a friend to come with a truck, I sharpened my shovel, and we dug them all up and pitched them out." Jane nonetheless recalls the "rose period" as enormously valuable to her ability to grow a diverse range of plants today, observing, "If you can grow a rose, you can grow anything." Admittedly, a few roses, "which *must* be fragrant," like *Rosa* 'Sombreuil', *R.* 'Yves Peuget', and David Austin's 'Heritage' and 'Mary Rose', have crept back into Jane's heart and borders.

After the rose parterre was expelled by Jane's determined shovel, the Overesches laid out the perimeters of an English-influenced garden at the suggestion of a local landscape architect, John Philip Baumgardt. Sited in the area directly below the house, the garden is enclosed by a six-foot-high block wall covered with stucco, which, Jane says, "provides soft color and a textural background to plants." It also creates a microclimate, allowing her to grow some plants that would not otherwise survive a Missouri winter. Within the walls,

worked like crazy in the garden, often together. I fed the children and had them in bed by eight, and then Bud and I would work until ten or so and have a late supper."

A menagerie of pets, spurred by the unleashed desires of six children and two parents who are "nuts about animals," quickly swelled to include dogs and cats, two ponies, two horses, chickens, geese, and goats. "The goats were marvelous pets," Jane says, "but they are browsers, and so were the geese. We had to choose between them and the gardens." These days, with the children grown, only the cats,

Jane planted herbaceous borders around the edges and carved graceful curved shapes for planting beds into the grass using patterns she cut from pieces of plywood and laid out in the space. The areas where grass was removed to create the parterres' shapes were bedded out with colorful annuals, such as 'Scarletta' begonias and ageratums.

Jane attributes the garden's current incarnation to an epiphany that came during a September 1985 trip to England and Scotland run by the American Horticultural Society. In a chilling rain the group of "plantaholics" visited the garden of "a Mr. Frank Lauley in Northumberland. Even on that dark, dreary day, the garden was so beautiful," Jane remembers. "He had six-foot walls around all the gardens to protect the plants from the winds. Very little was in bloom, but so many of the plants had foliage of color and variegation. I determined to come home and do likewise. We changed the garden the very next spring."

Out came the grass parterres. The new quadrants were raised and edged with six-inch-square landscape boards, "dressier than railroad ties," Jane observes. Where the quadrants meet is a diamond-shaped area, edged in Korean boxwood, with a 37-inch-high olive jar at its center. Jane first saw an olive jar used as a focal point in a monastery garden in Sicily and subsequently found one at Harrod's in London. "Not very practical, really; the shipping cost more than the jar. But isn't it perfect here?"

Paths were lined with gravel. Jane believes a formal structure enhances informal planting "with lots of plants. I love to see plants spilling over gravel paths." She adds, "The architecture must be definite, the design strongly shaped." An antique lavabo with a cherub's mouth constantly dripping water was installed in the south wall at the end of the north-south axis. A rustic arch terminates another long path. Other ornaments, sited with subtlety, have been placed around the garden. "My latest addition," Jane says, pointing to a cast concrete ball placed at the edge of a path.

ABOVE: The English Garden began in 1971 with the building of a six-foot wall. Traditional design devices such as enclosure, formal structure, and strong axial lines complement Jane's exuberent planting style. "Bloom period of most perennials is short. I rely heavily on the purple, gold, gray, and variegated foliage of trees and shrubs to make my garden exciting throughout the season." LEFT: A rustic arch, used like an exclamation point, terminates a long path. "The neutral color and texture of a stucco wall acts as a fine background for ornaments as well as for a variety of foliage colors," Jane observes.

RIGHT: The presence of peacocks in the Overesches' garden meant banishing chickens, which can pass disease on to larger birds. The peacocks' bold treks have forced Jane to barricade the front porch with swathes of plastic deer netting against their advances, "small hazards for the pleasure they give." With names like Agamemnon, Ajax, Diana, and Cassandra, these birds have attitude. "You can't beat a peacock displaying in a garden for pure color and atmosphere."

OPPOSITE: Maintaining the two reflecting ponds requires effort. Jane used to purchase tender plants just for summer display in her ponds, but now she limits herself to hardy water lilies and lotus, which still demand care, particularly in the fall. The water lily's foliage must be cut off and pots turned on their sides for the winter. Fallen tree leaves have to be removed, although a black nylon net is laid on boards over the pond in October before autumn leaf fall to prevent the heaviest onslaught. Because the leaves can suffocate the fish, yearly Jane dons her fisherman's waders and jumps in. While the ponds are less than three feet deep, they are "slippery as heck. Not my favorite task, but somebody has to do it. And that somebody is me."

With the garden's heart established, other gardens spread out farther from the house over time. "We never do anything on a small scale," admits Jane. In making the designs, Jane always thinks about creating "rooms." "Besides the separations, and different qualities of different rooms, intimate or open, I want to have views from one garden to another. So I put a good deal of thought into the arbors, gateways, and entrances. And I always try to think about the scale of each space and how it relates to the next."

Jane favors purple-, gray-, gold-, or variegated-leaved plants, and she researched the colored-foliage plants that she thought would survive the Missouri climate. Some, such as the 'Cherry Frost' birch, she purchased locally. "That birch is the only one like it I have ever seen in a nursery, and I bought it immediately." Other plants she purchases mail-order, often growing trees and shrubs from "nothing more than rooted cuttings. I am addicted to catalogs and buy my plants all over the country, coast to coast." She points out that horticultural education has often come through reading catalogs. Specimens of *Robinia pseudoacacia* 'Frisia', a *Cercis canadensis* 'Forest Pansy', *Cotinus coggygria* 'Velvet Cloak', *Daphne* × *burkwoodii* 'Briggs Moonlight', a variegated *Cornus kousa* var. *chinensis* 'Snowboy', and the shrub *Acanthopanax sieboldianus* 'Variegatus' have all started as small mail-order purchases. Infant trees are babied to maturity. While, for the sake of stimulating plant combinations, Jane tests variegated plants' tolerance for sun, she reminds that most prefer some shade.

As she strolls through her walled English Garden, it sparkles as the late afternoon sun highlights the filmy and delicate yellow foliage of the robinia. At its feet stand stiff,

OPPOSITE: The white fiberglass gazebo situated between the perennial border and the reflecting pool was purchased at the garden booth of the local country fair. For a recent Christmas, one of Jane's sons gave her a blue gazing ball, which sits in the middle of the table.

upright spikes of *Yucca flaccida* 'Golden Sword'; the two plants, both golden, offer extremes in texture. Jane ruffles the rosy foliage of the *Betula* × 'Cherry Frost' birch and the silver leaves of a weeping pear (*Pyrus salicifolia* 'Pendula'). She touts the purpleleaf sand cherry (*Prunus* × *cistena*) as a real workhorse, "tough and every bit as pretty as the Japanese maples at one third the cost. It holds its color all season, a job at which some purple-leaved plants, like *Sambucus nigra* 'Guincho Purple', fail."

Jane points out that her garden retains its diverse color palette, the living framework of her garden, throughout the growing season—from early spring to late fall. Flowers in the pinks, lavenders, and blues she prefers come and go, but the trees' and shrubs' colors remain. She indicates a blue spruce (*Picea pungens* 'Baby Blue Eyes'), which is scheduled for a move out of one of the quadrants. "It has outgrown this spot, but as a dense, gray accent, its color could not be beaten." Regretfully, Jane could have kept the spruce under control had she pinched its new growth each year. "Learned that lesson too late for this tree," she says. Artemisias 'Silver Queen' and 'Valerie Finnis' are earmarked to go into the spot to compensate for the gap of gray that the spruce will leave.

She insists she has grown more aggressive in her monitoring of plant growth; other trees that have the potential of outgrowing their sites are now given judicious pruning each

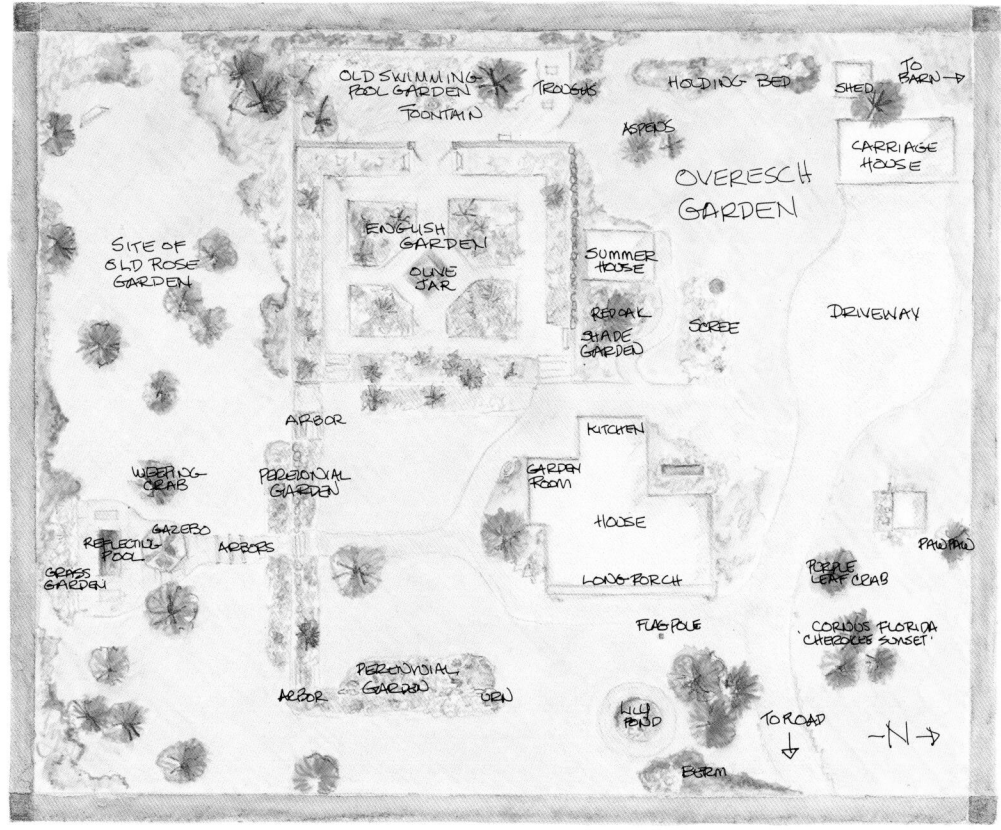

JANE OVERESCH'S RECOMMENDATIONS

FOR PLANTS WITH PURPLE, GOLD, GRAY, OR VARIEGATED FOLIAGE

Jane Overesch reminds that categorizing foliage with unusual color is arbitrary. It has to do with how a plant appears next to its neighbor, how it reacts to its shady or sunny location, and how it is seen by its viewer. For example, *Rosa rubrifolia* is now called *Rosa glauca*—one day a taxonomist decided that the foliage was more gray than red, and the name of an old familiar plant must be relearned. A number of plants are placed in the Variegated section here, but *Carex morrowrii* 'Goldband' could probably be in the Gold section as well, as it is green with a gold edge. Where does the red-veined, gray-leaved Japanese painted fern (*Athyrium nipponicum* 'Pictum') belong? It could be classified with the Purple to Red plants, Gray, or Variegated. A list of recommendations, Jane says, is merely a starting point for a gardener's experimentation with combinations of foliage to achieve special effects.

PURPLE TO RED

TREES

Acer palmatum 'Bloodgood'
Acer palmatum Dissectum group 'Red Filigree Lace'
Betula × 'Cherry Frost'
Betula × 'Tricolor'
Cercis canadensis 'Forest Pansy'
Prunus × *cistena*

SHRUBS

Berberis thunbergii 'Crimson Pygmy'
Berberis thunbergii 'Golden Ring'
Berberis thunbergii 'Rose Glow'
Corylus maxima 'Purpurea'
Cotinus coggygria 'Royal Purple'
Cotinus coggygria 'Velvet Cloak'
Sambucus nigra 'Guincho Purple'

PERENNIALS

Cimicifuga simplex 'Atropurpurea'
Euphorbia amygdaloides var. *robbiae* 'Rubra'
Euphorbia dulcis 'Chameleon'
Heuchera americana 'Ruby Veil'
Heuchera 'Chocolate Ruffles'
Heuchera 'Palace Purple'
Heuchera 'Persian Carpet'
Heuchera 'Plum Pudding'
Heuchera 'Ring of Fire'
Heuchera 'Ruby Robe'
Heuchera 'Velvet Knight'
Imperata cylindrica 'Rubra'
Lysimachia ciliata 'Atropurpurea'
Oxalis triangularis
Pennisetum setaceum 'Rubrum'
Penstemon digitalis 'Husker Red'
Sedum 'Mohrchen'
Viola labradorica

ANNUALS

Abelmoschus esculentus 'Burgundy' (okra)
Brassica oleracea 'Rabine' (brussels sprouts)
Capsicum annuum 'Peruvian Purple' (ornamental pepper)
Ipomoea batatas 'Blackie' (sweet potato vine)
Ocimum basilicum 'Dark Opal' (basil)

GOLD OR YELLOW

TREES

Chamaecyparis lawsoniana 'Minima Aurea'
Robinia pseudoacacia 'Frisia'

SHRUBS

Berberis thunbergii 'Aurea'
Caryopteris × *clandonensis* 'Worcester Gold'
Cornus alba 'Gouchaultii'
Ligustrum ovalifolium 'Vicaryii'
Philadelphus coronarius 'Aureus'
Sambucus canadensis 'Aurea'
Spiraea japonica 'Goldflame'
Spiraea japonica 'Limemound'
Weigela florida 'Variegata'

PERENNIALS

Carex elata 'Bowles Golden' (formerly *C. stricta* 'Bowles Golden')
Chrysanthemum parthenium 'Aureum'
Hosta sieboldiana 'Golden Sculpture'
Hosta 'Kabitan'
Hosta 'Piedmont Gold'
Hosta 'Sum and Substance'
Lychnis coronaria 'Angel Blush'
Tricyrtis 'Golden Gleam'

ANNUALS

Coleus × *hybridus* (many varieties)
Helichrysum petiolare 'Limelight'

GRAY

TREES

Picea pungens 'Baby Blue Eyes'
Pyrus salicifolia 'Pendula'

SHRUBS

Rosa glauca
Salix purpurea 'Nana'
Salix purpurea 'Pendula'
Buddleia alternifolia 'Argenta'
Caryopteris × *clandonensis* 'Blue Mist' and 'Longwood Blue'

PERENNIALS

Artemisia ludoviciana 'Silver Queen'
Artemisia ludoviciana 'Valerie Finnis'
Artemisia stelleriana 'Silver Brocade'
Artemisia versicolor
Artemisia 'Powis Castle'
Dianthus alpinus Allwoodii group
Echinops bannaticus 'Taplow Blue'
Erodium chrysanthemum
Festuca glauca 'Elijah Blue'
Helianthemum nummularium 'Wisley Pink'
Lavandula angustifolia 'Hidcote'
Panicum virgatum 'Heavy Metal'
Salvia officinalis 'Berggarten'
Stachys byzantina 'Countess Helene von Stein'
Stachys byzantina 'Silver Carpet'
Teucrium chamaedrys

VARIEGATED

TREES

Acer negundo 'Flamingo'
Cornus kousa var. *chinensis*
  'Snowboy'

SHRUBS

Acanthopanax sieboldianus
  'Variegatus' (now *Eleuthe-*
  rococcus sieboldianus
  'Variegatus')
Buddleia davidii 'Harlequin'
Cornus alba 'Spaethii'
Cornus sericea var. *occidentalis*
  'Silver and Gold'
Cornus sericea var. *occidentalis*
  'Sunshine' (formerly
  C. stolonifera)
Cotoneaster horizontalis
  'Variegatus'
Daphne × *burkwoodii* 'Briggs
  Moonlight'
Daphne × *burkwoodii* 'Carol
  Mackie'

Enkianthus campanulatus
  'Tokyo Masquerade'
Euonymus fortunei 'Harlequin'
Euonymus fortunei 'Sparkle
  and Gold'
Forsythia 'Fiesta'

PERENNIALS

Ampelopsis brevipedunculata
  'Elegans' (vine)
Arachniodes simplicior 'Varie-
  gata' (fern)
Armoracia rusticana 'Variegata'
Athyrium nipponicum 'Pictum'
  (fern)
Carex morrowii 'Goldband'
Chrysanthemum pacificum (not
  reliably hardy; may have
  to be treated as an annual)
Filipendula ulmaria 'Variegata'
Hakonechloa macra 'Aureola'
Hedera helix 'Buttercup'
Houttuynia cordata 'Variegata'
Hypericum × *moserianum*
  'Tricolor'
Iris pseudacorus 'Variegata'
Miscanthus sinensis
  'Gracillimus'
Miscanthus sinensis 'Strictus'
Miscanthus sinensis
  'Variegatus'
Miscanthus sinensis 'Zebrinus'
Oenanthe javanica 'Flamingo'
Phalaris arundinacea 'Picta'
Polygonatum odoratum
  'Variegatum'
Polygonum virginianum
  'Painter's Palette'
Polygonum virginianum 'Varie-
  gatum' (formerly *Persicaria*
  virginiana, Tovara
  virginiana)
Pulmonaria 'Excalibur'
Symphytum grandiflorum
  'Variegatum'
Tricyrtis hirta 'Variegata'
Yucca filamentosa 'Bright Edge'
Yucca filamentosa 'Color
  Guard'
Yucca filamentosa 'Gold
  Guard'
Yucca filamentosa 'Gold Heart'
Yucca filamentosa 'Variegata'
Yucca flaccida 'Golden Sword'

season. About the artemisias' aggressive behavior, which could lead them to march horizontally, where the spruce stretched vertically, Jane says, "I'll just keep cutting them back. There is no way I will let them overshoot their territory. But the extra effort is worth it for the color." She seeks other gray-foliaged accents, recently planting cardoons for their "great blue-gray leaves."

Water features also figure prominently in Jane's gardens, and at last count her recirculating fountains numbered six. They run, from fast flows to delicate drips, 24 hours a day. "The sound of water in a garden shuts out the rest of the world and gives the garden a restful feeling. Very, very important," says Jane, who believes that the sight of water is as much a part of a garden's atmosphere as is its sound." The fountain that anchors the Swimming Pool Garden, for instance, is located directly in the east-west axis, where it can be viewed through the gate of the English Garden. While the fountains more or less care for themselves, "on the rare occasion when they're clogged, I pour Clorox in them, run a wire through the openings, and they're off again."

Jane loves her hometown, but she concedes that the climate—"not a simple zone 5, but one with extremes"—is a challenge. The heat and humidity in the summer—temperatures may reach 100, with the humidity trailing not far behind—can make even a stalwart plant stumble. Often winter offers little moisture from October to March, and when the cold winters do not provide snow cover for protection, many plants succumb or are weakened beyond acceptable performance levels. Out they must go. Jane acknowledges, however, that one of the dangers of the nurturing she offers her plants is that they can do "too well." For instance, the weeping pear in the English Garden is growing fast; it may outgrow its location—and its welcome.

Jane is the only one who tends her garden. Like the head nurse she once was during her stint in the army, she is in charge, and she likes it that way. Clearly, the subject of additional help has been broached more than once. "Bud tries to get me to hire someone to come in here and weed. I do *not* want anyone else weeding my garden," she says firmly. "This is my garden, I know every inch of it by heart, and I love it.

"There are parallels between nursing and gardening," she maintains. "But beyond that, everybody has the urge to create. I can't paint or write music, but I can do this. I couldn't stand to have anyone else messing about in it. It's my thing, and that's that."

"Even when my husband was in charge of the

vegetables and I was in charge of the flowers, I was always the picker. I used to say,

'If you aren't going to pick, don't plant so much.'"

Marianna G. Paulson

The Fruits of Her Labors

MARIANNA G. PAULSON

BARRINGTON, ILLINOIS

Marianna Paulson's four-acre vegetable garden and orchard sits on top of a prairie hill in northern Illinois. Laid out in an L shape and fenced against the deer, the garden is surrounded by open fields. The orderly rows are overflowing with lettuce, carrots, beans, peas, broccoli, basil, and stalks of feathery dill. Red, black, and gold raspberries along with blueberries and currants stretch in long, ordered rows, like necklaces lined up in a jeweler's window. A cutting garden, a colorful ribbon of pink, blue, and yellow, divides the garden down the middle. Battalions of new corn stand at attention in beds, edged to razor sharpness. Insects and birds fly about their business. Eighty-five groomed fruit trees complete the picture-perfect scene.

For a home garden, Marianna agrees, hers is large. But working in it has been a way of life for so many years that to her its size seems perfectly natural. Gardening is a passion that Marianna and Merritt Paulson shared throughout their 50-year marriage until Merritt passed away in 1995. "We loved to work the land. It was a big focus of our lives. We stayed close to it and worked in it every day of the season." Although the couple did make time for travel, particularly to Europe, "since we couldn't leave until October, we never saw any of those great gardens in bloom. But I don't think I ever regretted that."

When Marianna and Merritt were married in 1944, they lived on a ranch in Florida that Merritt and his father, a watchmaker in Illinois, had purchased as a joint venture.

the farm as a fresh kid out of a Milwaukee suburb," Marianna chuckles. "I'm not sure I had any idea what I was getting into. But I have loved every minute of it from day one. It's always been an adventure." Many gardeners, she realizes, trace their earth-loving roots back through their own parents and grandparents. "My mother did have a garden of mostly annuals, and she allowed me to weed the paths, but I learned every bit of my gardening from my husband. He truly loved the land." Marianna notes with pride that this love has been passed on to her son, Henry M. Paulson, Jr., and daughter-in-law, Wendy. The couple took over five acres of the Paulson property in 1975, and their land is under restoration as a refuge for native plants and wildlife species.

To make their first farm profitable, Marianna and Merritt rented additional land to bring their total to about 150 acres. They raised soybeans, alfalfa hay, field corn, and 50 to

60 pigs a year. "We kept two acres for ourselves. We grew vegetables. Pretty quickly, the garden was huge. We also had a cow, sheep, and chickens. We made our own butter and ice cream." She pauses, "And I peddled eggs—twelve to fifteen dozen a week—to my friends."

The Paulsons raised most of what they ate. Marianna learned to can tomatoes and applesauce. She still uses the

PREVIOUS PAGE: Marianna Paulson's garden yields a glorious profusion of vegetables and fruits from June through October. "The garden," Marianna modestly claims, "is utilitarian in design, not meant to be an elegant showpiece. It is just a private, well-loved garden. We laid it out with two main goals in mind: the best orientation to the sun for plant production and efficiency of upkeep. It really is straightforward and simple." Called Merimar Farm, the name joins the Paulsons' first names as a celebration of their joint plea-

sure in gardening. ABOVE: Marianna grows nine different kinds of lettuce, including butterhead, red leaf, romaine, and oakleaf. She plants it at two-week intervals throughout the season, ensuring a constant harvest of tender, young leaves. RIGHT: Cabbages fit for kings. OPPOSITE: In the summer, Marianna is "almost one hundred percent vegetarian," tossing together sugar snap peas, kohlrabi, herbs, and lettuces for salads each day. "To me there is nothing so satisfying as gathering dinner from the garden."

same pressure cooker that she purchased at Montgomery Ward in the early 1950s. "I've never even replaced a gasket." Besides canning, Marianna filled a large freezer with vegetables, fruits, chicken, and meat.

The Paulsons worked the farm for ten years until the effort, coupled with Merritt's daily commute to his management consulting position in Chicago, became too demanding. Yet they were determined to continue their lifestyle. In 1958 they sold the farm and purchased the home where Marianna still lives, only eight miles from the old farm. Sited on 15 acres, it abuts the 500-acre Cook County Forest Preserve, affording privacy without pressure.

The Paulsons immediately started a vegetable garden outside the kitchen door. Besides growing vegetables, Marianna cleaned out an adjacent perennial garden, backed by

There the Paulsons raised cash crops of zucchini and strawberries for the Palm Beach market until the failing watch economy forced Merritt's father to surrender his investment in the ranch. The couple moved back to the north. Still, Merritt hankered for the farm life he'd seen as a young boy summering at a lake near the Wisconsin border, where he counted the local farmers his friends and helped them at harvest and threshing time. He determined that he would raise his family close to the earth, and Marianna agreed.

The young couple bought a 75-acre working farm, "with a charming little Cape Cod bungalow," in Barrington, Illinois, an old town established in 1865 on the Northwestern Railroad run. By that time, the Paulsons had a two-year-old son and another baby on the way. They became farmers overnight.

"I didn't know beans about gardening then. I landed on

a curved hedge, that had been made by the original owner and neglected for years. She strives to have successive bloom throughout the season, cultivating daffodils, day-lilies, Oriental and Asiatic lilies, phlox, alliums, yarrow, delphiniums, and chrysanthemums, mingled with prairie plants—filipendula, liatris, coneflower, *Asclepias tuberosa*, and prairie smoke (*Geum triflorum*). A hosta collection spreads in the shade of the nearby woodland canopy and an arbor opens to inviting paths.

As the trees above the vegetable garden matured, the site became shaded and too small for the Paulsons' plans, which grew a little like Jack's beanstalk. They moved the vegetable garden to its present location 50 yards east of the house in a flat, sunny field. They built a barn and planted an orchard. "You know how gardeners are," Marianna says, glancing across the long rows of crops coming to maturity. "We just kept adding." The veg-

Marianna cans her abundant harvest of tomatoes, often inviting young friends to help. "I supply the tomatoes; they supply the companionship. It's fun for both of us, and they go home with their own supply."

etable garden covers two acres, and the orchard another two.

The northernmost portion of the enclosure is planted in annual vegetables, except for corn, cucumbers, and toma-toes, which own their own beds. The rows run east to west. Each spring and fall the whole vegetable garden is rototilled and fertilizer is hand-turned into the soil. The Paulsons kept horses for many years; the family rode together, and the children competed in local horse shows. When they cleaned out the barn and paddock each spring, they used their own aged manure in the garden. After giving up the horses ten years ago, they began purchasing mushroom compost, well-rotted horse manure in which mushrooms had been grown.

Marianna explains that mushrooms use very few nutrients from their planting medium, leaving it a rich, aged fertilizer. "It just looks like lovely black dirt when we get it."

The land itself, she claims, is a potential gravel pit. "Every time we dig, we turn up stone.

But the advantage is that the soil has great drainage." Over the years, amending the earth throughout the garden has paid off in happy crops. "No doubt, we do have great soil now."

The garden's abundant production is ample proof of that claim. Spinach, lettuce, beets, cabbages, peas, peppers, beans, brussels sprouts, and herbs such as parsley and basil, often several varieties of each, are grown from seed. As for onions, Marianna purchases these as plants—'Redman', 'Walla Walla', 'Yellow Sweet Spanish', 'Granex'—plants, not sets, she specifies. "Onions, if grown from sets, tend to put up seed stalks and fail to grow as large. Onion plants grow a much larger onion, because they do not go to seed." The seedlings arrive, 100 plants attached together, "looking like a bundle of grass." She also purchases asparagus as plants and she recently added 100 plants of 'Jersey Knight' to her 15-year-old bed, as many of the old plants had ceased to be fruitful. All 'Jersey Knight' plants are male and hence do not set seed, making them more productive. To ensure a good

harvest, she was careful to buy plants that were northern grown; these arrived from South Dakota. "As soon as one vegetable is finished, another starts. We have asparagus for six weeks, and when it stops the peas are ready." Quick crops —arugula, kohlrabi, spinach, and lettuce—are planted three or four times throughout the season. In the cutting garden, Marianna plants cosmos, coxcomb, snapdragons, zinnias, marigolds, and celosia to be used in arrangements for the house. "Which I rarely have time to do," she laughs.

A double row of raspberries runs in the same direction as the vegetables. After trying many varieties, Marianna now touts 'Sceptor', a late-bearing variety developed in upper Michigan that is cold hardy and withstands her Zone 5 climate. It is also immune to anthracnose, a disease that attacks raspberries and is spread by the wild black raspberries in the area. In addition, she grows 'Titan', a summer bearer; 'Autumn Gold', 'Royalty', and 'Lowden', which are purple; and the black-berried 'Jewel', 'Illini', and 'Bristol', to fill out the season.

The blueberry beds run perpendicular to the raspberries, with 13 varieties in 10 rows—approximately 80 bushes. The harvest begins around the Fourth of July with early producers, like 'Northblue', 'Northland', 'Earliblue', and 'Patriot', is followed in midsummer by 'Berkley', 'Herbert' and 'Bluecrop', and continues until the frost with 'Burlington', 'Putte', and 'Elliot'. Blueberries are treated with an annual application of a soil acidifier, Miracid, in the spring, and the soil under the bushes is consistently monitored and kept close to the recommended pH of 4.5. The blueberry patch is the only area where an underground watering system of drip hoses has been installed. It was put in place when the blueberries were planted, to aid in taking the acidic fertilizer directly to the plant roots. The rest of the garden is watered with overhead sprinklers as needed. "Theoretically," Marianna says, "the overhead sprinkler must run for twenty-four hours to provide the garden with one inch of water." Fortunately, the well has always supplied an unlimited flow, so the garden's thirst is quenched.

To keep up to date with the best and most current corn varieties, Merritt yearly researched commercial growers' choices, establishing relationships with growers to discuss the benefits of yellow, bicolor, and white varieties. As with the blueberries, once corn starts, in mid-July, harvesting continues until frost. Between the ten different varieties the Paulson planted, the maturation time runs from 70 days for 'Sweet Green' to 89 days for 'Pegasus'. The corn is planted at two-week intervals, eight rows at a time. It, as well as other crops such as peas, is covered with a floating row cover when planted. Made of 64-inch-wide rolls of polypropylene, the row cover is anchored with metal fence posts laid along the lengths of its edges. The blanket allows sunlight and rain to pass through, moderates cold from the late frosts, and helps keep insect pests out. When the plants reaches at least a sturdy three inches, the cover is removed.

OPPOSITE: Garden beds are maintained by monthly rototilling between the rows "and lots of hand-weeding on our knees." Since the rototiller is two feet wide, crop rows are planted to accommodate the machine's path. Marianna does not mulch the garden, as she believes bark mulches "rob" nitrogen from the soil, and has simply never used the hay or salt hay preferred by many vegetable gardeners.

With the help of Warren Hansen, who lives nearby, Marianna continues the garden as it was when she and Merritt worked it together. Luckily, she says, Merritt kept good records. She picks up a poster-size layout of the orchard indicating each tree's location and name. "Every tree has a label at its base. Merritt kept a chart listing the variety's parents, when each was planted, the time it bloomed, the details of the spraying program, and the dates when the fruit was harvested.

"This is apple country, and the apples do fine," says Marianna. Peaches, nectarines, and apricots are subject to nature's vagaries. In spring, if a cold spell follows a warm one that has induced buds and the buds freeze, all fruit is lost for the season. For a successful crop of these "iffy" fruits, the weather must remain consistently cold, so that the buds do not come too early. "We went into this with our eyes wide open," says Marianna. "In the years that it works, it is well worth it. I can wait for those. However, I am glad this is not a commercial venture."

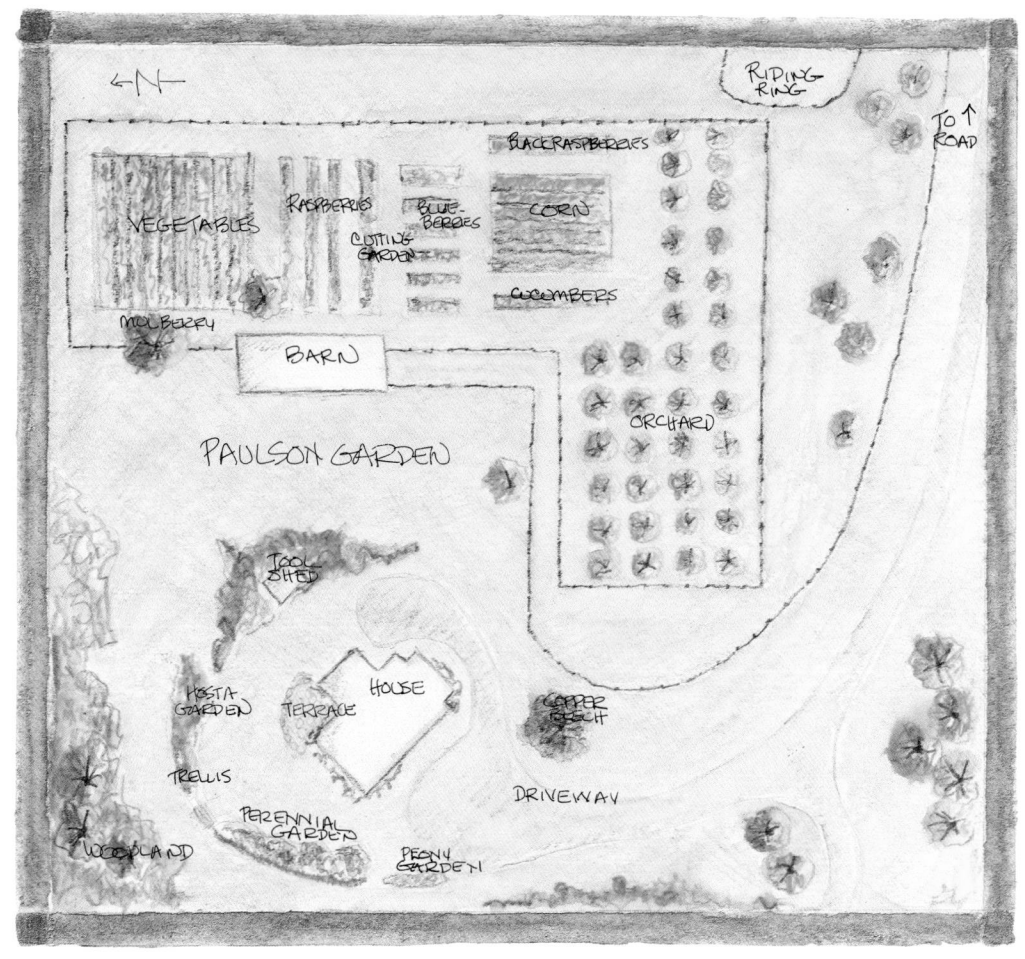

In the spring, generally in March, an arborist is hired to prune the whole orchard. He removes the water sprouts and redirects growth. The goal is to maintain the trees at the same size and with an open structure, allowing air circulation. The fruit trees are fed a slow-release 12-12-12 fertilizer in early spring only if they need it. If they are bearing well and look healthy, no fertilizer is applied.

The spraying program begins with a dormant oil spray in early spring at the time of bud swell. The next application, a mixture containing fungicide and insecticide, is applied at "first bud" or a stage called "showing color," where a flush of pink is visible. After "full petal fall"—"you don't want to interfere with bees and pollination"—the trees are sprayed again, and then again at ten-day to two-week intervals until mid-July. Cherries launch the season. 'Early Duchess' apples begin ripening at the end of July, and Marianna says they are her choice for pies and applesauce. "But maybe 'Golden Nugget' is my favorite for eating."

The kitchen, with its long, wide counter down the center, is a workshop. Big windows face the forest, and a decorative gas stove, to take the chill off the room in the winter, sits in a corner. Marianna determines the garden's planting program at the table; she manages its yield at the stove. As she has done for five decades, she cooks for pleasure and practicality, using the fruits of her labors, from cultivated black raspberries to 'Lutz' beets—"Mrs. Burpee's favorite, which just get sweeter as they get larger." Fruits and vegetables, often blanched; blueberry, cherry, and apple pies; and Marianna's specialty Blueberry Bunch Cake and black currant sauce fill the freezer. Red currants and raspberries become jelly.

The whole garden is fenced with a 4½-foot-tall, three-strand electric fence. Eighteen inches of chicken wire is joined to the lower portion; six inches is below grade. Above the chicken wire, the first two rows of electric wire are set only 12 inches apart to deter raccoons, the bane of many local farmers who have given up on corn owing to the animals' voracious habits. The top wire is a gentle reminder to the deer that they may look but not touch.

The lovingly tended plants, bushes, and trees on Marianna's property yield so prodigiously that she has introduced her own Harvest Festival, an annual September event. Members of the Illinois chapter of The Nature Conservancy and their families have a standing invitation to collect seeds from the prairie grasses—little bluestem and Indian grass—and to climb ladders to fill baskets with apples. "One of the joys of this bounty is sharing with family and friends. The love of gardening is a great unifier."

MARIANNA PAULSON'S RECOMMENDATIONS
FOR FRUIT TREES FOR HOME GARDENS

APPLES

NAME	HARVEST	DESCRIPTION
Ashmead's Kernel	Late October	Antique, 1700, England, golden-brown russet skin, yellow flesh, crisp, juicy, delicious, an excellent keeper
Blushing Golden	Mid-October	A beautiful apple, delicious, good keeper
Burgundy	Early September	Dark red skin, white flesh, crisp, juicy
Cortland	Late September	Large, red skin, white flesh, cut apple does not turn brown, good for salads, pies, and sauce
Cox's Orange Pippin	Late September	English, 1830, medium-size, red/yellow slightly russet skin, juicy yellow flesh, aromatic, mellow, a favorite for eating fresh
Crispin or Mutsu	Late October	Yellow-green skin, semisweet, juicy, best eaten fresh, freezes extremely well
Duchess of Oldenberg	Late July	Tart, juicy, best for pies and sauce
Empire	Early September	A McIntosh × Red Delicious strain
Freyberg	Early October	A Cox × Golden Delicious strain, small, excellent eating
Golden Nugget	Early September	Small russet type, cream flesh, luscious eating, a short keeper
Grimes Golden	Mid-September	Antique, good for eating fresh or cooking
Hawaii	Mid-September	Large, yellow-green skin, delicious eating, a hint of pineapple
Indared	Mid-October	White flesh; crisp, juicy; good for eating, pies, and sauce; a good keeper
Jonagold	Mid-September	A Jonathan × Golden Delicious strain, red skin, excellent eating
Jonalicious	Mid-September	Red skin, sweet but tangy, good eating
Karmijan de Sonneville	Late September to early October	Excellent eating and cooking, good winter keeper
Lodi	Early July	Large; green skin; good for pies, sauce, and eating
Lyman's Large Summer Apple	Mid-August	Green, good for cooking
Macoun	Late September	Crisp, juicy, flavorful
Melrose	Late October	Excellent flavor, tart, good for cooking or eating fresh, an excellent keeper
Northern Spy	Late October	Purple-red skin, large, crisp, a biennial, good for cooking or eating fresh
Red Astrakhan	Late July	Bright red skin, excellent for cooking
Red Gravenstein	Late August	From Denmark, excellent for sauce
Red Staymen Winesap	Mid-October	Large, excellent dessert apple
Ribsten Pippin	Late September	Classic dessert apple of England
Rome Beauty	Mid-October	Excellent for baking and for sauce
Royal Gala	Early September	Skin yellow-orange with red stripes to solid red, deep rich flavor, excellent for eating fresh
Sinta	Mid-September	A Yellow Delicious × Grimes Golden strain, yellow skin, good eating
Snow Apple	Early October	Dates from 1730, small, red skin, white flesh
Spigold	Early October	Large, yellow skin, crisp, excellent keeper
Spitzenberg	Late October	Antique, Thomas Jefferson grew it
Summer Rambo	Mid- to late August	Antique, 16th century, yellow-green flesh, juicy
Thomkins King	Late October	Large, yellow-green skin, good for cooking or eating fresh
Ultra Mac	Mid-September	A McIntosh cultivar, very good
Vista Bella	Mid-August	Bright red skin, good for cooking and eating fresh
Wealthy	Mid-September	Outstanding eating and cooking
Westfield-Seek-No-Further	Mid-October	Antique, skin streaked red, creamy yellow flesh
Winesap	Mid-October	Deep red skin, spicy, mildly tart, good baked or for sauce, a good keeper

CHERRIES

NAME	HARVEST	DESCRIPTION
Heidelfingen	Mid-June	Sweet
Meteor	Late June	Pie cherry
Montgomery	Late June	The best pie cherry
North Star	Late June	Pie cherry
Starkrimson	Late June	Sweet
Sunmist	Mid-June	Sweet
Van	Mid-June	Sweet

PEACHES

NAME	HARVEST	DESCRIPTION
August Alberta	Late August to September	Yellow, a late Alberta
Belle of Georgia	Late August	Sweet, white flesh
Canadian Harmony	Early August	Yellow flesh, nonbrowning
Earlyglow	Mid-July	Red, freestone
Elberta Queen	Late August	Large form, sweet
July Elberta	Early August	Bright red skin, yellow flesh, sweet
Madison	Mid-August	Firm, yellow flesh, sweet, very hardy
McKay	Late August	Freestone, large, orange flesh, very hardy
Polly	Mid-August	Small but top quality, white flesh
Red Haven	Mid- to late August	Freestone
Reliance	Early to mid-August	Top quality, takes 25°F
Rich Haven	Mid- to late August	Freestone, yellow, resists browning
Starking Delicious	Mid-July	Large to medium form, sweet

NECTARINES

NAME	HARVEST	DESCRIPTION
Nectacrest	Early to mid-August	Tangy, hardy to −28°F
Red Gold	Mid-August	Red and gold, belemish free

PLUMS

Delicious	Early August	Clingstone, red flesh
Earliblue	Early September	Prune-plum
Elephant Heart	Early September	Large, juicy
Imperial Gage	Mid-September	Dull green, small, round, juicy, sweet
Imperial Epicure	Mid-September	Antique, 1883, from France
Red Heart	Early August	Red skin and flesh
Santa Rosa	Late August	Purple skin, red flesh
Shiro	Late July	Yellow
Yellow Egg	Late August	Yellow, large, sweet

PEARS

Buerre Anjou	Mid-September	Yellow, big, juicy
Chapin	Mid-August	Seedling of Seckel but larger, smooth, juicy, sweet
Honey Sweet	Early to mid-September	Yellow, Bartlett type
Moonglow	Early September	Firm, juicy Bartlett type
Red Bartlett	Early September	Buttery smooth, sweet, juicy
Rescue	Late August	Huge, fine-flavored, rescued from oblivion by a horticulturist in Sumner, WA
Star King Delicious	Early to mid-September	Superior Bartlett type

Unlimited Possibilities

JOANNA McQUAIL REED

MALVERN, PENNSYLVANIA

Early in the fall of 1939, Joanna McQuail and George Reed went house hunting. Newly engaged, they dreamed of an old house with a little land where they could raise a family. A realtor drove them to a neglected farm, available through a sheriff's sale. The 1780 stone house was run-down, the waste line clogged, the rooms smoked gray from a fire in the furnace, but the young couple was enchanted. "It had little cubbies and a lot of charm. A grand Kentucky coffee tree stood in the yard, and we loved the barn. It was the one house we could afford, and it had forty-three acres instead of two or three," Joanna recalls. "We thought the possibilities limitless."

The place, which the Reeds named Longview Farm, became theirs the following January. From then until April, Joanna and George, often persuading friends to help, worked on the house in every spare moment. Days, Joanna sold books at Wanamaker's and George sold cars. Nights and weekends, they scraped, painted, shored, and patched.

From the beginning the garden was an integral part of their renovations. When Joanna and George, both keen on old houses, went on their honeymoon in 1940, they sought to learn restoration techniques at the historic sites in Virginia. But they went to visit the gardens, too. The shapes of the formal Colonial gardens; the herb gardens; the long sweeps and allées; the combinations of flowers, fruit, and vegetables—all made deep impressions on Joanna. She bought seeds and a book that became her bible—*Herbs: How to Grow Them, How to Use Them*, by Helen Noyes Webster. Joanna had never gardened before, but George's father, an accomplished gardener, came to help, and his advice was invaluable. He taught Joanna how to prepare the soil, to ready a seedbed, to thin seedlings, to hill up the corn, to watch for insects. Though a town-bred girl, Joanna took to country life. No task was too hard, no idea impossible.

Those early years were devoted to clearing and "earth moving," a subtle shaping of the land around the buildings. In preparation for planting vegetables, Joanna says, "We pulled the rough clods of grass and weeds off the top and threw them down the hill, and thus leveled off the area." She recalls that their best crop seemed to be stones, uncovered at every turn of the spade. Economy-minded Joanna turned the bounty of stone into walls, which she built mostly by herself, throughout the gardens.

"I've always thought big, but reduced things down to a homey level."

Joanna McLeod Reed

begin." Perhaps to make amends for his remarks about her house, Dr. Barnes promptly insisted, "You must come to my wife's school." Laura Barnes was launching her legendary tuition-free school of horticulture at the Barnes Foundation Arboretum in the fall of 1941; Joanna Reed enrolled in the first class. She credits those classes as fundamental roots of her gardening knowledge and style—and her plant collection. "I was exposed to world-class botanists and plantspeople as teachers," she remembers.

Each spring and fall, Laura Barnes instructed the staff to save seedlings, correctly labeled and wrapped in newspaper, and place them at the school's entrance for the students' taking. "To this day, I consider Longview Farm Laura Barnes's annex. I went to Barnes for three years; I took all they offered"—both in education and in infant plants.

At home, Joanna practiced what she was learning. The vegetable garden took shape. "It was just a plot the first

year," Joanna recalls, but by the second year she decided that if she were going to "continue this drudgery," she would make it "visually pleasing." Trained as an artist, she had absorbed the design schemes of the Colonial gardens from her Virginia visits. Thinking particularly of Wakefield, George Washington's birthplace, she staked

PREVIOUS PAGES, LEFT: Corn-cribs form the background to ebullient planting in the Old Veg. RIGHT: Grass paths in the parterre, which extends the length of Joanna Reed's house, were replaced with locally quarried "Avondale" stone; it holds the heat, affording tender plants an extended growing season. Joanna chose many Mediterranean, gray-leaved plants, particularly herbs, which thrive in the baking sun. THIS PAGE,

ABOVE: The Courtyard Garden outside Joanna's "typical Pennsylvania German 'bank house'" has a floor of gravel, as grass succumbed to visitor traffic caused by the Reeds' open-door policy. RIGHT: A sculpture by Patrick Radebaugh stands in a bed of *Hosta sieboldiana* and ajuga at the edge of the woodland. OPPOSITE: Each morning, Joanna dresses in her uniform: jeans, a turtleneck, and tall rubber boots, no matter what the temperature.

A serendipitous meeting that took place during Joanna's second summer on Longview Farm changed her life. One hot day, a man having car trouble knocked on Joanna's door and asked to use her phone. Authoritative, opinionated, and less than complimentary about the state of the Reeds' home, the man, Dr. Albert C. Barnes, took stock of the Reeds' few horticultural inheritances—a silver maple, an apple, some dying arborvitae, a privet hedge, a lone forsythia, and the coffee bean tree—and said, "I suppose you're going to have a garden." Straightforward as always, Joanna answered, "I want to, but I don't know where to

out an axial path through her vegetable garden and divided the space into quadrants. She remembered a central dipping pool at Wakefield, where the paths intersected, and she made herself a more modest one.

The paths of the vegetable garden began as dirt, but by the middle of the summer, they had sprouted a carpet of grass and could be mowed. The beds were later edged with brick, set into a poured cement foundation three feet deep, to keep the grass from penetrating the barrier. Fondly called the Old Veg, as a nod to its origins, the garden remains today as Joanna laid it out in 1941.

Within four years Joanna's gardens had started to take their permanent form. "It looked like I was going somewhere," she says. She instinctively took advantage of the lines the buildings on her property suggested and extended them into the surrounding hillsides in accordance with her own advice: "Follow the lines of something in existence and project out." The walls of a crumbling garage were repaired and a nearby dumping area was cleared, filled, and terraced on two levels by a U-shaped stone retaining wall to become the second garden. Seen from the entrance drive, the Bench Garden stands as a focal point in a vista that sweeps up into the meadow, ending at a refurbished corncrib. The barn was repaired and repainted a majestic red. The bold form of the original farm was never changed—it was just enhanced, enlarged, and brought into sharp focus.

"The driveway," Joanna observes, "is like someone split the whole place in half with an ax." Yet it creates an axial path, extending from the property's entrance, ever narrow-

ABOVE: Joanna's latest development is her meadow, a decade old. In October the meadow is a blaze of fall color, making a dramatic stage for the refurbished barn. The golden leaves are the previous year's suckers of *Sassafras albidum*. LEFT: An opening in the fence, framed by *Chrysanthemum* 'Sheffield', *Lonicera sempervirens* 'Sulphurea', and *Macleaya cordata*, leads from the Old Veg to the Meadow.

Late summer flowers, fruit and seeds
make splashes of color throughout
Joanna's garden.

A. *Anemone japonica*
B. *Salvia* 'Indigo Spires'
C. *Dolichos lablab*
D. *Magnolia tripetala*
E. *Helenium* 'Bruno'
F. *Coreopsis verticillata* 'Zagreb'
G. *Lobelia cardenalis*
H. *Polygonatum commutatum*
I. *Prunus*
J. *Viburnum dilatatum*
K. *Lunaria annua*
L. *Dahlia* unnamed cultivar

ing, to the opening into the woodland; from there it seems to stretch to infinity. A network of curving paths crosshatch in a playful pattern, as though drawn in an artist's sketch.

Meanwhile, the Reeds' babies arrived: Franziska first, in 1942, and then Jane and George Jr., just 18 months apart. Susie was born in 1948. But children did not slow progress. Though Joanna missed one term at Barnes when Franziska was born, she quickly returned, juggling the raising of children, attending school, and gardening, all part of a rich menu that has become the delicious fare of tale-telling. "Everything wandered around, animals and children. There were no fences, no doors on the buildings. I guess we were all early hippies," Joanna recalls with a smile. "I tied sheep's bells on the children's pants' straps, so I could keep track of them." She pauses, then reflects: "It was a happy time."

The Reeds bought a relic of a tractor, with cleats on its big iron wheels so it would not get stuck in the mud. They disked and overseeded to grow rich pasturage despite George's double shifts in the steam turbine division of Westinghouse. During the war years, the Reeds rented additional land and farmed about 100 acres. With the help of a neighbor, Isaiah Cuff, who gave freely of advice and time, "we had surprisingly good results. Pigs, straw, eggs, and turkeys were our

cash crops. We grew everything we ate, except dairy products. We never had a cow; I knew it would be even tougher to find a cow-sitter than a baby-sitter."

In 1948 everything changed. Surveyors for the Pennsylvania Turnpike arrived like storm troopers, complete with machinery that, documented in old photographs, looked remarkably like tanks. By eminent domain, the turnpike was constructed just 200 feet from the Reeds' house, altering the isolated farm on a quiet lane with "long views" forever. The Reeds' land was divided on both sides of the turnpike. Trees were destroyed and natural drainage interrupted, leaving the Reeds with "an enormous challenge."

The first priority was to screen this "interloper" from the house. Joanna looked to native trees and shrubs whose natural habitat was wet meadows. She added sour gum (*Nyssa sylvatica*), sycamore (*Platanus occidentalis*), eastern larch (*Larix laricina*), mulberry (*Morus alba*), and American arborvitae (*Thuja occidentalis*). She planted red and black chokeberries (*Aronia arbutifolia* and *A. melanocarpa*), *Baccharis halimifolia*, *Clethra acuminata* and *C. alnifolia*, buttonbush (*Cephalanthus occidentalis*), hollies (*Ilex laevigata, I. glabra,* and *I. verticillata*), northern bayberry (*Myrica pensylvanica*), viburnums (*V. acerifolium, V. dentatum,* and *V. prunifolium*), and witch hazel (*Hamamelis vernalis*). Red maples and ash were sown by the birds. Perennials such as *Asclepias incarnata, Chelone glabra, Eupatorium maculatum, E. perfoliatum, E. rugosum, Euphorbia palustris, Filipendula rubra, Helleborus foetidus, Lobelia siphilitica, Rudbeckia nitida,* and *Vernonia noveboracensis* provide huge bursts of color, like firecrackers—to Joanna, "A garden is not a garden without color." Nor does she believe in the power of single plants, except for large tree specimens. "For me, the effect is better when I plant in masses." So, like the loaves and the fishes, Joanna acquires one plant to multiply it into many. She also follows Vita Sackville-West's advice to try a new plant in three different areas to see which it prefers. To that wisdom she

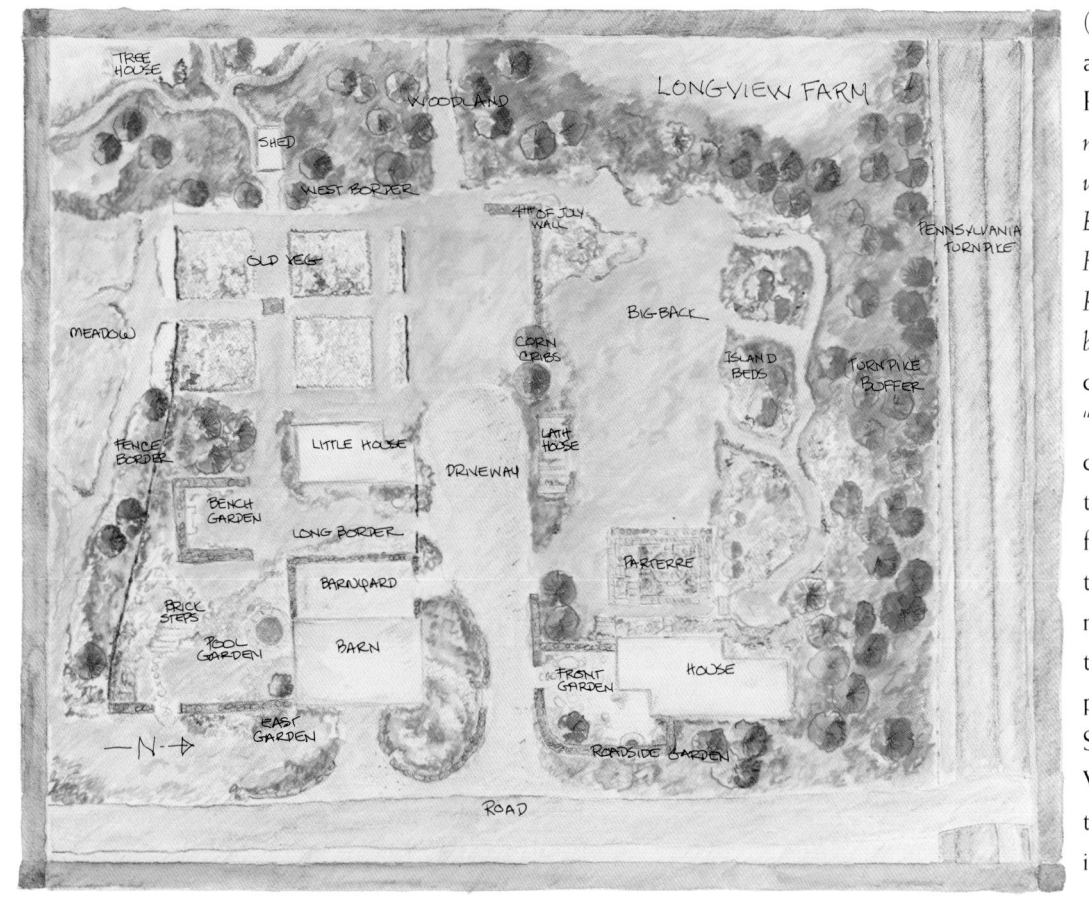

adds her own hints: "If a plant doesn't do well, move it. Plants adapt to extremes in weather if they are not coddled. Often a plant in decline is asking to be divided."

After the turnpike's completion, the Reeds' front yard, which was already close to the road, needed to be privatized. They built a 4½-foot-high stone wall to enclose what is now the Courtyard Garden. A fountain, with a lead fish, gurgles in the corner. Nooks were formed by plants, often in pots, such as bay and myrtle trees, rosemary, agapanthus, and assorted pelargoniums. All spend the winter just inside the doors of the house's contiguous glassed porch.

With their property truncated, the Reeds ceased active farming—except for "a few chickens, the occasional pig, and the children's horse and pony"—but the ornamental gardens, which had thrived despite farming and family, continued to take shape. An

BELOW: Joanna used the existing architectural elements, such as the stone barnyard walls surrounding the barn, to determine the lines and interlocking network of paths of her garden. The rich burgundy foliage of *Hydrangea quercifolia* offsets a collection of hostas and epimediums inside the gate. OPPOSITE: In October the scarlet foliage of a winged euonymus (*Euonymus alata*) is set off by the aged stone foundation of the barn.

eight-foot-wide cistern next to the barn that had once been creatively employed as a playpen was restored. Collared by *Anemone japonica, Geranium sanguineum* var. *striatum* 'Lancastriense', iris, lavender, and sedum and planted with hardy water lilies, it became the Pool Garden. Winding steps of crushed brick were added on an adjacent slope to create a connecting link between the Bench and Pool Gardens, one of Joanna's smooth transitions that entice a visitor to wander from garden to garden. Called the Dry Garden, this offers the natural drainage that welcomes *Allium tuberosum, Ceratostigma plumbaginoides, Sedum* 'Autumn Joy', *Santolina virens, Verbena canadensis,* and *V.* 'Homestead Purple', which make a glorious September exhibition of white, blue, rust, bright green, and purple.

Over time, Joanna began to crave a more formal garden close to the house, and the ideas

for her parterre germinated. In order to create the parterre, which she laid out just under the second floor porch, the land had to be leveled and terraced. Earth was moved by wagon to the site, compost was generated on the spot, and manure was added to the mix. Joanna was 40 and pregnant with her last child when she started building the parterre walls, which at one end are four feet high. George was trav-

eling, and she determined to complete the project by the baby's October birth. She ruefully notes that it is her least tidy wall, as some rocks she could no longer lift. But with *Alyssum saxatile, Campanula poscharskyana,* dianthus, euphorbia, gypsophylla, iberis, and nepeta spilling luxuriantly over the wall's edges, Joanna says with a laugh, "Who would know?"

The parterre was laid out in quadrants around a central circle. Additional long beds define each side. Joanna rejected the idea of a tightly woven knot garden, because, as she notes, "for every plant you have in a knot garden, you have to have two backup plants at the ready, or else the knot can look like a pumpkin without teeth." Boxwood (*Buxus sempervirens*) was trimmed to form borders and punctuation points. Its evergreen forms provided strong shapes in summer and winter. At age ten, however, the box declined, as the voles ate its feeder roots. Finally pronounced dead, it was removed. "If something isn't working, I see no reason to keep it," Joanna observes, "I don't change just out of

JOANNA REED'S HERB PARTERRE PLANT LIST

Joanna Reed's lifelong interest in herbs was first sparked by the gardens she and husband George observed on their honeymoon trip. Gradually, Joanna's knowledge and collection expanded. She studied herb history and folklore, sought plants used by Native Americans, and grew medicinal herbs. She joined the Herb Society of America in 1964, served as its president from 1980 to 1982, and remains an active member. Joanna is often asked to advise others on planting herb gardens, and she prepared the plant list for the Fragrant Garden, one of ten specialty herb gardens, at the National Arboretum. "I love herbs," she says. "As you work and rub against them, they smell so good." Below is a listing of the herbs Joanna has planted in the glorious herb parterre that extends the length of her house.

Achillea filipendulina

Achillea millefolium

Achillea 'Taygetea'

Agapanthus umbellatus var. *minimus* 'Peter Pan'

Agastache 'Fire Bird'

Agastache foeniculum

Ajuga reptans (white)

Ajuga reptans (blue)

Alchemilla vulgaris

Allium aflatunense 'Purple Sensation'

Allium cowanii

Allium giganteum

Allium 'Gladiator'

Allium karataviense

Allium moly

Allium rosembachianum

Allium 'Summer Beauty'

Allium tuberosum

Allium unifolium

Allium zebdanense

Aloysia triphylla

Alyssium saxtile

Anemone vulgaris

Aquilegia vulgaris (self-sown)

Artemisia 'Huntington'

Artemisia splendens

Asclepias tuberosa

Calendula (self-sown)

Campanula poscharskyana

Chenopodium botrys (self-sown)

Chrysanthemum leucanthemum (self-sown)

Chrysanthemum parthenium

Chrysogonum virginianum

Consolida delphinium (self-sown)

Crocus sativus

Dianthus caryophyllus

Dianthus deltoides

Dianthus plumarius

Echinops ritro

Euphorbia myrsinites

Geranium macrorrhizum

Gypsophylla paniculata

Hedeoma pulegioides (self-sown)

Hypericum frondosum 'Sunburst'

Iberis semperflorens

Iris florentina

Iris germanica 'Sangruel'

Lavandula angustifolia

Lavandula angustifolia 'Croxton's Wild'

Lavendula angustifolia 'Dark Supreme'

Lavandula angustifolia 'Hidcote'

Lavandula angustifolia 'Hidcote Giant'

Lavandula angustifolia 'Irene Doyle'

Lavandula angustifolia 'Munstead'

Lavandula angustifolia 'Rex Talbot'

Lavendula angustifolia 'Sharon Roberts'

Lavandula dentata (tender)

Lavandula heteraphylla, sweet lavender (tender)

Lavandula × *intermedia* 'Alba'

Lavandula × *intermedia* 'Dutch'

Lavandula × *intermedia* 'Seal'

Lavandula pedunculata (tender)

Lavandula stoechas (tender)

Lilium 'Enchantment'

Limonium latifolium

Mentha aquatica, orange or bergamot mint

Mentha × *piperita* 'Mitcham'

Mentha sauveolens

Myosotis sylvatica (self-sown)

Narcissus canaliculatus

Nepeta mussinii

Nepeta sibirica

Nepeta 'Six Hills Giant'

Nigella damascena (self-sown)

Origanum majorana 'Compact Greek'

Paeonia 'Garden Peace'

Paeonia 'Ludovica' (Saunders hybrid)

Pelargonium 'Apricot'

Pelargonium 'Chocolate Mint'

Pelargonium 'Clorinda'

Pelargonium 'Little Gem'

Pelargonium 'Peppermint'

Pelargonium 'Rober's Lemon Rose'

Perovskia atriplicifolia

Rosa gallica

Rosa 'The Fairy'

Rosmarinus officinalis 'Benenden Blue' (pine-scented)

Rosmarinus officinalis 'Golden Rain' ('Joyce De Baggio')

Rosmarinus officinalis 'Goriza'

Rosmarinus officinalis 'Majorca Pink'

Rosmarinus officinalis 'Mrs. Reed's Dark Blue'

Rosmarinus officinalis 'Nancy Howard' (white-flowered)

Rosmarinus officinalis 'Tuscan Blue'

Rosmarinus officinalis 'Wills Pink'

Ruta graveolens

Ruta graveolens 'Blue Beauty'

Salvia azurea

Salvia 'Buchananii'

Salvia caespitosa

Salvia coccinea 'Splendens'

Salvia dominica

Salvia farinacea

Salvia greggii 'Cherry Queen'

Salvia greggii 'San Antonio'

Salvia guaranitica

Salvia involucrata

Salvia involucrata 'Bethelii'

Salvia lycioides

Salvia murii

Salvia puberula

Salvia sinaloensis

Salvia × *superba*

Salvia uliginosa

Santolina chamaecyparissus

Santolina chamaecyparissus 'Bowles Form'

Santolina virens

Satureja montana, winter savory

Silene armeria (self-sown)

Sisyrinchium (self-sown)

Stachys byzantina

Stachys officinalis

Thymus capitatus, Greek thyme (tender)

Thymus mastichina, Portuguese thyme (tender)

Thymus praecox ssp. *arcticus* 'Albus'

Thymus praecox ssp. *arcticus* 'Coccineus'

Thymus praecox ssp. *arcticus* 'Green and Gold'

Thymus praecox ssp. *arcticus* 'Herba Barona'

Thymus praecox ssp. *arcticus* 'Pink Chintz' (creeping)

Thymus praecox ssp. *pseudolanuginosus* 'Woolly'

Thymus vulgaris 'Broad-leaf English'

Thymus vulgaris 'Narrow-leaf French'

Tulbaghia violacea 'Silver Streak' (tender)

Viola tricolor (self-sown)

a whim. Things change, and you have to flow with them."

The loss of the box opened the door "to a much more interesting plant list." Rosemary took the boxwood's place as the central accent plants. Joanna grows eight cultivars of *Rosmarinus officinalis*. The plants are brought into the winter porch during the coldest months (she has no greenhouse, preferring to devote the off-season to working on her renowned needlepoint creations), and then lugged back out and planted in the beds each spring. Joanna leaves them in the garden through the first few frosts, which stops their growing and retards their straggly winter growth, keeping them, she claims, healthier. More than a dozen different salvias, multiple varieties of santolinas, achilleas, alliums, lavenders, nepetas, artemisias, geraniums, and pelargoniums produce a palette of yellows, blues, pinks, and purples that sparkles throughout the season. Self-seeders such as the blackberry lily (*Belamcanda chinensis*), forget-me-not (*Myosotis sylvatica*), larkspur, *Silene armeria*, love-in-a-mist (*Nigella damascena*), and American pennyroyal join in spontaneous bursts, so the parterre takes on a different character each year.

Reminiscing, Joanna recalls interruptions, sometimes years in length, during which the garden seemed to take giant steps backward. Three and a half acres of intensely planted gardens demands constant vigilance. Weeds and wandering self-seeders never sleep or take holidays. When family demands prevented her from keeping up with the garden's maintenance, "it

would take years to get it back in shape." The seamless flow from garden to garden today belies those hiatuses. "I wouldn't call myself a patient soul yet, but gardening has forced some patience on me," she allows, her eyes twinkling with amusement. "I can't argue back."

Joanna is a one-woman show. She maintains the garden by herself since George passed away in 1982. Her children, three of whom are horticulturists, have families and careers of their own. These days Joanna works from first light to dark in the garden. She does try to time her program to be in the shade on hot days, the woodland in midsummer. She still mows the lawns, which, she says, gives her the opportunity to observe the successes and failures in a contemplative state. "It's a wonderful time to get an overall look at the garden. Go around and

around. When you see something nice, each time around, you appreciate it. Or I say, 'I have to keep my eyes on that.'" Often she crawls deep into beds and disappears, tracking down an obstreperous weed or nurturing a welcome seedling. She notes, "A lot of what gardening is about is recognizing what is happening." Perhaps that wisdom comes from spending so

ABOVE: In February's setting sun an espaliered pear makes a dramatic shape against a crust of snow. LEFT: The gray bark and plum buds of a magnolia (*Magnolia stellata*) contrast with the deep red of the barn. Joanna plans all of her gardens to have winter interest.

much time on her knees— "something helpful I learned in convent school."

She jokingly calls her house "the hotel," as visitors and grandchildren play musical bedrooms. "I'm rich in family and friends." Often nightfall brings guests. Dinners in July rarely begin before 9:30 P.M. After a meal of curried chicken or beef stew, peppered with anecdotes of the gardening world and analysis of plants' peculiarities, Joanna retires to the kitchen alone. She accepts no help with the dishes. It is her quiet time. She looks out into the lighted Courtyard Garden and defines a packed schedule for the following day. Which beds need attention? Which plants need dividing? Which plants need a little extra care? "I am always planning, visualizing, and projecting into the future," she says. "As a gardener, there is a certain degree of optimism in everything you do." She reflects, "I never manage to do all I hope and plan, but one might say my garden is the result of ambitious goals and a tolerant attitude toward the gardener—me."

Index

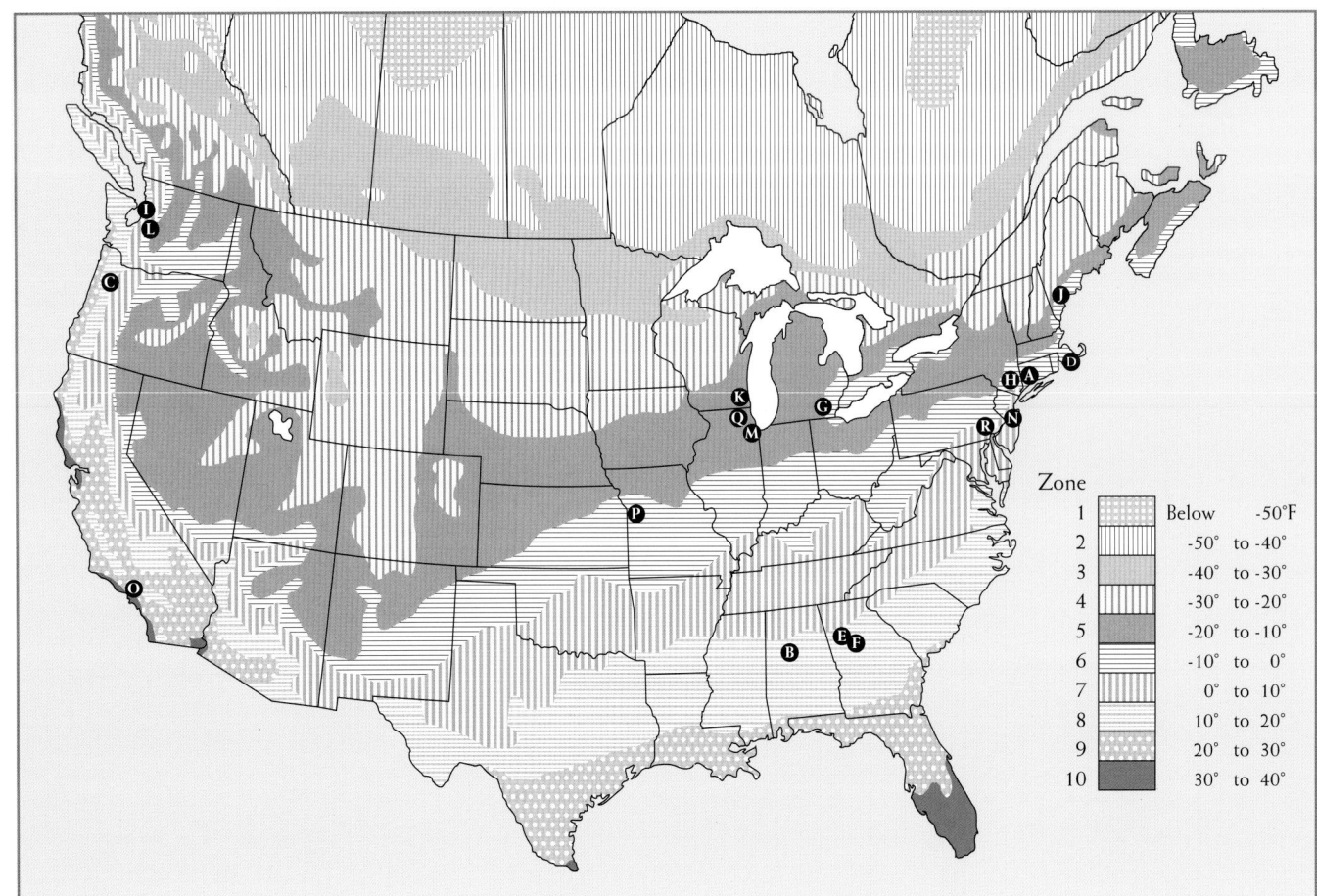

ZONE MAP

A. Eleanor Brinckerhoff Spingarn — *Redding, Connecticut*
B. Louise Agee Wrinkle — *Birmingham, Alabama*
C. Molly McGuire Grothaus — *Lake Oswego, Oregon*
D. Polly Hill — *North Tisbury, Martha's Vineyard, Massachusetts*
E. Anne C. Carr — *Atlanta, Georgia*
F. Louise Richardson Allen — *Atlanta, Georgia*
G. Betty H. Blake — *Onsted, Michigan*
H. Henrietta E. S. Lockwood — *Bedford, New York*
I. Jocelyn Horder — *Poulsbo, Washington*
J. Marion Prince Hosmer — *York, Maine*
K. Harriet McMahon Purtell — *Milwaukee, Wisconsin*
L. Ione Chase — *Orting, Washington*
M. Dorothy Hannon Gardner — *Winnetka, Illinois*
N. Jane C. Scott — *Locust, New Jersey*
O. Georgiana Bray Erskine — *Pasadena, California*
P. Jane P. Overesch — *Kansas City, Missouri*
Q. Marianna Paulson — *Barrington, Illinois*
R. Joanne McQuail Reed — *Malvern, Pennsylvania*

Louise Richardson Allen   Betty H. Blake   Anne C. Carr

Polly Hill   Jocelyn Horder   Marion Prince Hosmer   Harr

Eleanor Brumcherhoff Spingarn   Louise Agee Wrinkle   Louise Richardson

Dorothy Hamon Gardner   Molly McGuire Grothaus   Polly Hill

Harriet   McMahon Purtell   Jane C. Scott   Eleanor Brumcherhoff Sp

Anne C. Carr   Ione Chase   Dorothy Hamon Gar

Marion Prince Hosmer   Harrietta E. S. Lockwood   Harriet   McMahon

Louise Richardson Allen   Betty H. Blake   Anne C. Carr

Polly Hill   Jocelyn Horder   Marion Prince Hosmer   Harr

Eleanor Brumcherhoff Spingarn   Louise Agee Wrinkle   Louise Richardson

Dorothy Hamon Gardner   Molly McGuire Grothaus   Polly Hill

Harriet   McMahon Purtell   Jane C. Scott   Eleanor Brumcherhoff Spu

Anne C. Carr   Ione Chase   Dorothy Hamon Gar